FIGHT TO LIVE

SAREZAH LAKE

1st Edition

This book presents a personal journey, including experiences with weight loss, medical appointments, interactions with healthcare professionals and facilities, as well as a near-death experience. It is intended to be an honest and accurate account. The author is not a doctor, therapist, medical practitioner, or well-being coach, and the content does not constitute professional or medical advice. The experiences and choices described reflect what was appropriate for the author and may not be suitable for others. Everyone's health, body, and circumstances are different. A qualified medical professional should be consulted before making decisions related to health, treatment, diet, or well-being.

Neither the author nor any party involved in the production of this book shall be held liable for any damages, loss, or injury allegedly arising from any information or suggestions contained within this work. Readers assume full responsibility for their personal decisions.

ISBN 978-1-0369-2190-3

Control, consistency,
discipline and determination
will change your life

– Sarazah Lake

I dedicate this book to my three beloved sons
Rahim, Khaliq and Azim.
Love you all dearly and eternally,
Your Mama

CONTENTS

7/9/25

Dearest Lisa

Lots of Love

Sarah

xxx

INTRODUCTION

Ticking Time Bomb

"You are a ticking time bomb," my doctor said, staring directly into my eyes, as she continued, "Mrs. Lake, if you were to have a heart attack, it would likely end in fatality."

Those words instantly shook me to the core, because I knew exactly what she meant by that statement. My size had now escalated to the point that, from a clinician's point of view, it was life-threatening. There and then I knew I had to do something about it before it was inevitably too late.

Whilst I tried hard to avoid the doctor's look of despair – a look that spoke a thousand words, like *please, do something* – I couldn't look away. So we just stood in that silence for what felt like a lifetime, as that phrase *ticking time bomb* echoed through my head, forcing me to accept that with each passing day, I was increasingly putting my health and life at risk because, at any time, I could die from the strain on my heart as well as my other organs.

As long as I live, I will never forget that moment in the doctor's office. Nor that look that pierced through my soul, or that word *fatality*. That word, for many years, rang around my head. The truth is, you didn't have to be a doctor or a rocket scientist to understand that I was indeed a *ticking time bomb*. I had ballooned to a clothes size UK 32. My weight had completely spiralled, to where I was medically described as *super morbidly obese*, meaning the biggest there is – not ideal.

I had reached the point where I could barely move, let alone walk, due to the colossal size of my body. And by the sound of things, I was on borrowed time – time that was seriously running out. I guess it was sheer luck that, up until now, I had no obesity-related illnesses like diabetes, heart problems, or asthma. Any breathlessness I did have was mostly down to my size.

In truth, the only major issue I had was mobility problems,

obviously caused by carrying that amount of weight, coupled with a debilitating form of arthritis, which contributed to it being difficult for me to move around freely – which no doubt became another exacerbating factor to my size.

You would think my extremely limited movement would have pushed me to do something about my size, but for some reason, it didn't – or possibly I couldn't. Looking back, I think I clung on to the only hope I had in that desperate situation – that as long as my vital organs were healthy, I didn't need to lose weight, I was still fairly ok!

I mentally brushed off any kind of reasoning, telling myself many of us are big in my family, so being a big girl is part of my heritage and cultural background. Besides, the fuller figure was always celebrated, as it was an indication of being wealthy and therefore healthy because you could afford to eat in abundance. But, of course, my ignorance and cultural heritage beliefs didn't expand to the reality that my size was beyond being curvy or in any way healthy. The reality here was my weight had been putting a huge strain on all my vital organs – which, of course, I had conveniently turned a blind eye to, deluding myself with old wives' tales and propaganda so I didn't have to face the reality of my situation.

Until that crucial day when Dr Goel told me quite frankly, "You are a ticking time bomb," together with that haunting look of despair and concern that said, *Mrs. Lake, please, please, do something about being so dangerously overweight. Come on Mrs. Lake! Think of your life!*

That was the day that something snapped inside me. And in that moment, before she carried on with the consultation, I knew I was on my knees and had to find a way out of this nightmare.

To make things worse that day, before the doctor even continued, she offered me a seat, by making a signal with her eyes pointing towards a chair, with a slight nod as if to say, *Sit down*. But as soon as I saw the chair I was immediately horrified because the chair had arms.

Now, what that means for a big girl like me is no way will I be fitting my huge body in that tiny, confined space without getting stuck in it.

So, with a sickly grin, I politely declined, trying to hide behind my embarrassment saying, "That's ok, I will stand if you don't mind."

But she knew why, of course she did. She knew I couldn't fit my huge body in that standard-size square of a chair! *Standard* you know. *Standard*!

My doctor continued by asking a few more questions, namely about my family health history. I responded that both sides had a history of heart problems and diabetes. We continued to talk, as I shuffled from leg to leg, trying to ease my weight-bearing joints, pausing regularly to catch my breath because it took a lot of energy to talk, let alone stand.

It was at this point that Dr Goel began to break down what being a *ticking time bomb* meant.

She began by stating I was at an extremely high risk of having a heart attack, with dire consequences – adding that many people with a normal body size could survive a heart attack, because their hearts are strong enough to re-fire their body during resuscitation.

But for someone my size, it would be near on impossible for my heart to have enough strength to re-fire a body that size, simply saying, "Your heart isn't strong enough. So it is likely you will die on the hospital emergency table."

"Die? That's a bit final," I said.

To which she nodded: "Yes, it would be final, Mrs. Lake."

Immediately after that comment, a vision popped into my head of my three children who, in the event of a heart attack, would see me lying in a hospital bed with the nurse having to pull the sheet over my face because of a *fatality*.

Me gone, dead, finished, bye-bye, cheerio.

I can truthfully say that thought was unbearable. As a mother how could I put my children through that type of trauma, especially since I was familiar with losing a mum to tragedy? I knew I couldn't put them through that as they were all still young teenagers and needed me.

So I had to dig deep and find a solution to this insurmountable problem because, in the name of all that's holy, my last words before I die can't just be, *the bloody doctor was right. I was a ticking time bomb*. I had to change what I was doing to save myself from an untimely death.

So from then to every single day after that, I took action and absolute control as well as accountability of myself. There was to be no more room for excuses, no more *I will do it after the weekend*, or *I've screwed it now, being a Thursday, so I may as well start again Monday*. It was *start now*, because, for me, there really was no tomorrow.

Besides, deep down, I'd had a gutful of making excuses; excuses can be the curse of life, and they will keep telling you what you want to hear, just to keep yourself where you are. But eventually, there comes a point where the excuses run out and you have to stop what you are doing and make changes – or end up on a road that will only lead to doom.

Do this for us, Sarezah, I told myself. *For our poor burdened body, do it for the distress and the strain we have put on our heart and all our other organs, do it for our joints, for our poor skeletal frame that is struggling daily to carry this debilitating weight around. Enough is enough.*

I need to find a foolproof solution and find a starting point, to tackle this seemingly unconquerable task, to find the beginning to end a lifetime of being overweight. And that is how my journey began.

So let me take you on that journey, not only about weight loss past to present but the journey of life – with its many obstacles, trials and tribulations. A journey of sheer determination and, at many times, courage and the will to push past the tears and the agony throughout the decades of life! Where I survived from the depths of helplessness to hope, from success to survival, and ultimately, acceptance.

CHAPTER 1

The Beginning of the End

It may be easy, and reasonable, for some to question why on earth I let myself get that big in the first place. To be honest, it's not always a case of *letting yourself* get that big. It is something that gradually happens. I watched the weight slowly creep up over time. It takes years and years of being comfortably numb and blind to what you are doing to get to the size I was. Along with eating and eating with little to no control waiting for, someday, a miracle to happen.

And as I grew, so did my appetite. I realised the bigger you get, the more you must eat to satisfy your hunger. In the end, I would go from one packet of crisps to another. I then went to a family pack size. And when that wasn't enough, I went to a multipack of 6, or even, at times, I am ashamed to say I devoured a larger pack of 12.

And yes, of course, many could rightfully associate that with greed, but greed isn't necessarily the sole reason or even an answer to why you can end up consuming that amount of food (something I will explain in more detail later).

But I guess with those numbers it isn't hard to think, *she was greedy*, especially when you say you have eaten 12 bags of crisps in one sitting. However, let me shed a little light on that and let me try to elaborate on why being *greedy* as a large person is an easy concept.

Imagine there is a large hole in front of you, and you have to fill it back up with earth. Now you couldn't just put a couple of shovels in to fill it again, could you? It would need more than a few shovels to fill a big-sized hole, wouldn't it? The hole is not greedy, is it? It needs a certain amount to fill it up again – the bigger the hole, the more earth it will need.

So, if you have a big stomach that has been stretched over time, you are going to need a lot to fill it, too. Therefore, greed is not necessarily always a reason why some people need to eat a lot of food. They are simply eating what is necessary to sustain their body size.

Greed is one of the words I have a great disdain for. Many times in my life I have been told by various people that perhaps if I wasn't so *greedy* I would lose weight. Ooh and *lazy*. Yet another major misconception is that people perceive that so-called *fat* people are fat not only because they are greedy but because they're also lazy. It's as though fat and laziness go hand in hand. These are ignorant and biased beliefs, rather than the reality of one's true situation.

Of course, at times, I have been guilty of overindulging – like most of us have. At one time or another, we have all eaten more than we should have. But I soon realised that it wasn't as simple as overindulging. I recognised that there was a pattern in the way that I ate, which led me to conclude that over the years I had developed poor eating habits which, in the long term, led to me having a major problem with my weight.

I understood that this stemmed from having little to no portion control – literally eating until I was full. But there was a key aspect to this way of eating: I didn't eat regularly. I went extremely long periods of not having food, then scoffing all I could in one go. This is something we will go into in more depth later.

So whilst I didn't eat particularly unhealthily (I didn't eat crisps every day), my portions were out of control. So I knew this was going to be a tough issue for me because, unlike many obese people, I mostly ate fresh, unprocessed foods. I wasn't – and am not – one for fast foods or takeaways; I would have them, but on rare occasions, at most.

Fast food is also another misconception linked to *that's why you are fat,* which, again, isn't necessarily true. But if you are one of those people who regularly eat takeaways, then it could be quite easy to lose weight by simply cutting out those types of high-calorie, fried, fatty or sugary foods – and you would see results almost instantly by eating healthier food options. Especially if you only have a few pounds to lose.

Likewise, if you drink alcohol to excess, reducing your alcohol intake will help cut those calories and, before you know it, you've lost the weight you put on.

But if you are a person, like me, who was super morbidly obese, and eats regular healthy foods, that requires a different approach.

It's not a question of just cutting out – it's a question of cutting down the amount of food you consume and re-programming when you eat. And understanding that you have to be in it for the long haul. Just like the weight went on slowly over the years, it too would come off – slowly slowly.

"*Why didn't you notice how big you were?*" I hear you say. When things are gradual, it can become unnoticeable. The bigger I got, the more I adapted to that size, and before I knew it, I'd inflated to a UK size 32, questionably larger, seeing everything was stretchy elastic, which, of course, I just covered up with a baggy tee shirt, so I hid myself behind the reality of my situation.

I never took photos of my body, just my face. And if I did, I stood behind others, so I never saw myself. But, of course, eventually, I couldn't hide. Not just because of what my doctor said, but because I could no longer hide from the daily struggles of not being able to walk far or get up without help. That, too, was a gradual process. One minute lively, next minute you need help with day-to-day things.

Almost everything became challenging, to the point where the bigger I got, the less I could move and the less I could move, the bigger I got. It became a catch-22 situation. And, of course, the bigger I got, the bigger my appetite got. So I ate more to satisfy my hunger – and round and round the vicious circle went.

Anyway, like I said, even though I understood I had to take some sort of control of what led to the point I was at, I still didn't know where on earth to begin; it was all so overwhelming as I had been so used to just eating the way I ate to satisfy my colossal appetite that I didn't know what to change, nor how to control something I have always done.

Believe me, control is no easy feat – it's one of the hardest things I have had to do in my life. And control doesn't just apply to food. Ask a drug user or an alcoholic, they find it hard to control the amount they take or drink. Even if they try, the urge to drink overpowers their ability to control their desire not to drink – despite where it will lead to or what disasters it may cause. And before you know it, it's all spiralling out of control – and over time it becomes an addiction issue.

Some say food is an addiction. But I don't necessarily agree with that statement. In my experience, food is somewhat different, but it can have a similar thread to it. For example, take some sugary foods – once you start eating them you just can't stop. I guess it satisfies something inside of you, but you don't even know what that is.

However, when we don't exercise control, it leads to excess. And over time that excess leads to habits. Habits lead to addiction – whatever our vice, be it food, drugs, cigarettes (now vaping) or alcohol. We just use excuses for what we do and blame our actions on the fact that we have some sort of need or dependency, but fundamentally it is us that is responsible for what we do.

In my case, I was eating till I was full to the brim – again, is that greed? Maybe? Who knows? Some will think it's greed, others won't. To be honest, does anyone know why we do the things we do? We just do them, and whilst we're all different in many ways, we are fundamentally the same. I guess it's just *human nature*.

However, there is one thing I want to share – something that became very apparent during my weight loss journey – and that is the unsolicited advice on how to lose weight. Those who I endearingly refer to as the *fat brigade* – you know, the ones who think they have a God-given right to tell someone who is obese, how to lose weight, despite not having lost any themselves. They come up with notions like, *"Well, if you eat a bit of chicken and a lettuce leaf salad and cut all carbs out, you'll lose weight."*

Err, no actually, you're wrong! In fact, not eating enough, doesn't work either, because when you don't eat enough, your body will do the opposite and stop using food you consume as fuel. Its way of thinking is that no more food is coming so we better reserve what we have, as our body has gone into some sort of hibernation.

In fact, this is referred to as *starvation* mode, and yes, I do know – because after years of research I understood that is exactly what happened to me. However, this concept would generally go over the heads of people like that.

To be honest, the only thing the *fat brigade* seems to know is this adopted belief that being thin is the prerequisite of beauty. Therefore, despite what your face looks like, if you're thin, you are desirable! Oh, and it's not just diet advice you get from them either.

Diet advice tends to come hand in hand with the *"If only"* comments like, "*If only you were thinner, you would be so much prettier!*" I mean what, love?! I mean that's just rude, isn't it? Or here's another classic: *"Even though you are really big, you carry it well,"* or *"You've got such a pretty face. If only you lost weight, your size really lets the rest of you down."*

Of course, if I reacted to any of those comments with, *"What has size got to do with being pretty? And prettier than what?"* I end up getting a *"There is no need to be so aggressive"* response – but for them, wrapping an insult in a compliment is ok – ridiculous!

However, me being me, I do have a plethora of responses, but I will narrow it down to a few of my favourites like, *"Being thin is not the benchmark for beauty,"* or "*Actually, the problem with being thin is there is not much room for substance. Besides, my body is merely a vessel for my soul, and when I die, I won't be taking that with me, so I would rather nourish my soul because that's going wherever I go."* I generally don't get a response after that.

In all honesty, it is never the words I find offensive. It's the fact that people think they can bestow their opinions onto you, and you must adhere to what is acceptable under their labels. Thankfully, I'm not in the least bit interested in what other people think of me. To this day it really makes no difference to me whether you think I'm pretty or not, if you like me or not, or whatever else you might think of me. The only person's opinion that matters to me, is mine.

Besides, it's not always their fault. Unfortunately, there is so much misinformation out there, so most people are led by what they see or what they have heard some influencer on social media say, or read in some article in a magazine, about 'diets' that guarantee weight loss – so long as you've only got the odd couple of kilos to lose, of course.

Or you get some person who is pushing some paid promotion to *take this supplement to help aid weight loss.* Most of these platforms are just about making money and tend to prey on the desperation of people who are seeking hope.

Trust me, I know. I have tried every single possible diet over the years and failed every single one of them – from Weight Watchers to

Slimming World, the Atkins Diet to the Don't Turn Left on a Tuesday diet (that's a joke, by the way!).

I even tried taking something called Orlistat, a fat-burning tablet, which had horrific side effects, one of which was oily discharge from your anus, mate! My anus, you know. What that meant was oily liquid shit seeping out (sorry to be graphic). It got to a stage where I was stuffing wads of tissue in my backside to prevent it from leaking out on my car seats or the blooming sofa, I mean, for goodness sake, what a terrible and humiliating invention. But at the time, I was so desperate I carried on right up until the doctor took me off them because I was suffering from all sorts of other issues to the point where the risks outweighed the benefits.

No matter what diet I did, or how hard I tried, I always plateaued very quickly, and only ever lost a certain amount. For the many years I dieted and failed, I thought it was because of me. I failed because I didn't stick to the principles of that diet, which, after many years of my own research, I realised many diets prohibit certain foods like carbohydrates or are just too calorie- restrictive. Which simply leaves you starving due to the extreme low-calorie count, or by cutting carbohydrates to an unmanageable level so you end up with little to no energy – to the point where you give up. So when diets are too restrictive, you will fail.

Of course, not everyone will fail. Remember the people I spoke about earlier, the ones who eat takeaways etc. For them, it's generally sustainable because all they have to do is cut out the booze and takeaways, eat a piece of chicken and lettuce leaf salad for a couple of weeks, and bingo – they are at their goal weight (slight exaggeration).

But these are the same people who gloat to others about how they did – therefore so can you. Losing a few pounds or kilos is not the same as having to lose 300lbs. Like me. That is a different game altogether. The only action that works is changing your old eating ways and trading them in for new eating and exercise habits. Not just for a week or month. But for life. Better known as a *lifestyle change*.

And that is it – a *lifestyle change*. That is what one hundred per cent worked for me. Changing all my old eating habits into a balanced way of eating. Setting some limits and controlling the amount of food

I ate was the key to my success.

I didn't ever restrict my food to the point where I would cave in, because I knew from experience an extremely low-calorie diet would become unsustainable. Therefore my new lifestyle change incorporated all foods and even some treats. I promise you, if you do this, slowly slowly – bit by bit – over time you will have the success you have always dreamed of.

But to achieve a lifestyle change, there are several stages to go through first. One of them is taking an honest account of everything you eat. Start jotting down what you eat at mealtimes to build a picture of what your daily intake is.

Once this is done, you can start to enter the second part. That is to create a *calorie deficit,* which means calculating the number of calories you need for your body weight and then dividing those calories into proteins, carbohydrates and fats. Which makes up a balanced diet (something we will look at later). And lastly, it is imperative to incorporate some sort of exercise into your daily life.

At first, making those changes will be challenging – especially the food. For me, I had spent many years eating in a certain way, so trying to undo all those old eating habits was hard graft, and there were no shortcuts or quick-fix solutions. It took me a very long time to learn how to eat in a controlled manner.

But over time it got easier and easier and slowly, slowly I began to see results. It is certainly most doable for absolutely anyone – it just requires determination and patience which truly are the key, together with finding the correct information to keep you on track.

Whilst I learnt a lot from doing my own research, I did have to sift through a lot of rubbish that was buried in the *want to sell you somethings*. The first things I learnt was not only portion control, or foods with nutritional value, but also how I was cooking and preparing my food.

So instead of frying everything. I began to bake and steam more. I learnt how to get more out of my calories and split them up equally throughout the day – in other words, more for your money.

I quickly realised the reason why it seemed like I didn't eat much when I was a big girl was down to the fact that the foods I had been used to eating had a very high fat content, and a large amount of my diet was carbohydrates. Now, all carbohydrates contain a sugar content – be it potatoes or rice – making them extremely calorific. A high fat and high carb diet with little else and not using it as fuel will store as fat.

Combining that with no portion control and long periods of not eating is not ideal. In fact, sometimes I was so hungry I would raid the chocolate drawer and scoff all I could – which, of course, had little to no nutritional value.

Whilst it did the job at the time, giving me instant satisfaction, it spiked my sugar levels, and, as you know, the age-old principle of what goes up must come down means I'd crash. And once I crashed, I ended up eating again, then crashing and then eating. It was nothing short of yet another vicious cycle, and over time, the weight piled on and on. Things that are high in fat and sugar, not used and converted into energy, will be stored as fat.

So I learnt how to eat to stabilise my blood sugars and satisfy my hunger to keep me satiated for longer –without cutting out anything from any food group. I just learnt to control the amount of food I ate.

However there were a few things I chose to get rid of from my diet. Fizzy drink, fast foods, and I limited bread and very fatty foods. Fizzy drinks and fast foods weren't hard to give up as I didn't have much of them anyway. But there was one thing I gave up completely a few years after I started my weight loss journey, something that I loved with all my heart, but for love nor money, I just couldn't limit. So, in order to *reach your goals, Sarezah*, a term that has been embedded into my soul (something that will unfold later as I take you on my journey), I gave up chocolate.

One of the toughest things I had to adapt to at the beginning was getting used to being in a *calorie deficit*. In brief, this meant I could no longer eat till I was full, as there was a limit on the amount of food I could consume. This meant having to overcome that torturous feeling of hunger. And I tell you what, if you can overcome that, you can overcome almost anything in your life. Mate, being hungry sent me to hell and back more than once.

Many times during my journey I felt despair and anger due to hunger. And there have been countless times I just wanted to give up and concede to the emotional and physical pain of that feeling. But I didn't, I knew I just had to keep pushing through. And if I did cave in, I just got up, dusted myself off and started again.

It took time and patience. Like I said, there is no quick-fix solution. What you put in is what you get out. Trust me, day in, day out, it's hard graft. Yes, many times I failed – but many times I won. And in the end, I won more times than I failed and that makes you feel euphoric – especially when you reach a goal. But you have to start somewhere, and no time is better than now. Commit yourself and slowly, slowly you will get there.

Now a calorie deficit means consuming fewer calories than you expend – in other words what you burn in a day according to your size. Therefore in order to create what is known as a calorie deficit, it meant I had to do something I hate doing – getting weighed. But without that critical number, I wouldn't have known how much in the way of calories I needed to eat. It was the only way to kick-start my weight loss journey. So I had to bite the bullet and get on those dreaded scales.

CHAPTER 2

The Dreaded Scales

There is no love lost between me and the scales. The scales don't lie, do they!? The scales love telling you a few home truths that you don't want to hear – like how big you really are. So most of the time I avoided them like the plague. But now, with no choice, I needed to calculate what I needed to eat for my size and then create a calorie deficit (a key component to dieting).

Now before we continue, some of you may be wondering why I didn't get weighed when I was at the doctors. Well I did, but the scales only went up to a 25st limit. (I know, blooming only 25st!). Anyway, let me tell you what happened exactly.

See, when I hauled my colossal body on to the doctor's scales, not only did it make an excruciating sound under my feet, but the flipping dial went around and around, and landed on like a random single number, because – you guessed it – I was too blasted heavy. And yes, Doctor Goel just looked at me with yet more despair, before advising me to go to Boots the Chemist, as their scales go up to *big size*. Big size, you know.

So a few days later, I nervously made my way to my local Boots. I hauled myself out of the car with my husband's help. After finding a bit of stability I made my way towards the entrance.

I didn't really notice any of the stares from people – I had become so used to it that it was normal. It just didn't phase me and anyway I am of an opinion that you can think and stare all you want. But if I catch you looking or even hear you saying something, don't be surprised if you get a reaction. For fear is not one of my weaknesses.

Once inside, I searched for some coins in my purse and continued to slowly shuffle my heavy body towards the *big size* upright scales, stopping and holding on to anything I could to take a short break to catch my breath and rest my aching bones.

I eventually arrived at the machine and popped the coins in

the slot and waited for instructions. I clambered onto the scale with my trusted Crocs – the only shoes that could cope with my constant swollen feet and the easiest of footwear, as they simply slid on. No laces to tie up, because I was so big I couldn't even bend over to tie them myself – I had to rely on someone else to do it for me.

To be honest, even having to climb on the scales was hard enough as I nearly toppled over due to my lack of balance. But, thankfully, I didn't fall. I stood on the machine, which requested some info – height, age, etc. After I entered everything required, I anxiously waited for the printed results, which seemed to take for absolute ever, to the extent that I thought I'd broken it and all – like I did the odd toilet seat or seven.

Finally, and thankfully, the machine didn't break as the printed information came out, which I eagerly ripped off to see the results. Immediately a warm rush of absolute panic and complete disbelief came over me, because to my horror it read 32st 2lbs, (approximately 204 Kilos or 450lbs).

I was mortified. *How? How did I get this big… again?* Yes, I said *again*, because it's not the first time I have tipped the scales over 30st (more about that later). Because in that moment, I felt nothing short of absolute despair, anger and disappointed, in no-one else but myself. *How Sarezah? Just how?*

Well, that's when the internal committee started to chip in, you know the ones, when you are trying to rationalise and reason internally to find an answer to the question. The different aspects of your personality pop up and have a thing or two to say about any situation.

The first voice started off with a sarcastic tone, which always seemed to start with *mmm*, followed by a *well*, then back to *mmm, well of course you know how you got that 'fat' again, don't you Suzzz?* (using words it knows I loathe and Suz pronounced Suzzz is one of my many childhood school nicknames).

Gorging, isn't it? Hoovering all and sundry up, shovelling it all down the hatch like there's no tomorrow. We've watched you eat the kids' leftovers, crisps, chicken dinosaurs, turkey drummers – and that's all before demolishing your own heaped plate of dinner.

Another voice joins in agreement, *Well, that's right, isn't it Suzzzzz? We've watched you, scoffing it all, day in, day out, mmm.*

Interrupted by the balanced voice of the committee, who intervene where it can, trying to represent the defensive side of me: *Well it's not all her fault, is it? It was a bit of comfort eating, wasn't it? She been stuck in a rut. Life isn't easy, is it? Poor girl had to deal with all sorts of problems, with no help, which has contributed to her getting bigger and bigger – which in turn made her depressed. The more depressed she got, the more the poor girl ate. And the more she ate, the less she could move – the less she could move the more she ate.*

Comfort!? Bloody comfort? The sarcastic voices bounced back. *I've watched her eat a family fun size bag of pissing Bounty and a giant size bag of Walkers cheese and onion crisps – five bloody minutes after having six slices of toast, slathered in butter, of course – followed by God knows what else.*

The defensive voice came back with: *Come on, she's a big girl, big girls need food. She doesn't really eat much, does she?*

Well, said the attacking voice, *if she didn't eat much, how did she get that fat then?*

At the time, I had no answer to that. I just sat there and conceded, listening to my own personalities fighting each other in the midst of internal civil war – and the real me was completely defenceless, because I knew I'd let my eating slip away into complete chaos.

Eating too much. What a statement – one with little to no answer. What is even eating too much? Although I can say the answer to that question came a little later, during a lightbulb moment after many years of understanding and learning about myself. But right now, I was in the shits, mites (my father used to say mites instead of mate, due to his very strong Mauritian accent – so mites kind of stuck with all of us as did some of his other quotes).

Light-heartedness aside, the reality of the situation was I'd reached crisis point. I was a 44- year-old *ticking time bomb* woman, that had ballooned to just over 32st, who could barely move, who needed help with doing most everyday tasks and chores, like showering and dressing, cooking and cleaning.

I couldn't even take a shit without worrying if the bastard toilet seat was going to break, much less needing help on and off it. *For fuck's sake, what have I done to myself,* I thought. *How did I let myself get this bad? And where the hell do I even start to make a change? Fuck my life!* I thought. *Fml!*

That journey home was pretty silent. My husband isn't a huge conversationalist unless it's some nonsense theory he enjoys talking about. Therefore a day out at Boots is hardly riveting conversation. Besides, he most probably thought I was just picking up the usual cocktail of prescriptions, seeing I'd gone to the doctors recently.

I didn't feel much like talking, I was caught between being ashamed of myself, angry and upset, and bombarded with all kinds of thoughts, with that 32st echoing around my mind thinking *how did I get to this size again*, it was all so overwhelming that I felt sick to my stomach.

See, it's not my first time I've been over 30st. Once I was bigger than that when I was in my early 20's after I'd left home. I had the freedom of eating what I wanted with no-one to take my food away. Which of course meant I had no control of what I was eating and within a few years my weight ballooned to an all-time high – even bigger than 32st 2lbs.

In fact, I hit over 35 stone around 1991! Yes, I said, 35 stone! If that isn't bad enough, finding out I weighed that much wasn't as awful as it was getting weighed, because for me it was the height of an embarrassing experience.

It came after I'd been to the doctors who wanted to weigh me but was met with the same old story – he didn't have any scales fit for purpose. So the doctor said I had to go to *Parcelforce* to get weighed because there were no other scales anywhere to accommodate my weight other than there. I was like, "Parcelforce? Are you actually joking?" But he wasn't. So I went to Parcelforce to get myself weighed. That whole experience was nothing short of awful – not because anyone was rude, but because they weren't.

On arrival I was greeted by a few workers. One of them said, "Can I help you love," assuming I was there to pick up a parcel. That's when I took out the piece of paper the doctor gave me and passed it over to him. He looked at the piece of paper, remaining silent. To which I explained to everyone what he just read – that I had to get weighed here, at your depot, because the doctor said he didn't have any scales big enough to weigh me.

I looked at their faces and felt mortified as they all stood in shock, mouths wide open, until one of the young men broke the awkward silence and said, "Oh, ok love. Let's get you started then," in a jolly voice. But behind his eyes I could see the pity. Whilst the others did all they could to avoid my gaze out of sheer embarrassment of the situation, that young man didn't. He acted completely normally saying, "Ok, love, you just hop up on this, here give me your hand." He took my hand and helped me onto the scale.

As soon as my hand touched his I could have just cried for many reasons, one of them being, *how the fuck have I gotten this big*, the other, and the most hurtful to my soul, was that he was so nice about it.

Think about it, here I was, a young beautiful lady, who is having to climb onto *industrial size scales* because I couldn't be measured on anything else, helped by a person who didn't have a single ounce of judgment towards me. I just wasn't used to this type of sensitivity and understanding, it just wasn't part of the brief of my life. *Kindness!!!*

As I stood on those scales, I watched with absolute dread as that bloody arrow went right around that scale and stopped at just over a whopping *35 stone*. That's when I caught that young man's eyes and saw his sadness – sadness that he felt for me. Not just pity but *poor girl*. Because something made her like that and he was right, something did.

But he didn't say anything, none of them did, he just continued to help me off the industrial size scale, holding my hand as I stepped off, he then took the piece of paper and wrote the weight on it.

Without saying too much, I just smiled a little awkward smile as he said, "You take care of yourself, ok my lovely."

"Thank you," I said, trying not to make eye contact, to avoid any more shame. Not just because of my size, but because that young man didn't laugh or ridicule me – he was just a kind and polite person and that almost broke me.

After being back at the doctors and discussing the results, I came home, desperate to make a change. Although my doctor wasn't unkind or cruel, he certainly raised his medical concerns. He told me there would be huge consequences to my health as I got older due to being *super morbidly obese*, meaning I was dangerously overweight. But, even then, it just didn't sink in enough to make me snap, I guess I focused on the key words of *when you get older*.

Of course, initially I had taken some steps to losing weight by cutting out foods and drastically cutting how much I ate. I'd lost a fair amount but realised diet alone wasn't enough. So I took further action and rang a local small, but well known, gym. I chose this gym because it was a proper bodybuilders' gym. I understood a bit about this because from around the age of 14 I began weight training and knew it was something I could do to help myself as even at that age, I saw results.

I spoke to a wonderful man, Graham Hamilton, who was the then owner and manager of the gym, which is called Hamiltons. I told him about my plight over the phone. During the conversation I did say, "Look, I'm huge and I don't want anyone laughing at me or saying anything because I am not the type to not say anything back. I don't care what people say about me, but if I hear something there is going to be a reaction. But I don't want to come and cause a scene, if you know what I mean."

To my surprise, his reply shocked me as he said, "If someone says anything they will have me to deal with. This gym is a gym to help people get fit and healthy – it's not to a place to be judged in."

He then invited me to come in and have an induction. It was daunting at first, especially when I walked through those doors weighing a whopping 35st. But he was waiting to greet me and showed me around. I couldn't fault anyone in that gym – they were all fantastic, from the staff to the members. Everyone helped and supported me.

There seems to be a sad myth or even a bit of fear attached to walking into a gym – that everyone will laugh or make a comment, or stare at you to make you feel uncomfortable. I can tell you one thing – that has never happened to me in any gym I have gone to, even when

I was at my biggest. And even now, in the very unlikely event that one or two idiots do make a comment, there will be far more who won't and in fact will defend anyone who is trying to help themselves.

During that period, I managed to lose around 12 stone in that gym through exercise and diet.

I was still really big but because I did a lot of strength training, I built muscle, which made me look a lot smaller than I actually weighed.

Plus a lot of it was down to my body shape. See, some people are bottom heavy, some top; me, I am big all over, so the weight loss was even, whilst there was a marked difference in how I looked, to what I weighed, I still topped the scales at around 22 stone. But for some reason, no matter how hard I tried, I just couldn't get any lower than that.

Anyhow, back to the journey home from Boots after that nostalgic visit. I sat in that car feeling dazed, peering out of the car window trying to process it all, mulling over and over things, trying to understand where it all went wrong.

I even started to have a row with myself, saying stuff like, *no wonder you don't like getting weighed, ignorance is bliss isn't it. Why didn't you just stop. What did you think would happen, mmm? Eat without control and see what you get. 32st. That's what.*

I can't even express how bitterly disappointed and shocked I felt.

But this time I felt differently and was determined not to fail again. I think it was the shock of reading that printout in Boots, and what the doctor said that snapped something inside of me – and I knew I couldn't carry on like this or I would be a goner.

Like I said, at the time I was at an absolute loss as to what to do or where to even begin as every diet I did didn't work, but I somehow had to find it in myself to fight to save my life, before it was too late and that *time bomb* went *boom!*

I say battle for my life *again*, because it's not the only time I had to fight for my life to stay alive. Believe me, I've had a few close calls. However, one of those times came much later in my life. In fact, almost seven and a half years into my weight loss journey, a battle that was not in my hands, a battle that relied on fate and destiny; one that was out of my control.

That is something you will see as the story unfolds, but for now, in that moment at the age of 44, control was in my hands, so I said to myself, *Let's have some faith and find a way out of this terrible situation.*

CHAPTER 3

Faith

To me, having faith is not the same as being religious. Whilst I have a strong faith and believe there is a God, I don't consider myself religious, even though I was born and loosely raised as a Muslim. Which in my household was somewhat confusing, as you could do almost anything that is considered sinful – like cheat, lie, steal – as long as you didn't eat pork!

That was very confusing for me, growing up. It didn't help that my father would quite often tell me how to be a proper Muslim whilst he was drinking a glass of whiskey.

Of course, as I got older, I could see the hypocrisy of what he and others said. I mean, pork really is the easiest thing to give up, isn't it? Because the reality is you have lamb, chicken, beef and fish to choose from. But the consensus was, and still is among many Muslims, that as long as you don't eat pork, you can seemingly carry on with as many sinful acts as possible!

However, even though I believe there is a God, I am not the sort to bestow what I believe on anyone else. Whether you are religious or not, believe in what you believe, be it Allah, Jah Jah, Jehovah or a chair, or if you are Hindu, Christian or atheist, or whatever else you follow.

I don't question another person's belief, based on my opinions and what I think someone should be doing under the guidelines of my faith. My faith and belief in God have developed and strengthened because of my life experiences. And, fundamentally, I don't know if there is a God or not – none of us can be 100% certain.

But there is a 50% chance there is and a 50% chance there isn't. (Not the only time I've heard that statistic either). And I won't know if God exists until I die – which, believe me, I have come close to a few times in my life, one of those times being when I was fighting for my life and grasping onto my life in a hospital bed. I saw something that I cannot explain and can only describe it as *the other side.*

Anyway, throughout my life, in troubled times, I have always looked within myself, where I harbour my faith. It is where I look for guidance to find solutions to any problems. And in order to find those answers, I try to sit alone and silently, with a peaceful state of mind (which at that time was a luxury, as I had mid to late teenage boys to deal with during the day and my husband's incessant snoring throughout the night).

But I managed to find a moment to look within for some clarity. A short time later, my thoughts led me to take out one of my trusted books that contained quotes and words of wisdom by Sufi sages (Sufism, in short, are people who follow a pious form of Islam, who believe that a direct, personal experience of God can be achieved through meditation. Sufism has a more mystical feel to it, to which I am deeply drawn.)

Book in hand after drawing a few deep breaths, I asked aloud, *please help me* to goodness knows who – but I was so desperate to find a way out of this insurmountable problem and would do almost anything to find a solution. After a few moments, I closed my eyes tightly, then randomly opened a page and read the first quote that my eyes landed on, which said, *"You are your biggest obstacle, rise above yourself."*

That answer struck me like a lightning bolt, as I immediately understood the sentiment behind that quote – that me, myself and I, was indeed my biggest obstacle. I allowed myself to get to this point without any control, hoping and waiting for tomorrow to come, to bring some miracle to change my dire situation!

But that was just vain hope. It was a pivotal moment for me once again and in my heart, I knew it was time to be ruthless to the undisciplined me, and find a way out of what led me to become a staggering *32st 2lbs.*

I knew it would not be easy, Lord knows this isn't the first time I've tried to lose weight, more like the 1000th – and believe me I must have tried and tested almost every single diet known to mankind, and pretty much failed each and every single one of them.

Whilst they all started well, I couldn't cope with intensely restricted formula of these diets, so I would fail! And this happened time and time again. Over and over again. Year to year. *Fail, fail, fail!*

But it was failing that compelled me to take a more in-depth look into the context and the meaning of dieting. Because despite giving every diet I undertook my best shot, for some reason I just couldn't stick to it because each diet left me feeling extremely hungry and lethargic. And consequently, each time I ended up caving in on the diet – which then felt like failure pointing its fingers at me saying, *You haven't succeeded because you simply gave up.*

Arguably, at times, that was the reason, but in defence I have realised through my own experiences many so called diets are actually very difficult to maintain, because I realised most diets are marketed and targeted at those who only need to lose a few kilos or so – therefore these diets are easier to maintain.

For the bigger person, like me, these types of diets are extremely calorie restrictive, or very low in carbohydrates. Making them unsustainable for anyone who needed to lose more than a few kilos, like me. I understood I had to take a different approach other than a quick fix solution, as the *'Lose 7lbs in 7 days'* diet wouldn't and didn't work for me. I needed to find something that I could commit to but would also satisfy my huge appetite.

That meant a diet that is designed for the long-term user. I needed to find a diet that gradually reduced my calorie intake – similar to the likes of Slimming World and Weight Watchers, which adhere to this type of principle and offer support to those who want to lose weight as part of a team.

But I even failed those too. Because at the time I was dieting with Slimming World, they offered the *'red day, green day'* system (which is now discontinued). This included something called *'sins'*. Red day was about more protein and less carbs. Green day about more carbs and less protein. Unlimited fruit and veg on both days. Sins were the treats you could add to your calorie intake.

Unfortunately for me, it didn't help as I ended up in the same position – as I could eat as much as I wanted on a carb day with no portion control, which consequently led me to failing. I realised in order to succeed you need to have a long-term plan consisting of two actions, if you want results: *calorie deficit* and *exercise*. That is it and, simply broken down, a permanent lifestyle change (something I will keep going on about, so it is embedded into your conscious thought).

For me, in order to make those lifestyle changes, the first thing I had to undo was all the old habits that brought me here – to the point of being super morbidly obese. I then had to create a foolproof plan that was sustainable and doable. In order to do that it meant having to look at a few home truths – one of those being my relationship with food.

I needed to understand my eating patterns, where I went from starving myself when I woke up until late morning, then I would gorge until I was full of whatever I could get my hands on – then crash, eating what I could again – then starve until late evening, then eat until I was full then carb crash and fall asleep.

It led me to question whether I had some sort of issue with food, was I some sort of an emotional eater? Or could I even possibly have some sort of addiction to food?

Neither of those questions are particularly easy for anyone to answer, let alone me. The truth is I eat at any time, be it if I am happy, sad or angry! Therefore, how do you even test to see if you are an emotional eater?

Most of us will find that eating is a pleasurable experience; food that we love tastes so good, so it gives us that feel good factor. In all honesty, eating will automatically make me feel better regardless of what mood I am in. If I am happy, I eat. Angry, I eat. I eat if I am alone or with people – I just love to eat.

In fact, every meal was a production. It was never a case of have a quick sarnie. It was a baguette (usually half or more – I know, alright it was a long time ago!) filled with all sorts be it chicken, cheese, mayo, salad or anything else I fancied. So how could I know if that was emotional eating?

I then looked at the notion of being 'addicted' to food. Food addiction isn't really linked in the same way as drugs and alcohol, because unlike food, drugs and alcohol are not a necessity. You need nutrients to survive. Understanding and deciding if I had an addiction to food was another really difficult question to answer. I mean, for the past 10 years, I've eaten porridge most days – it doesn't mean I am addicted to porridge, does it? So what is a food addiction?

Conversely, like I briefly mentioned earlier, some foods can actually have addictive properties, for example foods with high sugar or fat content.

Let's take chocolate, for instance, it is both high in sugar and fat, or crisps and ice cream, hence why these things taste so good. That is why once you start eating a bar of chocolate, or a big bag of crisps, or a packet of biscuits, it's hard to stop.

Trust me, I have demolished a whole pack of chocolate biscuits or a whole giant bar of chocolate! Done and dusted, just to be left with regret. However, regardless of this, it was still difficult for me to define if I had an addiction and/or if I was an emotional eater.

But after many years of changing my eating habits, I came to realise, it's not necessarily food itself that is the addiction, but it's the feeling you get from eating food because it gives you a certain pleasure and comfort. After a meal or something you enjoy eating, you get a certain fulfilment. It satisfies something inside of you that keeps you wanting more and more.

Much like that very first sip and taste of a beer, spirits or wine – it's like nectar. It's always the best, isn't it? It satisfies and pleases you in a way that you keep wanting it, so you end up drinking another pint or glass of whatever and then another – because it seems like you are always chasing that first sip, looking to get that same feel-good factor.

Just like some drugs, for example cocaine. I have heard users say the night starts off just drinking, then a bit later, the bag or packet comes out (slang for cocaine). The first few bumps are OK (bumps being a snort of cocaine powder). Soon after, you are agitated because you are overcharged, then you crash. Then you need more, because the urge is so ridiculous and before the first bag has finished you've bought the second bag.

And you've completely forgotten that before the cocaine came out you were having a great time just drinking. But now, with the coke freely flying about, it becomes a different type of party and before you know it, you are a complete mess. Food addiction might not have the same outcome as alcohol or drugs. I mean, Lord knows you aren't out of control eating some rice pudding, are you? Nor are off your face after you've had chicken bhuna!

Therefore, to me, food addiction must come from the senses and in the feeling of pleasure that food gives you – so you want more and more, which leads to lack of control of the amount you eat, which in turn results in consequences.

For example, let's take that roast dinner; after you've stuffed your face with as much as you can, or for those of you who have controlled eating, there is a sense of pleasure and enjoyment, you feel satisfied and content. It's given you a certain pleasurable experience.

From the first time you put food in your mouth, the taste and feeling gives you a certain sensation and, over time, you start to associate that feeling of pleasure with eating. So you think that food is what makes you happy. So you keep eating and eating – turning to it each time you feel troubled or down.

So when you eat chocolate or biscuits, they are something that make you happy, from both the sugar rush and the pleasure you feel, releasing your serotonin. Also foods like these don't just make you happy – they can also satisfy the taste for sugar.

For example, if you have what they call a sweet tooth, eating sweet things will satisfy that craving. Therefore you can almost liken a sugar craving to those who crave a cigarette due to their addiction to nicotine. Many would call sugar an addiction as they would call cigarettes and booze.

Either way, I learnt and understood, no matter what your vice is – sugar, drugs or drink – if you don't have some control over it, it will control you. And you will soon suffer the consequences of your actions.

So I questioned: *If I feel good after eating, does it mean I eat to feel good?* And I honestly don't know, to me it's almost an impossible question to answer.

All I knew and know is food is absolute life (oh, and coffee). Like I say, I eat at any old time, when I am happy, sad, angry, excited, low, high, you name it, any occasion, I just love eating and appreciate food! I mean who doesn't? But I am quite sure someone out there with some sort of ology degree, would happily pigeonhole me into something they learnt in a textbook.

Personally, I think terms like *'emotional eater'* are often used as an excuse to hide behind. People tend to use that, along with the endless list of excuses, to justify their poor behaviour. I often hear, *"I did this or I do that because I have had a trauma. And my trauma response is to do this or that."*

And I guess at times there are valid reasons for what some do. But ultimately if or when it starts to affect your health or wellbeing, you have to stop doing what you are doing.

I realised no matter what the cause of my obesity was – be it indulgence or trauma – I had to stop and change my eating habits and control the fine line of eating and overeating. Because if you continue to do the latter, you will end up getting burnt – which at the age of 44 I was truly sizzling in those hot embers of getting burnt – and taking action was my only remedy as my obesity was now, indeed, knocking on the door of fatality!

The first action was to look at what and when I ate – in other words my eating patterns. Now whilst I am of the opinion that there are no healthy or unhealthy foods, you obviously still have to be sensible and wise with what you eat.

I learnt to eat smart, I still eat almost everything, but I learnt to recreate healthier versions of everything I ate – which included roast dinners, curry and rice, lamb, chicken, steak – and on occasion I still have some foods like bread, crisps, and fried food, but it's limited, and I make sure I control the amount I consume.

And honestly, there is nothing wrong with having a little treat or something special that you enjoy once a week; I mean you've got to live, right? It helps in many ways as not only does it give you some fulfilment, but it prevents you from depriving yourself from anything. My advice is just try to keep it within your calorie count, have some control over it. It won't matter too much here and there, just don't make it the entire weekend or allow it to spill into the week.

To control my food intake, I began to log everything I ate on a daily basis in a journal.

Writing down what I ate gave me a massive insight and understanding of my eating behaviour. It was clear that the foods I ate didn't have much in the way of nutritional value, because my diet at the time consisted of high fatty foods and a lot of carbohydrates.

Carbohydrates are divided into two types, complex carbohydrates such as potatoes, rice, vegetables, which take longer to digest and are a more staple source of energy, and simple carbohydrates which are largely found in processed foods, baked goods like cakes, biscuits and soft drinks like cola. Either way, carbs are sugars and if not used as energy will be stored as fat. And I ate little in the way of fresh vegetables or salads. So I began to look for ways to change my eating habits.

This is when I came across a word I'd not heard before, *macros* (more about that as we travel further). But it was at this point I also realised that whilst I enjoyed eating a more varied diet, I had compromised what I ate to suit my husband.

See, I was raised to eat salads and vegetables, but my husband didn't venture past carrots or peas. In all honesty he is a nightmare when it comes to food. He doesn't eat tomatoes, peppers, courgettes, aubergine, soups or salads. Man likes simple carbs – in fact anything with sugar, sugar and more sugar! He is proper basic, no frills. Which didn't encourage the children much – until they got older, and I made them eat certain foods, only for them to realise it's actually nice.

Of course I could have made my own dinner separately, but I didn't (well, not at that time, anyway) because there was a family household budget. Fresh foods are a luxury in cost compared to processed foods. It is criminal that a small bag of apples costs over £2 and a packet of biscuits is 30p.

And, if I'm honest, I just didn't have the enthusiasm to cook several separate meals, let alone fight for fridge space for the vegetables and salads amongst the copious amounts of other stuff crammed in to meet needs of the rest of family.

Coupled together with my limited mobility, there was no *just nipping* anywhere, or standing cooking for long periods of time, let alone running to the shops to replenish a fresh food stock regularly as there were no food deliveries like there are now.

I guess some of you might think, *"She just couldn't be bothered"* or *"That is just another excuse, that's why she ended up becoming so fat."*

Well, not being bothered doesn't actually make you overweight or *fat*. Having no discipline and lack of calorie control is the problem.

Fat! Gosh what a bloody word, a word that gets chucked about relentlessly, yet this word is somewhat ambiguous and has different meanings, depending on the way in which it is used as to how the word *fat* will be interpreted.

CHAPTER 4

The Word 'Fat' and the Trouble with Perceptions

Let's take a few moments to analyse the word *fat*. *Fat* can be a term that pertains to either nice or not nice. For instance when we describe food, we often use the word *fat* together with words like *juicy*, for example, fat and juicy prawns or a big, fat, red, juicy tomato, and so on.

These types of descriptions are expressing our passion and love of those things, we are not insulting prawns or tomatoes – we are admiring them for what they aesthetically look like, how pleasing they are to the eye, knowing the joys they are offering us.

We often call round fruits like peaches big, fat and juicy – or plumptious. Or perhaps a fat, cuddly puppy, or a child – a cute chubby toddler, like me. As a child, my family constantly told me I had big, fat, juicy, rosy cheeks that they wanted to bite. Or perhaps, like when someone offers you a big, fat piece of cake.

It's not insulting to say those things because we are capable of looking at fat in a loving way and with admiration. In fact, never in the history of my life, have I ever heard anyone say, *"Look at that fat ugly prawn," or "Jesus Christ, look at the size of it. It's disgusting, look,"* pointing at a round, juicy fat lemon, have you? More than likely not.

Then please answer me, why oh why when some people look at someone who they consider to be so-called *fat*, does it turn into something vulgar and insulting?

How on earth did it get to the point where people judge those who reach a certain size at a certain age with utter disgust? How does a word like *fat* transpire from a nice description, if it's a type of food, or something cute, to absolutely degrading and humiliating to a human being who is seemingly bigger than what is considered to be *normal*?

I guess a reasonable explanation is we have been conditioned into thinking like that. From a certain age, you are told, *you don't want to be fat. No one will want you if you are fat and ugly* – like the two go hand in hand.

Nowadays, there are even more ways of communicating that opinion through platforms like social media, where it reaches out to even more people – with even more expectations as to what you should or should not be, to get a *like*.

The top of the hated list is being *fat* – to most of the world, *fat* is undesirable. Even in modern times, with the evolution of diversity and inclusion, any big girl or boy that tries to say *I'm comfortable being a plus size* usually gets slated and shut down by the same argument – *being fat is not healthy*! When really, the concern is not health. It's just the excuse used to continue hating on fat people.

Because I can tell you right now, being slim is not a guarantee or carte blanche for being healthy either, mate. Trust me, I know that for a fact.

Besides, I certainly didn't lose weight to look *nice*. I did it because my doctor said I was dangerously overweight; using words like *fatality* and *ticking time bomb* will push you to do that. Those words forced me to change before my weight killed me.

Being overweight isn't like being a drug user or alcohol dependent; with those types of issues there is a more tolerant acceptance that they do what they do because they have become addicted to them. Or they have an addictive personality, or a trauma led them to block out the pain.

Fortunately for them, there isn't as much stigma associated with those issues the way there is with obesity. There isn't always the same assumption that those with addiction issues are just lazy with no self-control, discipline or motivation. But if you are obese, you could not *ever* have any underlying medical or mental health problems that led to your obesity – you would simply be pigeonholed as *they just couldn't be bothered*, OR *greed led them to become obese*.

Seeing I have been a big girl for most of my life, I have the vast experience of what it feels like to be described as 'fat' – from both sides of the spectrum. Be it good as a child and bad as an adult. See, as a child, I was absolutely adored for being a chunk. But from the young age of around 10 to adult, I heard every type of *fat* insult under the sun.

So over the duration of my life I have become accustomed and somewhat resilient to abuse which has led me to be somewhat tough skinned – be it my size or the colour of my skin, so if and when I was ever insulted, those words don't actually offend me.

What really gets me is people thinking they have the God-given right to say what the hell they like because of what they believe the right size is or the correct complexion of someone's skin. It's silly. At the end of the day think what you want – but if I hear or see you, don't be surprised if you get a reaction.

Being exposed to many types of abuse, prejudices and violence – both inside and outside the home – led to this resilience. At home I was limited to what I could do, but outside of the home, I did not allow myself to be a victim, otherwise I would have been subjected to a plethora of constant attacks, namely due to my skin colour – and my size was just a bonus for the many racists.

And back then if you didn't fight back, you would have been smeared. Violent retaliation isn't something I enjoyed – it was a necessity and something I had to do in order to protect myself as well as others, as I can't just sit by and watch any animal or any person get hurt, even if it means me getting a bash.

However, in some situations I have had to gauge whether or not to react. *Is it life threatening? Am I outnumbered? Do they have a tool?* (Yes, I did say tool, tool being a weapon). See, there is a reason for that.

As a teen, I was stabbed in a racial attack, by a pack of scumbag, maggot skinheads, who decided to jump me on my way home from school. I was around 14 and they were 18 years plus. You know the types – all on the dole (benefits), don't want to work, just hanging around sniffing glue.

This event happened after I had left my best friend Lisa Diles' house late, so instead of getting into trouble at home – which didn't take much – I decided to take the short cut home down the folly, through the local council estate to where my road was. The only catch – it was where the skinheads hung out. Even though I knew better not to go down there, it was that or get a severe beating from my dad.

As I approached that danger zone area, my heart sank, because they were inevitably there and as soon as they saw me, they shouted out 'Paki' then began chasing me, then cornered me and attacked me, kicking and punching me indiscriminately. In all honesty I was already used to that sort of assault and, by now, the old adrenaline was pumping.

Anyhow, even though I was completely outnumbered, I somehow managed to grab one of them amongst the brawl and slammed him against the brick wall of the garages, using all my weight to pin him with my forearm. I crushed his face and head as hard as I could, grinding the skin on his face against that rubble as he screamed in agony.

I then consequently got jumped from behind by his scummy mate. All I remember is this arm pulling me back around my neck and, as he did so, he stuck a fair-sized blade downwards into the fleshy part of my tummy.

At first, I thought it was a punch. I only realised it wasn't when I felt this rather warm syrupy liquid soaking through my school uniform skirt and running down my stomach to the top of my leg. That's when I also started to feel a bit wonky as the realisation of what had just happened hit me.

Those little pricks ran off laughing and left me there, holding onto my bleeding stomach.

But I somehow managed to hobble myself to the door of my house and banged as hard as I could, shouting, "Open the door!"

My dad opened the door, saw the blood and said, "What the fucking hell is going on, mites." To which I responded, "Dad, I've been stabbed."

"Crumbs, mites," he said – *mites* being *mate* with a heavy accent.

Gasping for breath as the pain escalated, I said, "It was skinheads. They jumped me." And ever the opportunist, I added, "That's why I'm late."

My father, being a charge nurse, attended to my wound. He began by gently cutting my skirt, which by now was congealed with blood. He then began cleaning the wound and proceeded to stitch it with the bits from his first aid kit.

After he finished, he said, "You're lucky, mites, your fat gut saved you. If you weren't so fat it might have been worse, mites."

Thanks, dad! But I guess there is some truth in that as my weight was my armour.

Fighting was unfortunately very normal back then. Whilst I have always been one to fight back and defend myself, some of my fellow people of colour found it difficult to defend themselves. I guess it is that age old principle of *fight, flight or freeze.*

Depending on your personality and situation, which one would you do?

None of those reactions are good or bad – they just are. However, my personality dictates that even if I am frightened, my response is to *fight*! Besides, I am accustomed to violence as it has been in my family since the day I was born, so to me it is my *normal.*

From single figures in age, I watched my father frequently pummel my mother. Until one day, she left him – but in doing so she also left us behind. That being me and my only sibling, a brother called Farhad – leaving us to be his punch bag, with my father turning most of his rage onto me, both physically and mentally.

This started at the age of 9 years old, where I was completely defenceless, right up until I was 19. It was over ten years of hell where, during that time, I was almost always covered in bruises.

But growing up in such a household made me extremely tough and resilient. Within the home I was unable to retaliate, so I had to learn how to cope with the violence. But when I was outside the home, I wasn't defenceless, nor did I fear the consequences of my actions. So when I fought back, I had no limit as to what I would do. I followed this principle because that is what my father did – he had no limit, so at the time neither did I.

Besides, no one could ever hit harder than my dad, who was a big 17st man, so when I said those skinheads were kicking and punching me, I wasn't fazed by it – they didn't have that man strength my father had because they were only 18 and they were far weaker than him.

It didn't even hurt when one of them stabbed me – it was only the realisation that I had been stabbed, and the blood seeping through my uniform, that made me feel a bit wonky.

So I grew up pretty fearless, knowing they would get smeared if they came near me. From an early age, people would just leave me alone because I became what is known as *a bit of a nutter* – someone who had no fear and nothing to lose.

Fear – that's another word that is ambiguous, isn't it? There are different types of fear, from the fear of getting hurt, to the fear of making a change in your life. There's the fear of being alone, which may keep you in a loveless – or worse – violent controlling relationship. Fear of death, fear of heights, fear of losing someone, the fear of failure. I mean, the list is endless.

Fear is a word that can truly imprison you.

I know I'm no counsellor but since I was a child, I saw fear for what it was. It's an extremely unpleasant emotion which can be the biggest hindrance in life. But if you can sort your fear out, you can be free of its chains. For fear will control your behaviour and prevent you from being the person that you really want to be. Fear is a predatory illusion, it just sits there, building a picture of a result that is not real.

Let me share with you a bit about that.

As an adult, I developed an irrational fear of spiders. Until one day, a friend of mine came over with her children, on a rainy day during the summer holidays. So, unable to go outside, we decided to go to a local garden centre which had a pet shop inside.

We were looking at the exotic pets when a worker came over and began showing the kids the lizards and snakes etc., which we were all gently handing. Everything was lovely until my girl brought out a some big ol' tarantula. A tarantula, you know.

Mate, my heart started racing as this irrational fear overcame me and consumed my whole being and I thought, *Nah, forget that,* so I backed off a little bit.

But not my tiny little 5' foot nothing friend. My friend now starts holding this big hairy, almost as big as her head, tarantula like it was nothing. I ain't gonna lie – I shit myself, mate.

Then the worst thing that could happen, happened. The girl asked me, "Do you want to hold her?"

Her!!!

"Nah you know, I'm ok. You know." Smiling. But in my head, I was like *I'm not touching that fucking huge monster, that thing is so big, it looks like it's going to rob me.*

My mate now – my little mate – starts saying, "Oh look, your mum's scared of a little incy wincy spider."

Little?! It was the size of a dinner plate, mate. Internally I was beside myself – in fact *fear* was an understatement. But I couldn't let my children see I was scared of something because that's not fair. Bestowing your fears on anyone else just is not good, let alone your own children.

So I said to myself, *Right Sarezah, take a deep breath, of course you're not scared of it.* As I proceeded to hold out my hand, albeit trembling, I painfully watched the assistant transferring that massive spider from her hand onto mine. Mate, in that moment my mouth was dry and everything as that thing approached me, my eyes fixated on that gargantuan spider thinking, *Shit, she's massive, what if she bites me?*

As she touched my hand I winced slightly as I watched her slowly and gently climb into my palm, and within a few moments all those irrational thoughts I had melted away as I realised how bloody beautiful and elegant she was. Soon after, I found myself getting more comfortable with her and, as I did, so did she with me.

I watched her as she delicately walked over my hand and I said to the assistant, "Oh she feels so light."

This little spider that I thought would be all creepy crawly was the complete opposite – she was delicate, graceful and elegant. She danced around my hands and explored up my arm before settling back in my palm.

To be honest with you, I was falling in love. I think she was, too. Even the assistant said, "She must like you, she completely settled on you, look she's spinning a web on your hand, you must be warm."

I was completely mesmerised by her. So much so that I bought her. I know it's bad because they should be in their own environment, not kept as an exotic pet. But she was already here, and I did give her the best I could and looked after her. I named her Sophia after Sophia Loren because she was as beautiful as her. She lived for nine and a half years. When she passed away, just like all my other pets, I cried for THE friend that I had lost.

See, that's the trouble with perceptions, isn't it? We over think, don't we? I know I have at times. Let me give you a fine example of that.

One day, some years after I had reached my weight management goals, I decided to go shopping on my own to a city in Essex called Chelmsford.

And for some reason I decided to dress in some sort of SWAT/ military police style outfit, which was all black with big black menacing boots and a black bomber jacket, and off I went thinking I looked nice. But I guess I did look like a bouncer – which wasn't particularly unusual for me, seeing in most of my late teens to late twenties, I worked as a doorman in clubs (more about that later).

So there I was, casually looking around the shopping centre when I was suddenly struck by hunger. Now I'm one of those hangry people, so it's best to get food swiftly. So off I went to one of my favourite shops in the whole world – Marks and Spencer – to get some grub.

Now as it wasn't my local M&S; I had to meander around before I found something edible, that wasn't too calorific. Once I found something suitable to eat, off I went towards the pay as you go tills.

Oh lovely, I thought, walking up to someone finishing up at the till, and said to him, "Have you finished here, mate? I'll have your till."

He looked at me – quite questionably, might I add – before saying "Errrr sure," and proceeded to walk off laughing.

Strange, I thought, *What's so funny*? Shaking it off, I then began scanning my items. But within a few moments, I noticed an elderly female member of the M&S workforce watching me, somewhat intently! It looked like she wanted to say something but didn't, so after a few more uncomfortable moments of making eye contact with her, it then dawned on me that perhaps it was because I had headphones in, so I took one out.

But she still didn't say anything, she just continued to dither around, staring at me somewhat hesitantly. Then it dawned on me as to why and in my head, I thought, *Oh here we go.* She thinks *'cos I'm 'BLACK I'm gonna nick stuff.* Mate, that's when I began scanning each food item with immense exaggeration, then slamming them into the carrier bag – to show I was scanning and putting them in the bag and not my pocket –snarling as I did so!

Well that's when it got worse! Listen, yeah, even though that dusty old lady could see I was scanning and putting those items in the bag, she went and got security you know, not just one, but two security guards! Mate, I was incensed – and I must have looked it, because her and the two security guards all stood sheepishly looking at me, at a far more rabid snarl! A snarl that said, *go on say something. Say something and see what is gonna happen!*

Of course no one said anything, but I continued to stare at them, with me and my internal conversation saying, *Bloody racists. Thinking I'm going to steal some chicken bites, like all black people steal, for God's sake!*

I proceeded to take my bank card out, eyes and snarl penetrating them, whilst somewhat theatrically scanning my card to show all and sundry that I am paying for the goods and not stealing them like they think I am, then ripping off the receipt, and holding it up directly at them, as they stood, like frozen statues.

I shook my head then picked up my bag, putting the receipt in it along with my paid for goods. However, as I looked up, something caught my eye.

It was a lady – a black lady at that – with a beautiful bunch of yellow roses in one hand and a basket in the other, and behind her stood another person, with a basket full of groceries and behind them, another!

In fact, there was a large number of people standing behind one another, all in an orderly queue – all waiting to use the self-service checkout tills. All looking at me disapprovingly.

Mate, my mouth went dry, and my eyes widened as I continued to scan the somewhat annoyed faces of those people standing there watching, as realisation hit me as to what I had done, accompanied by that warm rush of embarrassment, that I jumped the orderly queue. *For goodness' sake!*

Now, from start to finish, the problem here was pure perception.

Firstly, the bloke at the till. His thoughts were, *"Well, she doesn't care, she just pushed in and jumped the queue,"* turning back laughing as he walked away.

Followed by the mature lady worker who just wanted to say, *"Excuse me dear, there is a queue behind you."*

Now, if she had said that, I would have realised my mistake and apologised, saying something along the lines of, *"Oh silly me,"* (Chortle, chortle, trying to hide my embarrassment behind humour). *"I didn't realise the queue was there – so sorry, it's not my usual M&S – sorry, sorry,"* holding up my hands, acknowledging my mistake.

But oh no, that didn't happen because of my own personal perception – where I thought that

dusty old woman must think I'm a thief, because I'm black.

Because *all black people steal* in the eyes of white people – especially the older ones! Which of course was only exacerbated by the fact she went and got security.

Not because she thought I was stealing, but because she thought, *"F… this. I'm too old to be dealing with Miss Jump-the-Queue Angry over there – security can deal with this."*

Then security comes over, wanting to say the same thing, *"Excuse me love, but there is a queue behind you."*

But of course, on arrival, they were greeted by Godzilla – resulting in neither one of the security guards wanting to get involved because of *their* perception of me … A stocky-looking, pissed-off, more-than-likely security guard herself (*Lord knows, she looks like a security guard*), who is probably on her lunch break having, by the looks of it, a bloody bad day – so they thought, *This is not worth it. Just let her pay and go.*

Meanwhile, the black woman in the queue behind me, holding the beautiful bunch of yellow flowers, had that disappointed and scathing look on her face that said, *"See, it's a blooming small minority of black people that give the rest of us a bad name. These 'road man' ghetto lot are just good for nothing."*

As she shook her head with the same disappointed look a parent would give a child, they all watched me scurrying off with my shopping, whilst putting up my hands repeatedly saying, *"Sorry, sorry, I didn't realise there was a queue."*

Honestly, you couldn't make it up – what a scenario, and the shame of it all. Flipping perceptions! It could have easily been resolved!

Anyway, I digress, so back to the reality of my situation. At 44 years old, my weight had reached a colossal 32st and 2lbs. My eating was out of control. I knew I had to make a change but was at a loss as to where to start, I was extremely hesitant to go on yet another diet which, historically, had always led to failure. So I then decided to take good look at the philosophy behind the word *diet*.

CHAPTER 5

Diets and Retrospection

I came to realise one of the problems with the word *diet* is that there are certain expectations we have with regards to its meaning. The word *diet* offers us what we want to hear – and that is *success*!

But modern-day diets tend to follow trends that target an audience that is looking for a short-term fix, like the *'Lose 7lbs in 7 days diet,'* or the *'All you can eat on a Wednesday diet,'* or the *'Don't look left on a Thursday diet,'* or the *'Lose 10lbs in a fortnight diet.'* (Yes, I am being flippant!).

Now, diets like this sound promising to an audience who especially don't have much to lose.

These quick fix type diets operate in a way that focuses on drastically cutting carbohydrate and calories from your daily intake.

Therefore, when you revert to a normal way of eating, the 7lbs ends up straight back on – and quite often, even more. This focus is on the restriction of certain food types and drastically cutting down the amount of food to where it is too restrictive and ends up being unsustainable. So I realised I had to find something that was achievable.

And I did, finally, at the age of 44 years old, after much past failure, together with plenty of independent fact-finding research along with experimentation, find the perfect solution: *calorie deficit*, together with *exercise,* which slowly, slowly, wins the game.

Failure is another word that is often viewed quite negatively. Remember earlier when I used failure as a learning curve, and found what worked and what didn't work for me? See, in the end my countless failures led to my eventual success. But failing wasn't the difficult part for me.

What was difficult was finding out the root causes that led to obesity – something that unravelled during my journey when I revisited my childhood. Which all began when I received some advice that helped put things into perspective from one of my favourite doctors of all time, Dr Huw Morgan-Davies – a philosophy that to date I still adhere to.

During one of many appointments, Dr Morgan-Davies exclaimed rather passionately, "LOOK, Sherrrezzzah'. (Incidentally, that's not how you pronounce my name, I'm afraid I have one of those names that is quite difficult to pronounce. The easiest way to say my name is *Sir Razor*). "It's not rocket science – eat less and move more!"

Now that statement stuck in my head, as never a truer word has ever been said! That is when the Doctor advised me to book in for a health check and have a chat with the lovely new nurse Jan, who could advise me further. Off I went to see the nurse, and, to my delight, he was right.

Jan is an absolutely beautiful person inside and out, and is one amazing, intelligent lady.

I clearly remember the day I met her, I was sitting in the waiting room when she called out my name in a thick Yorkshire accent, "Mrs. Lakeeeeeeee."

Well, there stood before me this saucy looking nurse, with long blond curly hair, and the most charming of smiles in little wedge shoes. I was like, *"Well hellllllooooo, there,"* back! Flashing my dimple cheek smile at her and raising my eyebrows, with a little giggle, she ushered me into her room.

From that day on we were both caught – hook, line and sinker. In fact we have been really good friends over the past 25 years, we've been through a lot together, as you will see as we travel through the chapters. Jan has always been a fantastic and supportive friend. And is most definitely one of my very few *ride or die* girls.

During that appointment she asked me a few questions about my health and checked my vitals – blood pressure etc; thankfully they were all normal. We spoke a bit about what I ate. And she said you don't really eat unhealthily; you just might have to watch your portions. Which, of course, wasn't rocket science. Remember – *eat less*.

But even though in my eyes I was eating less, in reality, with no real accountability of what was going in, I saw little to no progress. It was this constant yo-yo style of dieting. Eat less, lose a bit, plateau, cave in. Put even more weight on, blah, blah, blah! In fact it wasn't until Dr Goel said I was a *ticking time bomb* that I began noting and accounting for all my eating habits.

After a few weeks I came to the realisation that I had a major issue with portion control. A clear pattern emerged, where I'd get up and not eat until late morning; by then I would be starving, so I would proceed to eat anything and everything till I was full. And when I say *full*, I mean to the brim – up to my oesophagus.

So, on paper, a typical day usually started with no food until I reached a point of extreme hunger. Then I would go on a rampage – firstly by banging in four pieces of toast in the toaster, and whilst I was waiting for that to cook, I would shovel in some crisps, just to satisfy the gnawing feeling of hunger.

Once the slices of toast popped up, they would be slathered in butter and lashings of peanut butter, or swirling with marmite – followed by something sweet, usually some form of chocolate, as biscuits weren't really my thing – or whatever else there was available to eat.

I would literally eat until I couldn't eat any more. Then I would be buzzing from all the carbs and sugar I'd just rammed into my system.

Then after a few hours – or less – I would crash and hit rock bottom to the point where I was craving something carby and sugary because my energy was so low. So I'd gorge again as much as possible, until my stomach was bursting.

It was like I was doing my own type of intermittent fasting – but without any control of the amount I ate. I was eating till I was full, repeating this over and over again, day after day, week after week, month after month, year after year.

So why did I do this? It didn't seem *not normal* to eat like this. Was there a root cause? I have eaten like this since I can remember. So I asked myself a few questions like:

Do I eat because I am hungry? Or because I'm bored? Are there any triggering factors that lead me to eat until I am full? Am I filling some sort of void and emptiness?

I didn't even know how to answers to those questions because in my eyes I'm just doing the same thing since I was a child. I knew I needed a fresh pair of eyes who could guide me through the unknown, so I turned to my dear friend Jan, who was now a senior nurse practitioner, which included a senior role in the safeguarding department.

This is the time I began to realise that some of my eating habits stemmed from my somewhat traumatic childhood. This all came about one day when I recalled telling Jan about a birthday event I experienced as a schoolgirl.

My stepmother had asked me to invite some of my friends to add to the already invited family members for my upcoming birthday. Thinking she was showing me some kindness – which was rare – I agreed. So a couple of friends arrived along with the relatives on party day. Of course, when people visited, she put on a show of being a nice person. Obviously, when no one was around, she was nothing short of vile.

Anyway, to cut a long story short, it was time to cut the cake. Now the birthday cake is a big tradition for our families. The cake is an indication of how much you are loved so it is always a grand affair – which she knew. I guess that is why she went to the trouble of hiding the cake until it was time for the big reveal.

I was very excited, and thought to myself, *Will it be fresh cream, with fresh fruits, or maybe there will be big fat juicy strawberries on it, my favourite.*

Soon after, I was sent out of the room whilst my family and friends gathered around the cake at the table. I heard a few giggles along with a couple of shhhh's so I thought *Oooh, it must be really nice.* I stood patiently waiting for them to light the candles on the cake and waited for my signal to come in.

Off went all the lights, as the chorus of *'Happy birthday to you,'* started. I walked into the dark room guided by the glimmer of those lit candles, as they all continued to sing, *'Happy birthday, dear Sarezah. Happy birthday to youuuuuuuuu.'* I blew out the candles and the lights came on.

Whilst I closed my eyes trying to adjust to the bright light, I heard a couple of the guests laughing, one who's cackle drowned out everyone else's – that was the stepmother thing. At first, I was confused as to why there was this laughter, thinking I was missing something, then I saw my birthday cake, and my heart sank.

It was a Miss Piggy cake. For those of you who don't know, she was a character out of *The Muppets* and was known for being fat. I mean, on reflection, she was quite gorgeous really – glamorous, voluptuous, sassy and strong. To be honest, she was the original boss lady, so I can't really see how that is insulting, but as I was not an adult, I was a young teen, I didn't see that at the time. What I saw and felt was the humiliation of the sentiment behind it, because my stepmother likened me to Miss Piggy to shame me. See, whilst she was laughing, she was pointing at me and then the cake.

Screaming in her demonic voice, "Look it's you, Shezahhhhhhh," (her hideous pronunciation of my name). "A fat piggy. That's what you are – a fat pig, aren't you? Fat pig Shezahhhh. Miss Piggy. Hahahahahahah," she continued like that to the point where the guests began to feel embarrassed by her exaggerated prolonged laugh, whilst I just stood there looking down, red hot with humiliation, sadness and rage at the injustice of her actions.

But I couldn't do anything about it – I just had to suck it up and look within to find my own source of comfort. But unfortunately, from that day on, birthday cakes were never the same. This is also when Jan became quite emotional and said it out aloud, "Sarezah, that is child abuse," as the stories of my childhood continued to unravel, as did my understanding of child abuse – both mentally and physically – and where my lack of portion control manifested.

I buried and dealt with my childhood trauma a long time ago, knowing from the day I left that house I would no longer have to live like that. Besides, in my mind, once I had left the place that was harming me, why would I want to carry on and continue damaging and hurting myself, so I was never abusive to myself in any way. I never said bad things to myself or put myself down, nor did I ever believe what they called me was the truth.

The only benefit of revisiting those times helped me to understand my eating patterns. And instead of wasting my energy trying to fathom why they treated me like that, I already knew.

They were cruel, both my father and my stepmother were vile and malicious. They were drunken abusers, who enjoyed bullying those seemingly weaker than themselves. Most of the time they were either blind drunk or hung over. So I spent most of my childhood avoiding them – but they never let up and I became their target for everything that was wrong in their lives, caused by their alcohol addiction.

The worst of it started from when I was around 11 years old. They found satisfaction in tormenting and persecuting me – especially after a drink or nine.

At first it was just name calling and criticising me for being inadequate at something I was supposed to do. Then there was the physical abuse, under the guise of disciplining and correcting my so-called bad behaviour which, as I got older, inevitably turned to punches and extreme violence.

As time passed, things progressed from physical and verbal abuse to mental abuse. By the time I hit adolescence, they just wanted to break my spirit in any way possible so they would take away any form of enjoyment – from me listening to music to wearing fashionable clothing, anything that made me happy.

And by my early teens they began drastically restricting my food as, evidently, I was too fat and bringing shame on them and needed to lose weight, so I wasn't allowed to eat. I was forbidden to eat breakfast or take sandwiches to school. I was only allowed to eat one meal a day at night – or when they said I could.

It was part of their alcohol-fuelled narcissistic behaviour of control and degradation – to take something away from someone to punish them for the enjoyment they got from it. Food being the worst thing they could take from me because it was a true source of love for me.

At times I would end up so hungry that I wanted to cry from the aching and gnawing from the pit of my stomach. That's when I started to steal food at home – wherever and whenever I could. I would gorge on anything and everything I could get my hands on. Obviously, this created enormous problems, not just at the time but later in my life, as you will see when we travel through the chapters.

This is also the time when I began to self-harm. Many times I would slice my skin with a razor blade or scratch my skin with a fingernail till the skin scraped off (in fact, in our days it was called a *chicken scratch* and was a bit of trendy thing to do as kids).

But for me, it was a way of relieving the internal pain of not being able to get away from this hell and I could say I fell off my bike or something and scraped my skin off!

See, when you are only 13 or 14 years old and not permitted to do anything – from eating to wearing make-up, to talking to girls let alone boys, to not being allowed to go out – life felt like hell, let alone prison! All I was able to do was to go from home to school, back home, cook clean, scrub and repeat.

Unlike most kids, I hated weekends and holidays – because at least at school I was away from them. My father, whether drunk or sober, would beat me senseless to correct me! Usually for things like not cooking the food the way he wanted, or washing the clothes by hands properly, or there was something wrong with the way I stood, or I did my hair differently and looked like a tart.

And worse, by the time I was 14 – until the day I left home – he'd say things like, *"You are walking different – have you had sex with a boy, you whore bitch! I will smash you up you whore!"*

Or even worse than that, *"I will take you to the doctors to see what you have been doing."*

Do you know – I didn't even know what he was referring to until I was older, that he meant my 'hymen' which is a thin piece of tissue located at the opening of the vagina and can be stretched open the first time you have sex – which might cause some bleeding and discomfort – but it can also break during sports or riding a bike or even by using a tampon, which of course I was forbidden to use (sorry to be so graphic)!

Fundamentally, my father just wanted to break my spirit in any way he could. His favourite way of achieving that was to beat me until I cried – which, of course, when I was younger I did.

But over the years and by the time I got to around 14, I had become so hardened to it all. I had a ton load of defiance, which wasn't ideal because he could have killed me really, but I just wouldn't – and couldn't – cry. My soul and body, along with my mentality, would not let me.

I would just look straight at him with pure hatred. Which fuelled his rage even more. But my thought process was, *"Well, if I'm going to get a beating, it may as well be for a reason,"* so I stood my ground and used my courage to get through it. I was defiant to the end, even though I knew what would happen. As a result, many times I was left black and blue from the tirade of kicks and punches of a grown 17st man.

Whilst it was relentless, on rare occasions outside of school times – like weekends or holidays – I was allowed to go and see my best friend Lisa who I met when I was five years old; think *Pepsi and Shirley*, that's us! Or I got to take a neighbour's dog for a walk, a German shepherd called Prince. Plus, when I could, I would sneak out when they were out or at work.

I also used to listen to music in my room – and music was (and still is) my life (along with food, of course!). Which my stepmother knew and would tell my dad I was becoming *obsessed* with certain bands, especially bands with all men!!!

Knowing I was forbidden to speak to men, she said to my father that this might *encourage me to have a boyfriend.* She knew this was another way of taking away anything she saw me enjoy! Because, in the end, he took away my music. So I had to learn to hide the music I liked. Unlike normal girls I didn't have posters of men or pop stars. (In fact the only poster I ever did have when I was older, and it was of *Rocky*! One of my favourite films to date!)

It didn't stop there either, it spread to *anything* I enjoyed. I wasn't allowed to laugh or have any type of fun. One instance of this was with my beloved Aunty Rashida. When we used to visit her in Paris, I would have to help her in the kitchen – which, of course, I loved.

But if we were heard laughing or joking around, my stepmother would tell my father who would remove me immediately and make me sit down. Quite often my Aunty Rashida would stand up for me, saying things like it was her fault I laughed, or she would ask me to come back in as she needed more help in the kitchen. To which my father would either say *"No"* or grit his teeth and show me a fist and say, *"You better shut it, girl – or when we get back home, you'll get it."*

They truly couldn't bear me being happy. To make things worse – if that was even possible – the *step thing* was immensely jealous of my beauty and my personality, especially as I got older, so I was forced to shut up around people, and I wasn't allowed to wear anything that was remotely nice, as she would make me wear the ugliest smock style of clothing that hid every curve, saying I was *too fat* to fit into anything nice.

She oppressed my beauty and expression any way she could. But it never worked. See, to me, beauty isn't an item of clothing or a look. Beauty is you – and what you exude from your inner self.

But in order to survive, I learnt how to hide the things I loved, otherwise it would get taken away. Which seeped into my adulthood – until I had my children, because I could never conceal the love I had for them.

The only thing I couldn't hide as a child was the love and happiness I felt when I ate. The delight shone through my eyes and lightened my aura – which she hated. So, like I said, they took it away. So I ended up getting food where I could. Either my friends at school would share their lunch with me, or I would use my bus fare money to buy food seeing that I learned to befriend the bus drivers, just by being nice and polite – which often meant I got to ride for free. (I tell you, politeness and kindness can definitely go a long way).

I am ashamed to say at times – when I was desperate for something to eat – I used to steal a bit of money out of my dad's pocket. Whilst I never stole anywhere else, as my opinion of stealing is pretty low, when you are driven by hunger, you will do almost whatever you can.

Besides, I never took much, I would usually only take small change – 5p's and 10p's. Just what I needed to get by. Besides he was too much of a drunk to notice small change going but big notes would have been.

I would go to the dinner hall and ask what I could get for like 10p or 15p. One of the regular dinner ladies, Elaine, took a shine to me. She also had a son at the school – he was nice too.

Bless her, she used to really look after me and give me free food many times. Maybe she could see – behind the happy exterior – the sadness in my eyes. Little does she know how many times her kindness got me though the days.

But by the time I was 13-14 years old, having the fear of not knowing where I would get food from led me to developing a terrible eating habit – *binge eating*. Any time I was alone, I would eat what I could. In one sitting, I could eat up to eight slices of toast. Or rummage around the cupboard to find anything I could that was fairly unnoticeable to eat – be it a cold tin of mushy peas, sweetcorn, beans or even rice pudding. I would gorge on all I could, until I was full to the brim.

Unbeknownst to me, there were repercussions to eating this way. As it all intensified, so did the consequences – resulting in my body being thrown into *starvation mode*. My body ended up reducing calories out, to restore energy balance, and stopped me from actually losing weight.

It's almost like my body thought I was hibernating – having some sort of fear that it won't get the next meal – so subsequently held onto what it could as long as it could, reserving it as a sort of fat storage.

This is where I understood that this type of eating pattern and behaviour, where I had eaten for survival – seeped into my adult life. It had become so normal to starve for long periods then eat masses of food in one sitting that I hadn't really seen this as an issue.

At the time, no one really knew I was doing this – so there was no way of knowing what I was doing was right or wrong.

CHAPTER 6

Strength

I'd just turned 19 when I started my first ever paid job. It was with British Rail as a clerical officer. This is also the first time I had any type of independence, as well as freedom. It was absolutely wonderful! But even then, my father tried to take that away from me – by demanding that I put all my wages into his account, in an attempt to continue to abuse and control me.

But I refused – point blank – to his face. That's when he used his usual method of response and that was violence, so he lunged towards me, raising and pointing a clenched fist inches away from my face, and said, "You will, girl, or I will sort you out, you bastard. Or I will make you lose your job by ringing in and making false complaints about you!"

I mean, I was stunned! And I mean *stunned*. You would actually go to those lengths to get me the sack because 1, I wouldn't give you all my wages and 2, which is the biggest part of it – I was happy, and much more than that, I was liberated!

And that made me snap!

So instead of cowering away to protect myself from his punches, I felt my face change and my eyebrows narrow as I looked straight at him into his soul and snarled, "Go on then, hit me!"

That stopped him straight in his tracks, because he knew what would happen, there is only so much a person can take before they snap!

So, he didn't come near me. I stood there shaking my head and said, "Do you know the difference between you and me, I don't hit women! See, unlike you, I'm not weak, I only defend myself against those who are attacking me. You're a bully who only beats those that are no challenge to you," because not once in my lifetime had I ever seen him hit a man.

Then I walked away – and that was that. The end of a man who controlled my life for so long – but who was now powerless.

Whilst laying bare my upbringing hasn't been – and isn't – particularly easy for me, I am doing it with the hope that by being open about it, others in my position who may have been born into certain cultures, or any other circumstances, understand this is not acceptable.

Don't allow someone to treat you in a way that is in any shape or form abusive or coercive – whoever it may be. Don't ever be embarrassed or ashamed about what you've gone through. It's not your fault; you didn't do anything to make them like that. Sometimes bad people in life just happen to be your parent or partner or brother – or whoever!

What I never did was punish myself for what they did to me. Or take over where they left off, as the abuser. Whatever I went through, I never mentally turned against myself. It never made sense to me. Why would I want to continue hurting myself because of what they did to me? I used what I could to make myself stronger. I used growing up in that environment to help me understand some of the good and bad things about myself – to change what I could and let go of what I should.

One of those was learning how to control my anger, because I would often react aggressively. Instead of diving in headfirst – or even with fists – I learnt to assess the situation and understand how I needed to defend myself, depending on the circumstances.

Not like when I was younger. If anyone confronted me, they would encounter my wrath, but unlike my father, I had rules and limitations. Like I said earlier, I would never fight girls or women but, if need be, I would restrain them (which, at times, I had to during my days as a doorman).

By my early 20's, I managed to escape that house – albeit through a marriage. But it was someone I met and chose for myself, despite my father trying to marry me off when I was 16; thankfully being fat and common put a stop to that one.

However, this is when the issue with food got worse. See, there was no-one controlling what I could eat or how much food I could have. The love of food was suddenly freely available to me – and boy, did I love hard!!!

After all, food is my first love, and that had developed from as young as I can recall – probably around 2-3 years old. This is when I was fed, fed and fed! In fact my family on my mother's side would offer me food as a reward, because pre divorce, my family expressed their love to us this way.

It was my aunties that would entice me with food, by warmly addressing me as *"Sarezah darling."*

You know, I was called that for such a long time that I genuinely believed that was my actual name. I was absolutely horrified and disappointed when I realised my name was just *Sarezah!*

Back then, if a sentence began with *"Sarezah darling"* it usually meant some food was going to be offered. However, there was a tiny glitch! "Sarezah darling, do you want some cake?" "Yes, of course I do!" "Ok then – dance!"

That is when I unashamedly danced for cake, whilst all the relatives cheered me on, watching me rolling my big chunky hips, mimicking the adults when they put their Mauritian homeland music on – called Sega – or to songs like *Jonny Reggae*, *Peggy Sue*, or other songs of that era.

It was all for a big, fat, juicy piece of cake, or anything else that was on offer – be it a samosa, a bit of Mauritian onion bhajia or a fried bread bhajia, known to us as *du pain frier* or any other delicious Mauritian *gajaks* (street food snacks).

Now remember – before anyone starts getting all judgmental – this was the early 70's. No one cared about being fat as much as they did about seeing a child happy and laughing. Eating in my culture – and most cultures – was considered healthy. That was what was important back in those days – a healthy and happy child. With no hang ups about food.

To be honest, even though there were many hardships, our lives were a lot simpler and easier – unlike today, when there are so many pressures on everyone to act and look in a certain way, no matter your age.

Luckily for me I grew up to understand – and learnt by myself – that beauty is beauty, and beauty comes in many different shapes and sizes.

Beauty exists all around – in many different things and in many different ways. Beauty is not what society makes you believe what beauty should be – or what it should not be.

By the way – contrary to popular belief – please understand that I most certainly did not lose weight for aesthetic reasons. Not at all. I lost weight to save my life, as my doctor said to me, *"You are like a ticking time bomb!"*

I thought I was all right – even when I was at my biggest.

Besides, food was celebrated in the family. It was a reminder of being back home, as the Mauritians came from a Commonwealth country. They were invited to Great Britain, mostly to work in the NHS. So cooking was the main event of whatever occasion.

And from the age of about five – when I could pick up a knife – I started to help cook, firstly by doing the basics such as peeling, chopping and slicing. Then I progressed to cooking with none other than my father, who was an exceptional cook. He could make a meal out of absolutely anything.

In all honesty, my father, should have been a chef. However, it was not to be. But clearly cooking is in the blood, as my middle son Khaliq – a classically trained chef – is now a Michelin Star chef (proud mummy moment). I did not train as a chef, although my son says you learn most of your cooking skills on the job. I learnt to cook from experience, from my father and my grandmother – and then developed my skills as I got older. Then I created my own range of recipes under the name of *Mama Lake* so I could still enjoy healthier versions of my beloved food.

So whilst I learnt the basics of how to cook from my father, the one person who taught me how to understand and develop flavours was my *Nanima* – my grandmother on my mother's side.

Mate, she is the scariest person I know; she was the matriarch of the entire family. She commanded total respect from everyone. She was a force to be reckoned with, as I found out when I went to Mauritius in the summer of '77 – where another relationship bloomed with one of my closest blood relatives and developed into what it is today, pure love for my darling little cousin, Uzma.

We are so polar opposites, chalk and cheese. If we were Disney characters she would be Pocahontas. She is tall and slender; I would be Moana, short and chunky. She is a top scientist; I'm just a big mouth and blagger. My cousin Uzma excelled in her education and through those years we were able to meet in London where I worked, just outside Liverpool Street, when she was studying. We have always had a wonderful relationship and a strong bond. (It's funny, I've always looked out for her and looked after her, but that role changed in February 2021, when she became the one who looked after me).

It was during that visit to Mauritius '77, that my Nani taught me how to source the best ingredients to use. Whilst the island of Mauritius is small, it's a melting pot of many cultures that have all shared with one another their secrets of taste and recipes, which over time grew into what Mauritian food is now.

My Nanima, like my father, gave me the small jobs to do – like peeling potatoes and onions etc. But the worst job ever was having to sift through rice! Oh my days, it was long and boring. I had to sit in the morning – albeit under the sunshine and sweet filled air – on the back step of her house, picking out the grit and stones, not once but two to three times from one end of a massive round metal tray to the other. With the blooming beady eyes of my *Nani* watching from time to time to see if I'm doing it right.

Thankfully I soon progressed from the boring jobs to the most prestigious job of them all, collecting the right spices, then grinding them on a stone *roche*, to air the masala. That was a pressured job, goodness me, but I did get it right most of the time – out of fear, if nothing else.

The holiday was rather mixed in terms of enjoyment. My mother basically left us with our grandparents, with the odd few days out – most of which I have tried to blot out. But the last pleasant memory I had of that visit was an event organised by my grandfather, just before we flew back to England after a very long extended holiday. It was a whole day event that spread into the early hours of the evening. Food had been prepared by the local community members for us to enjoy.

That evening, after a full day of eating, the adults gathered around talking. I remember feeling a little sad that we were leaving.

Not because of the family – because I truly saw a very dark side to all my mother's side during that somewhat traumatic trip – but I had become very accustomed to the Mauritian simple lifestyle.

After all, I'd been there for almost three months, speaking mostly Creole, the Mauritian native language. Hence why I am fluent in Creole, to the point I had almost forgotten how to speak English and had to relearn when I got back home.

Anyway, that warm evening, I found a quiet place and sat alone. I remember the coolness of that wooden step, as I sat watching the insects buzzing around the lights, listening to the faint sound of the hustle and bustle of the gathering, whilst the chorus of crickets and grasshoppers sang for us.

I watched – for what was to be one of the last times – the wonderful sunset on this beautiful island. As the last red strips of the sun disappeared into the darkness of the night and the once warm air turned into a cool breeze onto my little cheeks I looked up in the sky, watching the beautiful evening draw nearer to nighttime. The silhouettes of the people at the gathering were shimmering in the background, under the makeshift light and candles, with sweet aromatic smells filling the air.

I chose that moment as I whispered a goodbye to Mauritius, knowing in a few days we would start our long journey back home after that extremely long holiday. But little did I know when we returned the end of that summer, my parents were to go through a very ugly divorce.

The problems started soon after arriving back home. There was a marked difference in my parent's relationship, and within a few months my mother left the house – in the most traumatising manner, which involved lots of screaming, fighting and a rather large police presence.

The most vivid memory I have is my mum going through the house, taking her jewellery, her pots and pans, ornaments, clothes etc. In fact, everything she wanted to take – except for us. The last thing I saw was her being escorted by the police to her car, where most of her family were gathered.

And as she did, she walked straight past me without a glance –

nor did she look back. She just looked ahead and never looked back again and that changed our relationship for ever, in fact after that I saw my mother only on a very few occasions. It was most definitely the end of our family – and the beginning of what was to become my hell.

Like I said earlier, home life was terrible growing up. And to top it all, outside the home, there was a constant barrage of racism. Which in some respects I didn't really mind, because I wasn't defenceless. See, anyone that opened their mouths and shouted out *paki* or *nigger*, I would be like, "Oi. Come over here and say that" then I'd be like, "Actually I'll come over there." To which, usually, they'd run away!

This violence carried on right throughout my schooling. The beatings got worse the older I got, but my father would never hit my face – in case it bruised – except during the summer holidays where it didn't matter as it was six weeks long and there was ample time to heal. So he would always aim for my body and legs. Occasionally my arms would get bruised, because I used them to cover myself as at times he would smash his fists into the top of my head.

However, one day a teacher – Miss Shepherd – noticed the bruises all over my back just before a Physical Education lesson. After the class, she pulled me over and took me to the headmaster's office. I was surrounded by my deputy headmaster and my form teacher who offered to help me after I initially denied anyone hit me.

But it wasn't that easy back then, I didn't have anyone else to go to. My mother had already refused me when I'd asked to move in with her because I just couldn't take it anymore. She didn't give a reason – but I suspect she didn't want the burden of a teenager, so I would have been placed in care whilst my father – like most bullies and narcissists – had a good way of hiding things as well as twisting and turning it back onto the accuser, like he always did. It was always my fault I got the beatings – or my mother's fault she asked for it. Thank goodness it's not like nowadays with safeguarding.

However, all these experiences have made me mentally and physically stronger and, in turn, made me extremely resilient. All the above – coupled together with the estate I was raised on, (which is ironically called White City, one of the roughest estates in Colchester,

Essex, back in the day) – led me to becoming one pretty tough cookie.

Over the years, after much soul-searching and self-analysis, I came to realise my weight had become part of my protection. My size was almost like my armour – shielding me from those beatings, whether they were in or out of the house.

These experiences also gave me a great sense of distain for injustice. It sickens me when I hear of anyone suffering at the hands of another, be it animals getting hurt or a person. I am also not an advocate for war and, contrary to what some may believe, I don't like violence. I've only defended myself and others – I have never hurt anyone without just cause.

Some of you may not understand that concept and others will, but as we continue this journey over the course of my life, you will see that a life-threatening situation – and even death itself – is not something I am unfamiliar with!

I have even come close to death on a couple of occasions, one being fairly recently when I had to literally fight for my life. Whilst I came close, and I mean close, it wasn't my time, because when it IS your time, there is nothing you can do!

CHAPTER 7

Death

I joined a health club called *Clarice House* in the early 2000's when it first opened its doors, and I have been there ever since. In the beginning, it was a private health club, then it was sold and became part of the Bannatyne Group. I often went with my family after my doctor advised me to go to the pool as it would help take the weight off my sore aching joints as being in the water was not weight bearing.

Even though I had help, it took me hours to get in and out, but it really did help both mentally and physically. In fact, this club and its staff have been there for me throughout it all, and they have most certainly helped me win the countless battles during my weight loss journey.

It's truly home from home for me. It is also where I met another member, Cathie, who became a great friend. She would help me a lot, in many ways. She is also a person who taught me one of the most valuable lessons of all time, *Keep your mouth shut, you won't be thanked for it!* Cathie's quote has even been passed down to my boys.

One day, Cathie and I had a coffee together and were chatting about family. She was aware my mother had passed when I briefly mentioned it in a previous conversation and, believe it or not, I can be a closed book. Besides, I never really spoke to anyone about my mother's death outside of my family and close friends, as it was somewhat traumatic. However, during that conversation, Cathie asked me, "How did your mum die?"

Ordinarily, to avoid going into details or answering any questions relating to her death, I would answer that according to the verdict at her inquest, the primary cause of my mother's death was a heart attack. But, to my surprise, Cathie expanded on the questions by asking if my mother was ill – which I slightly hesitated at, as I hadn't prepared for that type of scenario, so didn't have a ready answer.

So I told her more information than I would, saying yes, my

mother was ill beforehand, as she had diabetes and angina. But, to my astonishment, Cathie continued asking, to the point that I found myself telling her from start to finish how my mother really did die and how, for the second time in my life, she left me, but this time it would be forever.

It all started on the 3rd of November 2003 when I made countless phone calls in an attempt to contact my Mama, who for the second time in several weeks didn't answer. I rang my husband in despair, telling him she hasn't answered the phone again. I asked him if I should go to her house to see if she's ok, because inside me I felt a bit raw, like something just isn't right, I told him rather dramatically. I can feel death, which was true. I felt a part of something inside me had died.

My husband said, "You can't think like that. You don't know what's happened. She is probably asleep like last time when she took those sleeping pills, remember."

Then he continued to say that it was almost school pick-up time, *you will have to go because I am over an hour away, so I won't be home in time to collect the children.*

This reality meant all I could do was desperately continue calling my mum's home number, hoping and praying she would answer, like she did a few weeks back when I couldn't get through and had the same panic, only for her to tell me she took a sleeping tablet and was zonked out. Logically, I thought she must have done the same again, but my intuition and heart were saying something else, and that was DEATH!

Before I knew it, it was early evening, I had to make tea and get the kids sorted, so I wasn't able to drag the kids and hubby with me to go and find out what was happening. And my husband can't cope with the boys alone, so I decided to contact Kader, 'my good friend,' who is actually more than just a friend, he is one of my non-blood brothers. We grew up on the same street, his family have been in my life since I was 11.

The two older boys, Kader and Savash (Kad and Sash), have always been a massive part of my life. I have known them for the best part of 45 years! In fact, I consider them my true brothers, who I can trust implicitly with any situation. These boys would be there for me, as I would them. So with that in mind, I asked Kad, who lived very close to my mother's house, to go and check her place to see if there were any signs she was home, like her car on the drive or if any lights were on.

On arrival at my mother's house, on that cold November evening, after thoroughly checking the house, Kad gave me a call at 7pm saying he knocked hard on the door and called through the letterbox then proceeded to shine a torch through the windows to see if he could see anything, then said, "Sezah," (Sezah being my childhood family nick name), "I'm sorry but her car isn't on the drive and there are no sign of anyone at home, all the lights are off, in fact it's all a bit eerily still."

After that call, I thought of every single possible scenario. But I told myself *be positive* and pushed those thoughts aside, telling myself mum's probably gone to bed early – so let's just wait till the morning. But throughout the night I just felt something terrible in the pit of my stomach gnawing away.

So I just ended up clutching at any ol' straw or other possibilities of why she was not answering any attempt of contact. I even thought perhaps my mum had gone to stay with one of her friends, like Aunty Ruby. I would have called, but didn't have her number, so I rang another Aunty (none of these aunties are related to me, these were my mother's Mauritian friends, but out of respect we called them Aunty). Anyway, she didn't have it either, so I said not to worry as I was trying not to raise too much of an alarm.

Needless to say, that night I couldn't sleep. I lay awake scared to face the truth of what my heart already knew. Eventually fatigue consumed me and I must have dozed off. No sooner had I drifted off I was awoken by a strange feeling of a presence in the room. I sat up and saw something at the end of my bed.

At first, I thought it was one of my children who had come into my room, but it wasn't.

Instead it looked like a shadowy, human shaped figure that was filled with these different coloured circle-shaped orbs floating in and around the body shape.

I thought that it was my eyes trying to focus on the dark ambience of my bedroom. So I closed and rubbed them, and reopened them, thinking I would have better vision, but as soon as I did, I saw the same thing – which hadn't moved. So I did it again, and again, only to see the same thing!

So I woke my husband up from his snoring and whispered, "Oi, what's that over there?" pointing to the end of the bed. "There is something in the room!"

"You what love, who?"

"Look," I whispered so as not to draw attention to the strange presence, "At the end of the bed. There's something in the room."

He too stared directly at it, and by the look of his face he must be seeing what I am seeing.

He remained silent for some time before he said, "Nah, there's nothing there love!" "Yes, there is!" I whispered in despair. "Look!"

"No there isn't, just try to get some sleep, love!"

Then he rolled his back to me and drifted off back to sleep!

It is there! Why can't you see it, I thought! So I just lay awake, peeping from the top of my duvet covers, staring at that apparition. And in my heart, I sensed that was the spirit and presence of my Mama!

I awoke early from what little sleep I did get and together, with my husband, we got the kids ready for school, then made my way to mum's house, stopping to get money out for the locksmith, who evidently wouldn't come without a police presence. Which I get, as I could be any ol' someone spinning a lie, trying to break into the next man's house.

On the way I spoke to my husband about those orb thingies again, telling him I was certain I saw them. To which he replied, "Yes love, you did see them, because I saw them too and I felt something in the room. I didn't say anything because I didn't want you to worry!"

I was gobsmacked and said, "Oh ok, so you saw what I saw and instead of telling me then you thought you'd tell me literally three minutes away from my mum's house. Where I am just about to break into her house with the police and a locksmith, cos I don't have a key! Yeah, nice one mate!"

From that moment my stomach was churning even more, together with my heart pounding to the point I felt somewhat faint with fear and apprehension. My stomach even flipped when we turned into my mum's road. The first thing I saw was that the locksmith and the police officers had already arrived! That's when the reality of the situation hit me. Trembling with angst I introduced myself as they commenced the ordeal of breaking into my mother's home! We exchanged a bit of small talk, but in the back of my mind I was thinking all sorts – including these two are a bit young to be police.

In an attempt to distract me from watching the locksmith painstakingly trying to open the door, the police officer began a bit of a light-hearted conversation – in fact, this young man was really nice. Something I wasn't used to, since my memories and experience of police are not good. Because since the 70's and 80's there were often massive clashes between *them* and *us*. But he, Danny, was definitely the next generation of policing. In fact, whatever I went through that day, he went through too and was nothing short of brilliant.

Nonetheless with all the commotion going on, a few of the nearby neighbours began gathering around asking questions. The officer tried to disperse them, but they just ended walking past slowly as you do when there is any kind of incident.

Sometime after, the aunty who I considered my mother might have gone to stay with, turned up, obviously confirming she wasn't with her, and my stomach churned again as we drew closer to fate. Then my mum's neighbour came out to see what was going on, as she and her family were close to my mum. But even she seemed confused as to what we were doing as she said she saw my mum go to the post-box with a couple of letters and what looked like a card, only a day or so ago.

I paused momentarily and said to her that did make sense because my mum would sometimes send me a birthday card through the post as I would joke with my mummy saying I never get anything other than bills in the post. I went on to say, *and flowers*, as she would buy me some on every birthday, whether it was mine or my children's. Her philosophy being, when it's the children's birthday it's ours too, as we gave birth to them on that day.

Honestly, I could have cried in that moment, wondering will I see my mum on my birthday, which is in three days' time. But that neighbour gave me some hope that maybe she is ok. Hope, it really is the last thing we cling onto, when we are faced with uncertainty.

The locksmith was finding it difficult to get through the locks. So during that time, I tried to rationalise that my Mum most probably is in a glycaemic shock as she may have forgotten her diabetes medication or worse, had too much sugar, which she was prone to doing.

It was always a case of her saying to Hamza, (my husband's converted to Islam name so we could get married, pure English bloke doing the right thing), "Could you be a dear and pop some sugars in my tea and not my sweetener!"

"Yes, of course," good ol' Hamza would say!

Finally we were in and immediately I began manically calling out to my mum. I searched the downstairs whilst the police officer, Danny, sprinted to the second floor and then the third. Everything went totally silent. So I began to scream at him, and said, I'm coming upstairs. That's when he shouted back, in a very shaky voice.

"Sarezah, do not come up here."

"What, why?" I shouted. "What's wrong?"

"Just don't come up here. Please, Sarezah, just stay downstairs. Please… just don't!" his voice quivered. "I've found mum!"

Hearing that drained almost everything out of my body, as fear rushed over my entire being.

My heart was beating so hard, I could feel it in my throat. Seconds later, that young police officer came down the stairs in a very different way to when he went up. His eyes looked vacant, and his face was as white as a sheet as he shuffled his feet, trembling towards me, and lifted his arms landing them on either side of my shoulders, where I felt the weight of his distress drop onto me.

He looked straight into my eyes and took a few breaths before chokingly saying, "I found her."

I looked into his eyes and somehow saw everything he had just seen. It was like a film rolling and transferring what he saw from him to me.

"Mum has gone, Sarezah. Mum has gone." he said.

"What do you mean, 'gone?' Where has she gone? Has she gone out for a walk?" "No, Sarezah. Mum's gone. She's left us!"

Tears began welling up in his eyes as I continued to ask him questions but trying desperately to avoid the inevitable.

"Is she still in her bed, maybe she's sleeping. Is my mummy asleep? She has diabetes, perhaps she's in a coma.

"Danny!" I desperately cried out, shaking him, trying to snap him out of his shell shock. "Is she sleeping?"

"No," he said in a whimpering voice. "Mum has gone, Sarezah, she has passed away." "Did you check her pulse. My mum might be alive."

"I'm sorry, Sarezah. Your mummy has passed away. She, she…" He stammered as he tried to continue in a quiet voice, clearly traumatised. "S s Sarezah, your mum, she has taken her own life."

"WHAT?" I said, with a confused look on my face. "What do you mean, taken her own life?

What are you saying? It doesn't make sense, Danny, what are you talking about, taken her own life. How?"

Somehow that young officer pulled himself together and dealt with the situation at hand, as he continued: "Sarezah, I know it's a lot for you to take in. I found your mummy, it appears that your mum has taken her life as there is a noose tied around her neck."

"WHAT NOOSE, MATE??? What the hell are you bloody talking about, noose?"

"Sarezah, Mum had tied a noose at the top of her four-poster bed with some sort of scarf and and…"

But before he could finish I said, "What bloody scarf are you talking about, I'm going upstairs," then began making my way towards the stairs.

"Sarezah, nooooo, don't, please don't," as he grabbed my arm, and I gave him a look to say get off me, mate!

"Look, Sarezah," he pleaded. "It's horrific. Your mum is in a very bad way. I don't want you to see your mum like that, Sarezah. She has hanged herself from a four-poster bed. As she has slowly descended, the weight of her body has slumped down and crushed her legs. They are now contorted and all bent up on the floor!"

I was in complete shock and disbelief at what I was hearing.

"Sarezah, I have to seal off the area until the coroner comes to determine the cause of death so we can rule out any foul play, so please Sarezah, I beg you don't go up there."

But eventually I did go upstairs, and I did see my Mama like that. He was right, her body had frozen with rigor mortis and was twisted and contorted with a tormented look on her face. Mummy's eyes were also bulging and there were burst capillaries on her face from the pressure of strangulation. I was numb, dazed as I stood there, looking down at her lifeless body.

But somehow my survival mechanism stepped in and took over, because almost immediately I pulled myself together. I didn't even cry, well… not that day. I knew I had to be strong for the coming days so I put all I had in my faith within myself and God, who must have heard me as something came to hold me up, because only God knows how my legs were still standing.

On arrival, the coroner made his investigation and told us his finding. He was somewhat detached and rather blunt when he delivered his initial verdict of, "Well she has killed herself, by the looks of it!"

Killed, I thought. That's a choice of words, as he continued to say there would need to be a full investigation into what actually killed her first, as he couldn't quite determine if asphyxiation was the primary cause of death or if the heart attack killed her first due to her weakened heart. And yes, that man did use appalling words like *killed* and *hung* to the daughter of a suspected suicide victim.

His insensitivity didn't stop there, either. He even had the gall to bestow his own opinion and thoughts that any mother who hanged herself for her child to find is selfish. Then, after a quick glance around the front room, went on to say, "Well, of course, she is selfish. You only need to look around this house to see she is selfish, it's filled with expensive furniture and ornaments!"

Now whatever truth there was in what he thought, it wasn't his place to say.

Ironically, after all he said, he had the nerve to offer me a sedative, evidently to help with the trauma of it all. To which I had a few things to say to him in return.

Firstly, I said, "You don't know anything about my mum or her life, so keep your opinions to yourself. Secondly, no thanks. I don't want a sedative. This experience isn't going to just go away with a sedative, is it? What about tomorrow and the next day. Are you going to come round again and give me a sedative. No, you're not, are you?"

He didn't respond for a while, then said, "Well, it might help!"

"Help with what? She's not coming back is she? Anyway, I can see we are finished here, so see you later!"

And funnily enough I did, a few days later in Tesco, of all places. And, to my astonishment, he recognised me and came straight up to me. Firstly, he asked me how I was feeling. Then he said, "I feel I owe you an apology for being a little insensitive." He went on to say, "You are a very strong person to have dealt with that situation the way you did."

"Thank you," I said – and carried on with my shopping.

However, I couldn't help thinking what if that wasn't me he said that to. And it was someone who had never been through the same sort of trauma and this was their first crisis. Your words and opinions about what you think is and isn't true could have had an everlasting effect on them, especially at times like these when someone is vulnerable, so the best thing to do is *Keep your mouth shut, you won't be thanked for it.*

Despite my mother's suicide, we fulfilled her wishes and gave her a Muslim funeral, which is a fairly quick process. In fact, my Mama was buried the next day, 5th of November 2003.

That day was truly awful for many reasons, one of them being some people's truly despicable behaviour. I know, right? As though burying your mum after she committed suicide wasn't bad enough, some people thought they would take advantage of my vulnerability, believing this is the time I would be weak so they could attack. Wrong! In fact, it made me more detached, so in the end, after that day, I lost more than just my mother, I lost love and respect for a few people I didn't think could ever behave in the way they had, but that's an entirely different story.

One thing that is vivid in my mind is when the evening approached after my mother's funeral, which was held at her house. One of the funeral attendants stood by my mother's front door, watching the fireworks as they exploded and illuminated the night sky with their spectacular colours. Sensing someone behind her, she turned around and looked at me, she put her tearful arms around me, and she said, "Trust your mum to go out with a bang, hey!" A small smile appeared on my face as I more or less repeated, "Yeah, trust her!"

Two days later was my birthday, 7th of November! Remembering what the neighbour said about my mum posting some letters, I was convinced my mummy sent me a birthday card. I waited and waited for that card to arrive, but it never did. I stupidly even told myself maybe it got lost in the post, and one day it will just turn up, but it never did.

For the first few months after my mother's suicide I drank, and I drank heavily, literally out of the bottle. Each day ended the same, once the children were in bed. Out came the bottle, in an attempt to numb the pain of those daunting images in my head. Images that taunted me both day and night – from flashbacks of asphyxiation marks around my mother's neck, or the burst blood capillaries on her cheeks, or her bulging eyes and blue lips caused by the pressure from hanging herself. Together, with the image of her legs bent up and contorted from the rigor mortis that had frozen her in that tormented position.

Bedtime was the worst because, each time I closed my eyes, I would see nothing else but those horrific images. So I thought by drinking myself into a stupor, it would help. Because that is what we often do, isn't it, if we want to blot out the pain of something, we drown them with alcohol or drugs.

But more often than not it doesn't help. In fact, we end up even more depressed, because once you are sober the problem is still there, there is no escape. And whether I was drunk or sober, those impressions remained.

So I thought, *what's the point of drinking? I don't even like the taste of it!* I took some courage and faced up to what I had been trying to run away from. And I let it run its course, and watched those images take free reign, whilst I bore witness to the consequences of my mother's actions.

A few weeks after the funeral, I had a routine visit to my doctor to review and collect my prescriptions for my ongoing ailments. On arrival, he asked me if I was ok. I told him my mother died and, of course, how. His immediate reaction was "Fuck, Sherrrzah, fuck." I mean, that's my doctor. I really was not expecting that sort of reaction. But I guess it was a shock to hear your patient say that their mother hung herself.

Then he looked at me and said, "Sherrezah, do not turn to the fridge. You've done so well," – which I had. See, for the first time in like forever, I'd lost weight and was down to 19st.

Ironically, by calorie counting.

He went on to say, "Now I'm going to give you another prescription, it's something called Prozac, an anti-depressant. Now I'm not saying you need it. But I want you to cash it in and pop it on the top of your wardrobe and if you get low, it's there in case you do."

I never did use it. But it was the best safety net ever. It was a *just in case* fix. But it was my hand that pulled me out of the depths of darkness and the love of my children. And because of those three young boys, I somehow just pushed through. And slowly, you just learn to come to terms with what happened and somehow get through it all.

I didn't have much time to grieve, due to family problems and greed that came minutes after my mother's death (but that's another story). We did have to wait a long 18 months for the inquest when the coroner determined the actual cause of death. The primarily cause was by a heart attack, and asphyxiation by strangulation the secondary cause. Which, for a Muslim, is a relief because, like most religions, it is a sin, or for haram, to take your own life.

My aunty said, "God took her life before your mum could, as she died in the month of Ramadan." And it is said that those who die in this month go straight to heaven. I often wondered if perhaps that is why my mother did take her life then. Perhaps to absolve herself of the many sins that we can all commit during our lifetime.

Suicide! That's another word that prompts so many questions but has little to no answers. No one can ever truly know or understand why someone takes their life. But I think many of us at some point or another have thought of ending theirs, for whatever reason. I know I have, especially when I was living with my father and my stepmother.

But I never did because, even at that young age, I understood and had the hope that bad days won't and don't last forever – but death is final, and if I took my life, that would mean my suicide would have eliminated the chance of anything ever getting better!

Fundamentally, we are responsible for our own choices and our actions. And those choices expand in every which way. My choices at many times were to find something that gave me some happiness, especially in tragic times.

My motto is, in fact, when in doubt, carb it out. So I ate, hoping it would ease the pain of what happened, but that consequently led me to even more problems as I ended up gradually going back to my old ways of eating and the weight went back on in record time.

But I guess, at times, we all need something to get us through. If you are like me, it's food.

If you are a drinker, it's booze. If drugs are your go to, you will take drugs.

CHAPTER 8

Addictions, Judgments and Discrimination

Addiction is much like the word *fat* because it can be widely interpreted. Addictions come in many different forms and flavours, along with many ways of luring you in.

During my lifetime, I have understood almost anything can become addictive. Even certain foods can become addictive. I don't mean things like peas or sweetcorn (although I'm sure in some extreme cases this could be possible). But things like sugars. But in my opinion, like I have said before, it's not necessarily the food that is addictive.

What becomes addictive is the feeling it gives you – which leads to eating in excess, and that is when the problems arise, because eating in excess is not much different to any other type of excess. In the end you will pay the consequences of your actions. Unless you have control of what you are doing and have the discipline to stop, you will suffer.

Just like it did again, after my mother's death. Despite the doctor telling me not to turn to the fridge, I did at that time. I ate away what I thought was the despair, which turned into creating even more misery where I estimate I went up to around 25st again, not that I was certain because, of course, remember I don't like to weigh myself.

My clothes size was the indicator as I ballooned up to a UK size 26 again. Which led to more suffering on already painful weight-bearing joints. Literally every step was extremely painful, exacerbated by my debilitating arthritis, to the point where I needed to constantly go backwards and forwards to the doctors, trying to find some strong pain relief just to get me through the day.

The doctor put me on many combinations of strong anti-inflammatory pills and a cocktail of other drugs to help ease the pain. My huge legs and feet would swell up so much that I had to take water retention tables daily to reduce the swelling – which I didn't take unless my husband was at home due to the amount of pissing I did. I needed help on and off the toilet. I also had a cream to ease the phlebitis on the inside of my calves caused, in my case, by obesity.

In all honesty, it is easy for anyone to think, "Why didn't you do something about it!" The answer to that is, I couldn't! See, no matter what I tried, no matter what diet I did, nothing ever worked long term. Believe me, I hated not being able to find a way out of that nightmare. It was like I was locked into this vicious cycle and I just got bigger and bigger to the point that for many, many years I needed help doing absolutely everything.

Not only did I need help on and off the toilet, but I'd even broken several toilet seats. I can tell you, there is nothing more tragic than sitting on a toilet doing your business, to hear crick, as the toilet snaps, as you somehow you have to get off without the whole damn toilet seat sliding to one side.

Even though I have my own en-suite just outside my bedroom, I could barely fit into the shower quadrant. Even if I could bend, I wouldn't have been able to because there was not enough space for my gargantuan body. I never even considered having a bath! I couldn't fit in it or get in and out of it independently. And no one I lived with had the Goliath-type strength to help me in and out of that situation.

"You should have stopped eating cakes and all those takeaways," I can hear some say, like that's the only reason people are overweight, from eating doughnuts and takeaways. See, that would be easy then. wouldn't it? Just stop eating them and bingo, you'll lose weight! Wrong!

Unless you are a big size person, no one understands the difficulty you go through just to get through a day and not just mobility-wise either, but mentally.

Every day you wake up and don't want to be like this, but you can't find a way out of this hell. You are constantly beaten down and tortured by literally everyone and all the ideologies of how you should eat to lose weight, like *"stop shovelling it in."* It's relentless. The judgments, the should and shouldn't of what you're doing, topped off by the discrimination!

I can honestly say I have suffered more discrimination for being *fat* than ever for the colour of my skin or being a female, and I have had my fair share of that, too. I once told my husband, you can go all around the world as a fat person, and you will find that humiliation and discrimination will be exactly the same – no matter where you are. People will take the piss out of any fat person because we are perceived as fair game, no matter what culture they are or what language it's spoken in. An insult is an insult – and you will know when someone is doing that. Let me tell you a little story about that.

Once my family and I took a visit to London, one of my favourite cities. We usually go to Knightsbridge to Harrods – and that day was no exception. My boys were quite young at the time; they were between the ages of 6-10. Sometime during the visit, I said to my husband I needed to sit down and rest because my feet were swollen. So we found a café in Harrods and ordered coffee for me and snacks and drinks for all the boys.

Everything was quite normal until I noticed a Chinese family sitting slightly adjacent to us.

Out of the corner of my eye I could see a mum, dad and a boy in his early teens. Whilst they spoke what I am assuming was Mandarin, which of course I couldn't understand, what was a universal understanding was laughing, which I became aware was directed at me.

Now, like I said, no matter what language anyone speaks, you will somehow know when you're being insulted, as I did that day. And in the mother's defence, she tried to stop them. But they didn't and just continued to laugh and mock me.

It was so obvious that even some of the people in the café clocked on to what they were doing, some smirked along but others felt embarrassed at the situation – one of them being my husband. That's why, over the years, I have had to curb my reactions to situations like this, be it because of my size or even racism, so he doesn't feel terrible or anxious. Not ideal, but there you go.

Now it didn't mean to say I wasn't chucking filthy looks their way, which prompted the mother to try to stop them before it turned ugly. I tried to keep my composure as best I could, until I saw my children's little faces. They all looked down with heavy, sad eyes because some prick was encouraging his son to make fun of their mummy. Mate, that boiled my piss. I thought, fuck embarrassing anyone. Besides, what am I teaching my young impressionable children. That it's ok for someone to laugh at you because of what you look like, be it size or anything else? So I was like *Nahhhh mate, I'm not having that!*

So, leading by example, I turned around to face them both and in my best Essex accent said, "Oi, YOU! Yeah you mate," pointing my finger at the father, as he looked at me rather startled. "Ain't you supposed to be a Buddhist, ain't Buddha fat, not very f*cking Zen then, is it?"

They immediately stopped. The mum looked at him, shaking her head in disgust. As if to say, good, you got what you deserved. And he did.

Look, even though I was a big girl sitting on a leather cube-style sofa, which must have made me look like Humpty Dumpty sitting on a wall, it doesn't mean a grown ass man can make me, or anyone else for that matter, a source of their own amusement. Because if you are ready to open your mouth, then don't be surprised if you get a reaction.

So the next time you see a person of size, or colour or anything, don't take the piss, because you might end up getting a reaction you don't want, and you might end up being the one humiliated and embarrassed. So just remember, *keep your mouth shut, you won't be thanked for it.*

CHAPTER 9

Life Carries On!

Many more dark days followed after my mother's death. Nothing much really went to plan, one of them being the stark realisation that I was never going to be a metal guitarist in a band (oh, did I mention I played guitar?), together with my dearest drummer friend Ric (short for Ricardo), who is also someone that is like a brother to me.

Music is everything to me and is one of my best friends. So, for me, being graced to write music and play in a band with such a talented musician as my brother Ric was nothing short of incredible, but that is where it stopped, because the reality was I had a family that meant, despite the opportunity, I couldn't leave them behind and go off touring. Plus I was too big and with limited mobility to do anything more than just dream!

See, my obesity made me a prisoner in my own home – which more often than not drove me to despair! I needed something to stimulate my mind, instead of just sitting in front of that sickening, mind numbing television. Therefore I decided to embark on a law course through the Open University as it was something I could do from home.

But I didn't consider that my basic education from a child upwards would be limiting – which was down to my father's cultural approach to women and education. My father's belief was that my education in life was to learn how to cook and clean so I could be married off to the highest bidder, who would pay him a big dowry, hence after senior school I was forbidden to go to university as he made it clear he was never going to invest in my education.

Still, I went ahead with the degree. For two reasons. As a child I used to watch a programme called Crown Court and dreamed about being a Barrister. Secondly, I felt it was a natural progression for me because from a young adult aged 20, and having spent a year working in the ticket office at British Rail Colchester North Station,

I was a elected by the office to be the Health and Safety and Union Representative for the TSSA Union – which I did for just under ten years. After blagging my way through that and learning on my feet, I became a representative for workers in arbitration and complaints.

As I became more and more recognised for my success in this role, I went on to be hand- picked by the then director as a Racial Discrimination Officer for the Divisional Director of the Network Southeast Railways.

But after my first marriage ended, and I subsequently became pregnant with my first son, Rahim (whose dad left me holding the baby), I found myself as a single mother with little to no help from anyone else other than my ex-husband and his family.

Whilst I did still work part time on the railways, I had to step down from my work as a union representative because I could no longer commit to the schedule. That, together with a part time wage, meant I earned less money, and with no help from the government I had to look for a second job, so I returned to one of my in and out jobs – security, namely nightclub door work.

Locally, it didn't pay much so I took the plunge and went to London where I became a Head doorman, Westminster-licensed. It was easier to work nights because I could leave my baby, Rahim, with the person I trusted the most, my ex-husband. Even though we had split up, he stood by me and helped me look after Rahim, for which I was forever grateful for his kindness and support.

That time in my life was tough. I literally didn't sleep for the first two years of Rahim's life.

Most Fridays and Saturdays meant I would do a part time day shift, come home, sleep on the couch with Rahim when he had an afternoon nap, then get ready for an all-night shift on the doors from 8-8. I'd work all night, rush back in the early hours of the morning, clean, cook, sleep a bit. Then rush back to London for another all-nighter. It was long. But as a mother, you do what you have to do to survive.

I tell you something else and all. Being a bouncer (door supervisor, as it was called) in London was an eye opener. We learnt many things. One of those was loyalty, everyone had each other's back.

We were taught how to respond to aggressive behaviour and how to diffuse potentially dangerous situations. I teamed up and worked with both women and men but, as women, we had to be able to handle ourselves in the unlikely event a man who was charged up on drugs and alcohol decided to attack one of us girls.

Not that this happened much as most of my co-workers, male and female, were usually bodybuilders, boxers, martial artists, or all three. We were all the size of tanks which, in itself, was a deterrent! But I very quickly learnt that the best way to deal with anyone is to always be very professional and polite. You had to, because you really didn't know who you were dealing with and what they were capable of doing.

My professionalism paid off and got me promoted to work in clubs, trouble shooting. Oh my, that's where the eye opening happened. Think about it, I was a little no-one girl from Colchester, with no access to anything much out of the town I was born in. So to see flamboyant exotic dancers, gay and straight, strippers, pole dancers, back room private dancing where all sorts of seediness was going on – not to mention all the prostitution – was a little bit overwhelming, but I soon became accustomed to it all. As well as learning very quickly to always have my wits about me and have nerves of steel and stand my ground, which I did on a couple of occasions.

Whilst I was Westminster-licensed, I was not restricted to work just in central London, this licence enabled me to work throughout the city of London. For the most part, it was fun, but there were many dark sides too. It's not always a glamorous position – you get to see the good and the bad that people do. You get to see and experience all spectrums of life. Whilst there are too many to write about I have two experiences that stick in my mind.

The first one is a time when I worked in a club in Islington in North London. Once the club shut down I found myself having to wait outside for a lift that was extremely delayed. This was a few hours before the break of dawn. So I sat at the bottom of the steps of the nightclub at 03.00hrs and waited on a summer's night for a complete stranger to come and pick me up. I mean, as a door supervisor in those days, you placed complete trust in people like that.

Many passers-by stopped, asking if I was ok, to which I said yes so they left. However, there was this young couple who stopped by and the young lady said, "You are not sitting alone at 3am in the dark in this part of the city."

She refused to leave me on my own, despite me saying, "I'm actually ok, I'm security, I can handle myself," she wasn't having it. She was quite sassy, which I liked, she even ordered her boyfriend to get us a couple of coffees.

All three of us sat together chatting the night away, waiting for my lift to arrive. A bit later, we saw a few night time stragglers making their way home from the clubs. One of them said, "Woah, is this where the after party is?"

To which we laughed, and the sassy girl said, "We are waiting for her lift to come." So they said, "We will wait with you."

Before we knew it so did a few others, and within moments there were about fifty-odd people. Sitting, vibing, smoking, drinking coffee from the all-night café nearby, whose owner must have thought it was his lucky day. We were chatting and laughing, complete strangers, sitting all together on a summer's night, waiting with a lone female door security for her lift to arrive.

Wow, just wow! And when he did finally arrive, everyone cheered and clapped. To which he looked completely surprised and said, "What the hell is going on?"

I said, "Oh, they were all waiting with me." He said, "What?"

"We didn't want to leave her alone," the girl who initially started it all said.

I hugged that couple and many of the others as I said goodbye. I even felt a bit sad as I got into the car. The driver beeped and they all waved and began cheering as we drove off. I turned around to take a last look at these wonderful human beings, as they faded into the distance as we drove away, a little sadness filled my heart knowing I would never see them again – but the memory of that night has never left me.

It was one of the most beautiful moments in my life – total strangers coming together in complete unity. Just like it was back then, we all had each other's back. Be it people you knew or complete strangers, like when we were on the doors. Most of us didn't know each other, but anywhere you went as doormen it was an unspoken rule – loyalty! It was a true display of what humanity can be. I felt extremely honoured to be a part of that experience.

The second experience was New Year's Eve 1996. Just before midnight, the DJ began with the infamous countdown of 10, 9, 8, 7, 6, 5, 4, 3, 2, 1 – then he dropped this…

Today is gonna be the day

That they're gonna throw it back to you. By now you should've somehow Realised what you have to do.

To which the crowd erupted.

For those who don't know or recognise that intro, it's a song called Wonderwall by a band called Oasis. Whilst they were massive back in the day, they weren't – and are not – my cup of tea. But this song was absolutely rinsed anywhere and everywhere you went. Everyone knew that song. And since the club goers on that particular New Year's Eve were from the East End of London and this hotel nightclub was on the Isle of Dogs, they loved it.

Me, the only female doorman (the other 10 being 10 male doormen), stood on the side of the dance floor at ease watching the drunk partygoers swaying left and right. singing their little hearts out to Oasis – when suddenly, a small group of men began to move towards us.

It caught us off guard a little, so we were all on alert. After all, a lot of these are either West Ham fans or Millwall. But this group of men edging forward were singing and walking towards us, smiling. One of them made a gesture to me pointing at my arm, then took my hand, whilst the other men of the group took my fellow workers' hands.

They then raised our hands and theirs up in the air together with the rest of the very packed nightclub and guided us onto the dance floor, so we, too, could celebrate the New Year in.

Whilst we were a bit reluctant to start off with, they started coaxing us to sing along. By then, it was pointless to even try to resist. Or maybe we didn't want to resist. I know I didn't, because it felt like a truly bloody wonderful moment where, once again, we all came together as one.

Now bearing in mind we were the bouncers, the crowd were all sorts of colour, ages and sizes. But every single one of us knew that song. English or not. White or of any colour. All of us linked together, hand in hand, arms in the air, swaying from side to side, singing at the top of our voices the chorus…

Because mayyyyyybeeeeeeee

You're gonna be the oneeeeee that saves meeeeeee And after allllllllllllllll

You're my Wonderrrrrrwallllllll.

There can be no denying that song is a bit of genius. There is a power in certain songs that have that ability to unite people, no matter who or where they come from. As it did that night, in that nightclub, it brought the love of different people together, as one. It was a truly beautiful moment – one that still makes the hairs on my arms stick up when I think of that pure moment of humanity. That DJ knew what he was doing. He brought us all together.

It was also during this time that I met my husband Guy in 1996. He was introduced to me by someone I worked with on the door. He was their flatmate. We are an unlikely match. Totally chalk and cheese. But you know what they say, opposites attract. And through it all, we are still together.

Oh and I failed my degree in the final year, and I didn't resit it. I simply wasn't educated or good enough. My basic grammar was awful, and I was rubbing around the bottom, at most. I gave it my best shot – but failed. Nothing you can do, just move on. But it helped improve my diction, otherwise how could I write like this? Even though it's taken me over five long painstaking years.

CHAPTER 10

The Battles and the Solutions

Before we continue and delve deeper into the world of Sarezah, I will touch on something I said earlier, about a misconception that all fat people eat a lot of food, and why that isn't always entirely true.

Let me explain. Like I said before, getting to the size I was took a long period of time, it was a very slow and gradual process. Therefore, as I got bigger, so did my food portions get bigger, then I got bigger again, then the portions got bigger and so on.

This meant I ate what I needed to satisfy my hunger but, more importantly, I ate the amount I needed to sustain the size of my body. Which meant at 32st I was probably consuming in excess of 5000 calories a day. Hence popular opinions would be *you ate too much, that's why you're fat.* So let me explain why, by using the best example I know, I don't agree with that statement.

It came at the height of my success after losing a vast amount of weight, when at just over 17st I was invited to appear in some magazines and newspapers articles to share and celebrate my weight loss success story. One female journalist interviewing me asked, "Did you eat a lot?"

To which I replied, "No, not really," explaining to her that whilst I understood I consumed a large amount of food, I realise I didn't actually overeat.

To which she abruptly responded with, "Well, of course you did, otherwise how else did you get that fat. Surely you must have stuffed yourself with cakes, donuts, takeaway, chocolate and whatever else you could get your hands on."

At first, I was somewhat ruffled by her comment as it threw me off guard. For some reason I assumed she would be impartial, but I guess that was just wishful thinking. Besides, I should have known better as ignorant and rude comments like these are not uncommon when you are perceived by others as being *fat.*

It's almost like they wait for the right moment to pounce and project their feelings onto you because, to them, being *fat* is the most disgusting thing in the world and they will have no problem in telling you or fat body shaming you. So I took a few moments to absorb what she said before I responded!

And fortunately, I did not respond in my usual epic manner, which likely would have ended with me saying something quite obscene because – let's be honest – that comment was directed straight at me (look, I'm from Essex, it's normal for us to use colourful language)!

Thankfully, over the years I have learnt to have a bit more decorum. It's no good mouthing off and getting on the defensive at the drop of a hat, otherwise nothing will ever be heard. So I took the opportunity to re-educate this woman and, of course, the readers of the magazine.

Therefore, after a few deep breaths and searching for correct words to use (words being one of the biggest tools in life, so choose them wisely), I addressed the comment she made and responded back to that *You must have eaten a lot, because how else did you get that fat.*

"Like I said, love, not really. See, if you put that amount of food I ate when I was 32st in front of me now, I wouldn't be able to eat it all because I'm not that size any more, am I?

However, when I was 32 stone, I ate 32 stone's worth of food. So your understanding of eating a lot of food is incorrect, because you were judging me by how much you eat, rather than what I needed to eat in order to satisfy the body I was in when I was a plus size. See my love, you eat enough for the size your body is, therefore you don't eat the same volume to sustain a body like mine, when I was 32st. You eat enough for your weight, and I ate enough for mine. So no, I didn't eat much!" Silence prevailed!

Her ignorance is not entirely her fault. As I said earlier, these opinions are formed by available information, i.e. for those who are largely overweight, *fat* is likely to be due to them being greedy and/or lazy and they should exercise more self-control!

Sadly popular opinion doesn't necessarily expand to comfort eating – it's not possible someone may eat to console any type of pain due to some sort of abuse. And if someone does, there's not the same sympathy for *fat* people as there is for others with vices or addictions. You wouldn't usually advise an alcoholic on how to stop drinking, because it's commonly understood there's an underlying triggering reason that needs specialist advice. But when you're a *fat* person those tips come flooding in!

These can range from cut out the carbohydrates and eat a bowl of broccoli, or go keto, then you'll lose weight! That is almost all I have ever heard. Like that even works! And when you try to explain why it doesn't work, because drastically cutting your diet has other consequences, namely it will throw your body into starvation mode, they start to argue with you, often looking at the next person, because they all love an audience, rolling their eyes saying, *"See, they are just making excuses they can't be bothered, or they don't want to do it."* Honestly, sometimes I just look at their mouths moving and think, *Just shut up, you sound like an absolute numpty!*

Anyway, I now have the experience to help others understand the myths behind the many weight loss concepts. Remember, it's not rocket science. *Eat less, move more.* That is the basis of what I followed, including following a calorie deficit, nutritionally balanced diet of protein, carbohydrates and healthy fats. Put this together with exercise, consistency and determination and you're onto a sure winner.

There will always be some exceptions to this rule of dieting. Occasionally, you may see or hear someone who is slender, saying, *I don't know how I'm so slim, I eat like a horse. I must have a fast metabolism.* Or someone who is large say, *I don't know how I'm so big, I don't eat much, I must have a slow metabolism.* I guess there is probably some truth in both of those statements. However, metabolism is another one of those big questions that there isn't a definitive answer for.

I cannot discuss the concept of metabolism, because I don't know much scientifically about it and wouldn't want to say something that is not true. What I do know is what I did to lose weight – if that boosted my metabolism, then that boosted it. I lost the weight either way, and as they say, the proof is in the pudding!

Without going into too much detail about the calculations, I want to give you an outline of the basics – the best starting point to calculate the calories you need to focus on for a calorie deficit. You should firstly look at what your daily activity level value requirements are, this is known as a BMR (Basal Metabolic Rate) so you get your TDEE (Total Daily Energy Expenditure) according to your weight, height, age and sex – in other words what your body needs in calories just to give it energy to exist.

Now I know some people will argue against this method, but this is how I lost weight – and how I mostly kept it off! Therefore I am just passing on what worked for me. Anyway, in order to calculate this, I suggest you go online and find a free calorie deficit calculator. This will calculate your weight and – depending on your goals – once you have answered the questions, it will generally create a calorie deficit plan and provide you a number of calories per day for you to follow.

The best way I know how to explain this is using what I did as the example. My aim was to burn 1lb of fat a week, this meant creating a calorie deficit of 3500 Kcal's in that week. So if, for example, my calorie allowance a day is 2500, and I want to lose 1lb a week, I would have to divide 3500 by the total number of days in a week, 3500 divided by 7 gives me a number of 500. That means I would have to minus 500 calories of my daily intake of 2500 therefore creating a calorie deficit. My new calorie allowance would therefore be 2000 a day.

Once this is created, you can move to the next stage and look at what you need to eat to provide your body with healthy energy. Because, like I have said, if you don't have a balanced diet, it will be unsustainable. If you don't eat enough carbs you will be lethargic. If you don't eat enough protein, you will not build muscle. And of course good fats, which are essential nutrient for your body and for your brain function. And some sugars. Don't believe the hype, because you need sugars for your liver and brain to function properly. Of course, I don't mean smashing down chocolate or a tub of ice-cream. I mean in the form of fresh carbohydrates like fruits and vegetables, sweet potatoes or just potatoes.

Now remember earlier when I spoke about the word *macros*? Some of you may have already heard this word, but for those of you who haven't I will do my best to explain. But firstly macros are not to be confused with what is known as *macrobiotic*. This way of eating is something completely different.

The *macros* I am talking about are *macronutrients* – which are made up of protein, carbohydrates and fats. Each macronutrient will also be inclusive of vitamins, minerals and fibres. The aim here is to divide up your macros into percentages (something I will focus on later). But the essence here is balance.

So even when in a calorie deficit, please do not cut out carbohydrates from your diet as they are not the enemy (unless there is a medical reason, so always check before you embark on any type of change). So a typical day of eating for me would start with a carbohydrate breakfast and lunch, then a light protein meal for my early evening meal. I worked on the age-old principle of, Eat breakfast like a king, lunch like a queen and dinner like a pauper.

Remember, you have to be totally honest and accountable for everything you eat, otherwise it won't work. There can be no more turning a blind eye, no more an extra mouthful here and there, or I've blown it now so I may as well eat what I want over the weekend and start again on Monday. Because all you will do is undo the hard work you have already done.

And, yes, you can have some treats, after all you have to live. But just limit them.

Remember, there is no quick fix, it takes time to adjust and there will be a few hiccups and hindrances along the way, just don't make them habits – it is tough, but it is doable. Slowly, slowly, things get easier; you start by winning the small battles which eventually leads to winning the lifetime wars.

Even I had the odd hindrances, one of them was chocolate! It was the devil! Why? Because for love nor money, I couldn't control the allure and temptation of chocolate – and I am not one of these who can just have one square or just a mouthful. Once I started eating it, I couldn't stop – and before I knew it I'd sunk 2500 plus calories, drunk on chocolate and filled with regret. So the easiest thing to do was give it up, so I set a date, the 21st May, 2016, and that was that. I haven't eaten it since!

Anyway, once I had my macros in check and got into a routine, the weight start tumbling off. But eventually macros alone wouldn't suffice, and I began to plateau. Once that happened, it was time to move onto the next stage and to fulfil another aspect of my lifestyle change, move more!

That meant back to another age-old principle that most are afraid of, especially some of the ladies out there, and that is strength training, fearing they will end up looking somewhat masculine. But this is the one way I lost weight and the way I completely re-sculpted my body (with a little help from a legend and a hero of mine, more about that later).

See, strength training is focused on compound heavy movements and these movements will burn fat! Again, something we will explore a little further. So whilst I had experience in strength training, it had been a long time since I stepped in a gym and, like all things, it had moved on since my days. A lot of equipment had been modernised – there was more emphasis on cable machines and kettle bells, as well as other methods and ideas that evolved from the old ways of training.

I thought it was best to do some of my own online research to help me re-engage. But the information out there was vast, all with varying views and conflicting opinions – which flipping left me confused and none the wiser. So I decided to talk to someone in the know and went to my then health club, Clarice House, now Bannatyne's, for help. I told them my situation and that I was desperate to lose weight and needed help and advice. They were – and still are – so supportive and offered to help me as much as I needed and even gave me free Personal Training in order to help me get started.

A few days after, I met with a couple of the club's personal trainers. They were both extremely knowledgeable and had already been told to devise a weight loss exercise programme. That is the point I came across an all-important factor that I had never heard of before until I spoke to these two trainers and that is that different body types respond to different ways of dieting and training.

These body types are broken down into three categories, endomorph, mesomorph and ectomorph. A simple breakdown of these follow:

Endomorphs generally have a stockier bone structure and large midsection and hips, who carry fat throughout the body and gain fat fast and lose it slowly. They tend to have a slower metabolism, sometimes due to health problems or as a result of a sedentary lifestyle. Defo Me! (More on how one should train in a minute).

Mesomorphs tend to have a medium bone structure with shoulders wider than hips. They are athletic and muscular, with an efficient metabolism who gain mass and lose it with relative ease. Not me, mite – more like my son Rahim. (Incidentally, mesomorphs are naturally muscular. I know, sickening! They should do 3-5 weight training sessions a week and incorporate some cardio to prevent weight gain).

Ectomorphs have narrow shoulders and hips and are small in stature and muscle mass. They tend to have a naturally fast metabolism which makes it difficult for them to gain mass. That's absolutely not – nor never will be – me (most of the training here would revolve around gaining mass. And big basic moves, squats, deadlifts, bench press, shoulder press etc, with a high lean calorie intake).

It is safe to say I am an endomorph. The focus was on fat loss techniques that included a mixture of resistance (strength) training, using the basic compound movements, squats, deadlifts, back rows, chest press, and so on. I had to do this to help strengthen my muscles and stabilise my joints. This had to be incorporated with HIIT, high intensity interval training – with short rest periods, for optimal weight loss, as cardio. This form of training uses lots of plyometric resistance training, obviously within your own capabilities and tolerance. I gradually included – and built in as much as I could – a steady state of cardio. This is equally as beneficial and includes swimming, walking and cycling – which we will talk about later.

Whilst I touched upon macros earlier, I now want to incorporate it into how I lost my weight, so you can see how it works on paper, then incorporate it into your lifestyle change. Remember, for me this was a key factor in my weight loss.

It concentrates on calorie deficit, using an important factor in fat loss which is to focus strength/resistance training on building lean muscle mass. And in order to accomplish that, I had to focus on both a calorie deficit and a daily higher protein intake than what I had been having as my diet mostly contained starchy or simple carbs – but at no time did I ever cut them out of my diet, I just learnt to eat healthy complex carbohydrates and healthy fats.

Macros – or *macronutrients* – are needed for your daily calorie intake, which is split into percentages of protein, carbohydrates and fats. The simplest way of finding out your macro allowance is to find a user-friendly online macros calculator to calculate what your calorie deficit should be, and a percentage of what intake should be for those three types of body types.

As I was a big girl, the focus began with just ensuring a balanced amount of carbs and protein but quickly moved to a higher protein intake to build muscle and burn more fat. As a rule, this is calculated as 2.2 grams of protein per kilo of body weight to aid weight loss. So relating that to myself, after I ensured that daily intake of protein was met, the remaining pool of calories was to be divided into carbs and healthy fats.

Of course, much does depend on a person's individual tolerance level and preference. Some people find they have a tolerance to low carb diets like 'ketogenic' but that was not for me. I'd tried keto diets but ended up experiencing severe nauseating symptoms. For me, it's all about a balance! Besides, if I didn't have enough carbohydrates in my diet to produce the energy I needed to maintain my body and later on train I would feel lethargic. I needed carbs as both a source of energy and to help me feel satiated!

I'm no expert, I am only offering a basic understanding of things without becoming too technical, or overwhelming. Lord knows it took me forever to understand it all myself. The basic facts of successful weight loss are this simple, you need a calorie deficit, with a focus on a balanced amount of macronutrients, rather than just focusing on calories. By just having calories, you could not eat all day long and blow it in a pizza or take away. That's ok once or twice but in the long run, won't work. You must eat in a way to satiate your hunger throughout the day, so split your calories into three meals and two snacks in-between each main meal. Eat smart and get more healthy nutrients to nourish your body.

I generally like to stick to what I refer to as a balanced calorie ratio intake of 40-40-20, 40% carbs, 40% protein, 20% fat. Sometimes I vary it – especially if I need to reign it back a bit – then I will try to focus more on a higher intake of protein or good fats, then I will cut the carbs a bit. But to start off, balance is the best way.

One important tip I taught myself during my weight loss journey was how to use my calories as if it was spending money – and seeing I am the chancellor of the home, I spend money wisely. So, for instance, if I had 2000 calories to spend, just like money, I want to get the most I can for it. Therefore if I spend most of it before lunch, I would be calorie poor for the rest of the day.

However, if I ate smart and spent my calories wisely – and chose to have balanced meals focusing more on splitting my calories between three meals at roughly 500 kcal's leaving enough calories to eat snacks in between – I'm onto a winner.

Now, once you've got the calories sorted. You then have to focus on optimising your weight loss. I mentioned the principle of weight training a little earlier – which worked for me when I was 35st and went to Hamiltons Gym. There, I was taught to lift heavy – and I mean heavy. Back then I was leg pressing 340kilo for ten reps 5 sets – which for a 24-year-old young lady wasn't bad at all.

But almost 30 years later – at the age of 54, during summer 2023 – I broke that and got a new PB (personal best) of 400kilo leg press, 10reps, last set of 5! That was at another gym – David Lloyd in Colchester – which I joined to get away from it all, after yet another great battle for my life.

In all honestly, there is nothing that beats the feeling of training. It releases all sorts of endorphins and serotonin. The buzz I get after a workout is like nothing else. This – together with a calorie deficit – is the key to success, along with a few other aspects – control, consistency and patience.

CHAPTER 11

Control and Consistency

Control is something that is not in the least BIT easy – especially at the beginning of any type of journey. It takes time to become accustomed to any new type of regime or whatever you are doing.

For me, when I first started, I often failed. Sometimes it's because I caved in and had more food than I should have had, others because I was hungry. It took time for my body to get used to a different way of eating. It can be a bit scary when changing something you have always done – but determination and will to succeed always kicks in.

So each time I fell, I got up and dusted myself off and slowly, slowly – over time – I learned to control my hunger. I even got to the stage that if I had the urge to eat and had no macros left, I'd go to bed hungry, just so I wasn't tempted to eat. At times I even wanted to cry! Well, more of a whimpering and moaning – but I was determined to control myself and that hunger.

No matter how I felt, I just closed my eyes and went through the pain, I did what I had to do to get through. I often told myself *fail is fail, Sarezah*. You can change failure but you can't change giving up, that's being defeatist!

Control taught me to set some boundaries and say no. No more, you've had your allotted allowance for the day, that's it. The battle isn't actually with food, it's with you, your will, your determination and control of what you have will win. You against you – it's a simple statement but one of the most effective, the *you against you* principle has certainly worked for me. Just like when my doctor said *Eat less and move more Sarrezzah. It's not Rocket Science, is it!* He's not wrong.

You have to learn how to tackle the many mental hurdles that come up – all those vicious hunger cravings that will torment you. So you need to wipe the slate clean and re-educate yourself – not just physically, but mentally. Which I finally did at the age of 44 years old. Some people have asked me if I wish I'd done it sooner? I don't know. I didn't. So there's no point in wishing for something that didn't happen – it will just keep you in a dark room of despair. Do it now, no matter what your age. Do it for your health, do it for yourself, remember *you are your biggest obstacle, rise above yourself.*

Control, consistency and determination are the key factors, but another is *discipline*. One doesn't work without the other. From when I started to where I am now, that's what I have done. Those words can unlock success, not just in one aspect, but in absolutely anything you want to do. Be it a degree, play music, open a business or change your life. *Control, consistency, discipline and determination* – mixed in with a bit of stubbornness, blood, sweat, tears and the odd tantrum. Do that and you will get results! I've been doing just this for almost 11 years and whilst this was a massive challenge, it wasn't the biggest challenge of my life – but these principles got me through.

Finally, never ever talk to yourself in a negative or derogatory way. I would never put myself down, even when I failed. I would say to myself *Come on darling. Don't be like that. Don't get cross and angry at yourself. You made a mistake. It's not the end of the world. Let's just start again.*

See, I am a great believer that your body, mind and spirit can hear everything you say – and one day, you never know when one of those might hear what you have to say and it might just save your life.

CHAPTER 12

Set A Date

August 31st, 2013 is the date I set my timer for my weight loss journey to begin. You've got to start somewhere, I thought, so why not make it official so it can become a memorable date.

On that day, I gave myself a pep talk, and reminded myself, *Sarezah you are a ticking time bomb. Live or die, the choice is yours! No matter what led you to eating the way you did, it is now no longer relevant. So change it. Don't set unrealistic targets, adapt slowly, reduce your calorie intake bit by bit, slowly you will win the race. It took years to get this big, it will take years to lose it. Cut down bit by bit like you did when you gave up smoking – it was little steps over time.*

That is how I eventually gave up cigarettes – after trying a gazillion times. It took me so long because I set unrealistic goals. Each time I tried I failed because I didn't think about reducing them. Instead, I would just cut it out completely.

All day, I would crave nicotine – then end up smoking again. I realised I couldn't just cut them out altogether so slowly, slowly I began – by firstly cutting out the cigarettes I enjoyed, like the first one in the morning, or with a coffee and after a meal. Over time I went from 20 a day, down to 10 a day then 5 then 3. Until the last day I ever smoked. Which was the millennium – New Year's Day 2000 at 1500hrs.

So I knew it worked. With a bit of tweaking, I could take the same principle but this time, cut down my calories.

There is a big difference between eating and smoking cigarettes – as you don't need cigarettes to live – but to a person who is addicted to nicotine, cigarettes are the fix for that craving. Just as food can be a fix for craving certain foods – such as those with high unnatural sugars, like cakes and biscuits. But this is not to be confused with natural sugars that are in the form of fruits and vegetables – these type of carbs are not the enemy, they are indeed an essential part of your diet as they create energy in the body.

Like I say, I didn't cut out anything that had nutritional value but limited that which didn't.

But carbs are essentially sugars and when not converted and used as energy will circulate to other parts of the body and be stored as fat in adipose tissue.

So to ensure I was adhering to the correct portion control, I bought some electronic kitchen scales and began to weigh all my food and count calories. At first I thought this is going to a bit of a rigmarole, get the potato, put it on the scale, register it on the app, blah, blah blah. But in the end it was just what I needed to do. I found this was the best guidance and accountability tool that existed. In fact, it has become a total godsend in my life and a huge support. The app I use is MyFitnessPal – but there are many out there, so choose the one that suits you best.

I recorded everything in that all important food diary (albeit an eye opener, at times).

However, I was brutally honest and recorded everything I ate. No more 'guesstimating' what I ate. So if I ate 4 slices of toast, I ate 4 slices of bread. If I had 40g of butter or 50g of peanut butter, I had that. 3 teaspoons of sugar, I added it. 2 chicken thighs with skin. Rice, etc, etc, I wrote it all down. I'd look at the end of the day on the app at the calorific value of everything I ate and stayed within my allowance.

I also regulated my meals to eat roughly every four hours – and within a few weeks I really began to see results. Over time, my cravings got less and less and the more I got used to what I was doing the more the weight began to melt off- – especially the first few stone (of course, I realise much of that would have been fluid).

Soon after, I began to see a marked difference in my appearance, and I dropped several dress sizes. Usually, once I'd seen results, I'd slip back into eating a bit here and a bit there. Like I knew I had this invisible buffer zone to play around in. But before you know it, you're back to square one or worse, bigger! But for some reason, this time I didn't go back, I stuck to my calories. And as I did, I watched the weight tumbling off.

That's the point I knew in my heart of hearts it was different this time as I was going to smash it – which also made me realise I had not got a photo to compare it with when I reached my goal of being a size 16. (This was the initial goal I set myself so I could buy clothes from any shop).

So I asked my son Azim to take a photo of me. He looked at me with a rather questionable look, and said in a sombre voice, "Are you sure, mummy?" Poor kid wasn't being rude. He could just see what I looked like – which wasn't great because, firstly, I was wearing a blue stretchy nighty and secondly, I looked absolutely huge. I was literally spherical, as I was approximately 27 stone-ish.

See, I never took photos of my body. Like most obese people, I only had head shots or photos of me hidden behind someone or at the back of a group photo, or standing in front of something that hid the truth. *See no evil and all that.*

CHAPTER 13

Back to the Grind

Soon after, I plateaued. I knew it was time to take the plunge and start hitting the gym. So I booked a session with the PT I had already spoken to, who told me to book in when I was ready. That day I made my way to the gym. I clearly remember it, as I was huffing and puffing as I struggled to carry my huge heavy frame to that gym floor – a place I had not seen for the best part of 17 plus years.

I knew the task ahead was going to be monumental, impossible even, as I recounted my situation that had led me to ballooning to over 32st. I was in my mid-forties, I felt almost already defeated thinking *how am I ever going to change this*. But I pushed those thoughts aside and told myself, *come on, don't dwell, let's just give it our best shot, yeah.* And from that moment, I was determined more than ever to just keep pushing.

The induction started with trainer number 1, Jack- – because throughout my weight loss journey I have had a few trainers, including my own son Rahim. This trainer encouraged me from the word go – he even affectionately called me Saze (Saze being a cross between my real name Sarezah and my family name Sezah). He pointed out that we were going to *start nice and slow on the bike, Saze,* pointing at the recumbent bike.

Even though I tried to get on the bike myself, I just couldn't. I was so big and my joints were so immobile that at times it was impossible for me to get myself on it. The poor lad even tried his best to help physically haul me onto the bike by himself, but couldn't, so he called in trainer number 2 Kerry, a young lady, to help. Mate, it took both of them to help me on and off that blasted bike. She even had to put my foot into the pedal. Even though I was embarrassed, these two didn't even bat an eyelid nor make a judgment or comment.

I remember the first few sessions of being on the recumbent bike. Trainer number 1 Jack said, "Saze, let's see if you can do 10 seconds without stopping."

That hurt – 10 seconds you know- – because, in truth, I couldn't even manage 5 seconds without being out of breath. I could have – and even wanted to have- – given up there and then as it just felt completely insurmountable. But I dug deep, focused my mind and made myself bloody do it!

And when I did, they both cheered and praised me. Not because I made 10 seconds, but because of my will. That was one of the most prolific moments of my journey. From then, I knew I had the determination to do whatever it took to succeed – and bit by bit I got further and further, each time a few more seconds than the last, until 10 seconds became 20 seconds then 30, then a minute. Then I got to the point which was best explained in one of the sub headlines in a magazine article that I featured in after losing the best part of 17st, that read *From 10 seconds to 10 kilometres in 20 minutes!*

As I progressed over the years, team Sarezah did too – support and encouragement grew and grew. I felt so honoured that so many people were rooting for me. That support and love I got made such a difference to me. I guess everyone could see how hard I was pushing and training and how determined I was to succeed!

Well so I thought, until I met trainer number 3, a Russian pro boxer, hard as a bag of nails, ruthless, Baltic champ. The day I met her is most definitely the day I met my match – as well as my absolute nemesis. She took me to hell and back. I hated her with a passion and loved her equally. There is no doubt about it, she is the one person who completely changed my mindset and made me train the way I do today. Who is she? Natalija Dolgova, that's who, and this is how it all started.

CHAPTER 14

Give It Your Max

It was announced to the gym goers at the Bannatyne Club in Kingsford Park that a new trainer was going to start. On her first day, I saw her standing at the island table that was in the middle of the gym, as it was at the time before it was revamped. She was writing something down. Mate, she looked absolutely stunning, and she still is. She has the whitest blonde hair and the bluest eyes, high cheek bones, athletic and strong, like a bull. But she had a look that meant business. A look of no fear. And boy was I about to find out just how fearless she was.

I introduced myself to her – she was very professional and polite but I sensed she was a little shy, so I came in with the ice breaker and said, "I hear you are a boxer." That was it, best mates after that. Not for too long though (I say that in jest). We are still very close friends – but not on the gym floor. Think *Clash of the Titans.*

It all began when I occasionally felt her eyes penetrating into my soul when I was training.

My girl was now watching me like a bloody hawk, ready to swoop down for the kill. See, unbeknownst to me, she had approached management and asked for the go ahead to train me.

One day she approached me, with me all smiley, and said in a thick Russian accent, "Sarezah, I don't think you train very hard, all I see you do is talk, and ha ha hee hee with everyone, so now, I am going to train you."

Now that took a few seconds to sink in. I mean, *you what love?!* Thinking *that's rude* – to which I went off on one of my infamous hands in the air and everything speeches, talking about how I've lost this much, me, I, I've done it myself. I've had people get me through the door, but I did all the hard work, how dare you and all that.

Mate, my girl now was just standing there, expressionless, looking straight through me, and chillingly said, "I train you now."

My blood actually went cold. "Meet me tomorrow, Sarezah, 9am, don't be late."

Then she just walked off, walked off you know, she left me standing there, mouth open at the shock that no one had ever had the balls to be that direct, well not until now!

That's when the misery began, mate, this trainer pushed me to limits I honestly never knew existed! It was the complete breaking and remaking of me. Good God, this woman was brutal. No more *Come on Saze, let's see if you can do 10 seconds without stopping.* Every day, each session was f*cking gruelling! This beast was on me like a rash. There was no let up, it was just relentless, she kept pushing me to the limit every pissing day!

Push Sarezah, push, give it your max Sarezah is all I heard on f*cking loop, along with *You don't want to reach your goals, Sarezah, you're not giving it your max, Sarezah, you're making stupid excuses, Sarezah!* Every flipping day – even at night when I went to sleep, I could hear that wretched voice in my head and see that expressionless blank stare on her face as I tossed and turned in my dreams! Savage!

She knocked me out cold every damn training session, whether it was a HIIT session (high intensity interval training) or 3-minute boxing rounds. I've never known anything like it, I've even been close to tears because it was just so hard. I have even wanted to rip her face off, only to realise, if I did try to rip her face off, she'd rip mine off first – besides, I would come out worse, because not only would she rip my face off, she would also pick me apart and smash me to pieces – just for fun!

And if I ever had the gall to complain or retaliate, she would just say *You're doing it* or *Do more reps* or shove another 30 seconds onto my HIIT! However there was this one time, during one of my personal training sessions, I got so pissed off with her *You're not giving it your max, Sarezah* every blooming second, whilst doing sprint on the stationary bike (sprints involve cycling for two to three minutes at a steady pace, then sprinting for up to a minute as fast as you can, then back to the steady pace. Absolute killer).

At some point I just snapped and yelled at her to *Fuck off, mate.* The whole gym just stopped – together with a few gasps and shocks of horror! She just looked straight through me and replied without blinking an eye, "I'm not fuck off, you fuck off."

I was stunned, along with some of the gym goers, who were thinking it's going to kick off any minute between these two heavyweights. And she looked at me until I looked away – because she didn't. Because she knew, fundamentally, she could have smeared me across that gym floor, because she's as hard as nails. So I conceded and just did those sprints and kept my mouth shut. You wanna know why? Because *I* won't be thanked for it.

It's safe to say, from then on, I grew to despise her – but only in the sense of training. In fact, I love this lady because she did what no one else ever achieved. She broke me and remoulded me into a machine so I could achieve those goals that I once only ever dreamt of. She took the negatives and turned them into positives. She told me, *Sarezah, I awoke the warrior within you, that had long been dormant.* And my goodness, did she. Natalija has been a huge part of my success – as well as my beloved club, Kingsford Park Bannatyne's.

From the onset, they've invested their time and faith in me, providing free personal trainers and anything else I needed to get me results. And, in turn, I didn't let them down. To this day, both Natalija and the club are a massive part of my life. Bannatyne's is like my second home and Natalija is like a sister to me and, in my opinion, the best trainer since sliced bread. Even now when things get a little tough when I am training and occasionally think about skipping a few reps, in kicks her voice in my head saying, *You don't want to reach your goals Sarezah.*

But as the old saying goes, all good things come to an end – and sadly our training sessions did. After a session I noticed she wasn't her usual self. She looked at me and said, "I'm leaving, Sarezah." I instantly felt absolutely crushed. I was like *Noooooo*. *She is the best thing that has happened to me, please don't take it away.* We've only worked together for less than a year and I'm getting the results I have always wanted. I almost pleaded with her not to go – but she said she had to.

That last day arrived when we had our final session together. I walked up towards the gym door. As usual, Natalija stood waiting menacingly, holding her professional boxing Baltic champ gloves! Then announced, "Sarezah, today you become a heavyweight fighter, you are going to do 12, 3-minute rounds. No more 3 or 7 3-minute rounds, Sarezah. It's 12, Sarezah." Do you know what. I did not say a single word. I didn't make a discontented moan or a groaning sound. I simply said, "Ok!"

Rounds one to eight were not so bad, as I was already used to doing seven, 3-minute rounds.

Now just to clarify, each round of 3 minutes was split into 1-minute rounds where we did a minute on round one which consisted of combination punches. The second round was speed – where I had to run on the spot or around the bag, tapping the bag with left right punches. The last round was the power round – punch left and right as hard as I can. Mate, it's an absolute killer!

Each minute got harder and harder and by the time I got to round 10 I was literally dying – sweat was pouring off me. My hair and clothes were soaked though, to the extent it was dripping on the floor – oh my gosh, it was so hard. Think about it, I'm having to smash a boxing bag with everything I have inside me for one round. Then switch it up and change on the middle round to a soft tapping and running around the bag. Then back to smashing the bag with all my might.

And with only 30 seconds rest between those three rounds. Not a joke, mate.

Occasionally, I would try to stop out of sheer exhaustion, I would grab onto the punch bag, like a tired boxer who's had enough of being punched. I know it sounds a bit extra, but that's what it feels like training with Nat. It's bloody gruelling. And to make things worse, she wasn't having any of that – she grabbed my sweat-soaked clothes and pulled my arms up, to get my hands up and back smashing that bag! Shouting, "Fight Sarezah."

Every second that passed, my arms got heavier. Every round was tougher than the next, then we got to the final round. "Round 12 Sarezah, round 12."

She put her arms round me like a trainer would a fighter in the corner and she began giving me the last round mental talk. "Last round, Sarezah. You can do it. This is it. You want to win Sarezah, you want to reach your goals. You want to give it your max, Sarezah."

I want to, I said to myself in my head. *I want to do it!* With little to no breath left, along with sweat pouring out of every possible gland, I looked up at her through my wet dripping hair and nodded. She gave me a mouthful of water out of the bottle – as she always did when she thought I needed it. But I knew just to take a sip. Any more than that at that intensity level can often make you chuck it right back up.

After another sip or two of water, Nat stepped a little closer to me and looked me in my face. "Last round, Sarezah. After this you are going to be heavyweight champ. You give it your max, your everything Sarezah, pull it out deep from inside of you. You will win this last shitty round, Sarezah. It's nothing."

Ding, ding, the boxing app phone countdown alarm went off informing us we only have 10 seconds left before we get up and fight again; 30 seconds really doesn't feel like a lot of time when you are gasping for your life.

The final round began and she literally started shouting at the top of her voice, once again, in the 'ol family man gym. "That's it, Sarezah. 20 seconds left, Sarezah, on round one. Keep pushing Sarezah. Round two. Run Sarezah," she came closer to my ear and whispered, "You are as light as a feather, Sarezah, it's nothing. Run, run faster. Keep going. Sarezah. Round three, Sarezah, last shitty round Sarezah, give it your max," she shouted. "You are winner, Sarezah, you can do it, push yourself. You are a champ,' she said. I could feel the tears fill my eyes as I felt euphoric, she called me *a champ*! The toughest of trainers thinks *I am a champion!*

For that last 45 seconds I smashed that bag like my life depended on it. 30 seconds left, she shouted, then said, "Switch, Sarezah." Switch meant last round, punch that bag like you are going for a boxing title. Uppercuts, body shots, hooks.

"COME ON SAREZAH TEN, NINE, EIGHT, SEVEN, SIX, FIVE, FOUR, THREE, TWO, ONE. YOU DID IT SAREZAH! YOU THE FUCKING CHAMP SAREZAH," she shouted.

I victoriously grabbed my opponent, that bloody punch bag, and hugged it and shouted, "I DID IT!"

I looked at her and she looked at me. I'd never seen her look like that before – emotional, I mean this is Natalija Dolgova we are talking about, you remember 'Miss Emotionless,' hard as a bag of nails and tougher than tough!

Well, that was until she put her hands on my shoulder, and I saw a little tear in her eye, and in a slightly croaky voice she said, "You did it champ! You did it, my little warrior!"

I also felt the emotions in that, because I too shed a little tear, for this was the first time I caught a glimpse of my new self – I witnessed what she pushed me to become. A machine. She made me into a f*cking human machine. In that moment I broke that *same ol' same ol'* cycle of what I had endured and settled for all my life. I finally rose above myself!

Moments later, Nat turned around to face the others in the gym, who had pretty much stopped anyway as my performance was much like a free pay per view, and said, "I just want to say, I'm so proud of her, she smashed it, she is a winner, and a champ. Thank you for listening."

I don't think there was a dry eye or not a lump in the throat of those members present, because many of those watched me day in day out, smashing it, witnessing all the ups and downs I had gone through to get that weight off.

That day – when she called me a warrior – is the day I strived to continue her legacy and to this day I push and give it my max!

CHAPTER 15

Progression

After Natalija left, I did have another trainer. We made some progress, but I think we just ended up hitting a brick wall. Even though I loved Bannatyne's, I had outgrown the gym. In order for me to further my gains I knew I needed to make another change. I learnt you have to switch it up or else you will remain stagnant – and I knew I had to get out of my comfort zone.

In December 2018, I approached the general manager at the gym and of Kingsford Park Bannatyne and explained that I had found another gym – but explained I was not leaving, because I love this place. I was still going to use the spa and pool, because it's dreamy – but the majority of my weight training will now be done at Pump Gyms in Colchester. It's a much bigger gym with different equipment. The manager completely understood and was nothing but delighted for me. He said that the club will always continue to support me wherever I went. And they did and have. I could not ask for anything more.

Pump Gyms was a lot further to get to but was worth the journey as it has almost every type of weight training gym equipment, complete with a boxing area and a cold lift room a few steps down from the main gym area. It has all types of cardio machines. It caters for every level of training, from beginner to pro. Members and staff are lovely and they literally took over where Bannatyne left off. I really loved my time there.

From the moment I started, I knew I would progress very quickly – and quickly I did. I began to build muscle which, in turn, burned fat. This is also where I first began to train myself, under the watchful eye of the manager Meg, who I like to call beautiful Meg because that is what she is – beautiful, inside and out.

Since meeting Meg – another little warrior – she has continued to be a wonderful friend and support. It was also a time I met my soon-to-become mate Ross, a fellow Man Utd fan. In fact, both of them supported me from start to finish. This is the time I created a new motto, *Once you reach a goal then move the goal, until you reach that goal then you change it,* so you just keep evolving.

Within a few months I'd made fantastic progress. Meg showed me different ways to train and that's when I started to see all the right curves in the right places and really began to like what I saw – well, when I had clothes on anyway. See, I looked great in Nike leggings, all tight fit holding it all in, but take them off and everything went proper south mate, utter devastation. Let me explain why. There are consequences to losing that amount of weight, and that's a shit load of loose skin, mate.

Now remember when I was at my biggest – I was completely spherical, a globular shape, somewhat like a party ballon. Now think of it like this. The party came and the party ended. And the ballon has found its way into a corner and is left for some time, during which it has considerably deflated not just in size but visually too. The texture of the balloon is now somewhat crinkly and pastry-like to touch. Well that's what loose skin looks and feels like on someone who was previously a big size person.

It is the absolute dread of super morbidly obese people, who inevitably will experience this after a huge weight loss like me – loose dead skin. And boy oh boy, did I. It literally hung down. It was an apron of wobbly subcutaneous fat and skin. It didn't just affect my belly. It was my thighs, my arms, which looked like blooming saggy bingo wings. If I was asked to describe it in one word.... *Disgusting!* And, it's like having yet another responsibility. Mate, you've got to keep the folds of skin constantly dry as well as clean throughout the day to prevent it getting infected.

Simple things like going to the toilet was a task all in itself. It was like a juggling act. I would have to lift and hold the skin flap with one arm, so the belly wouldn't flop against the outside of the toilet bowl (I know, gross, right?). Every five minutes (slight exaggeration, like four or five times a day), I had to replace the kitchen roll that I had to place in between the flap of skin between my private parts and belly, where the fold of skin would collect moisture – which would cause it to itch.

The best way I can describe it is it's like athlete's foot – that constant moisture that causes itching. The skin would become irritated, then the skin would develop a primary infection, which would require the use of a topical cream. In due course, that infection would more than often develop into a secondary infection and that would require an antibiotic cream. It was a constant battle to keep the infection under control.

That wasn't the worst part of it. Not only did I hate it because of all the above. Visually it was unsightly – and seemingly repulsive to the outside world. I'll tell you why, shall I?

Remember when I said even though I was at Pump Gyms, I still used the spa at Bannatyne's because it was dreamy. Well, one day after a swim, I rewarded myself with a nice relaxing bubbly hydrotherapy session and sauna. It helped ease my hard-working sore muscles.

I would stand under the fountain that jetted out water and let it cascade onto different parts of my upper body. Absolute bliss. It was like a massage all in itself. Now remember, from waist upwards I didn't look too bad – bit of bingo wings, boobs didn't and don't look too bad (chest day helps with that). But my legs and belly were a totally different story, and I suffered from tonnes of loose skin – which looked like 'cooked' filo pastry (because I'm brown).

On that day, without knowing what would transpire, I decided to go from the hydrotherapy pool to the jacuzzi. As I stood up, the loose skin around the tops of my thighs began swirling around the water and my loose-skinned thighs were clapping together which caught the attention of these two women. The daughter decided to point her finger towards my skin and said quite audibly, in a deep South Essex accent, "Mum, muuuuuummmmm, look at her ffffffighs."

The mother looked round and both of them caught my gaze and I was somewhat snarling – and they instantly stopped. Now remember my motto, *If I hear you or see you don't be surprised if you get a reaction!* If you don't want a reaction, then what do you do? Keep your mouth shut! Why? *Because you won't be thanked for it.* But anyway, once again I was the victim of someone else's amusement! Fuck people sometimes, man!

Look I'm not always aggressive, it's usually only when some idiot acts like this lot did! I suppose it's easy to have that opinion of me because I do have a face that looks pissed off and angry and that's on a good day. Additionally, I am adorned with lots of tattoos – meaningful ones, might I add, not just some random Zeus on one arm with a sand timer underneath.

And I certainly didn't get tattoos because of any trend! See, I had my first tattoo as soon as I could – and that was when I was 19 and received my first ever pay cheque – that being a single red rose, due to my love of roses and butterflies, on the top of my back on the right-hand side.

Of course it was in secret, and I had to take great care in hiding it from my father, Farouk – otherwise he would have gone berserk. But seeing it was something I always dreamed of having, it was worth the risk! That dream started when I was a child of around 11, when a friend's father handed down copies of a magazine called Back Street Heroes – because I always used to talk to him about his bike, saying when I grow up I am going to buy one just like yours. I guess that was endearing to him and, unlike my father, he wanted to inspire me to do that by handing me those very precious magazines!

During the night, I would flick through the pages that were filled with pictures of bikers in leather jackets on Harley Davidson's with long beards and tattoos – which was so appealing to me, seeing I was a born and bred *metalla* – heavy metal being my love, then house music being a very close second, and a few other genres of music too, including some from my childhood like Sega and Indian music, along with Arabic. I do love a bit of Madonna – that is because of my beautiful Azim. He loves her and when I say love I mean love! I love a bit of old-style rap, ragga/dancehall and dub/reggae, classical, all sorts really – just not country music. I can't get my head around any of that business! Anyway, tattoo wise I have one full sleeve on my right arm, and a half sleeve on the other, and most of my back, and one very dodgy one on my ankle!

Anyway, after that incident, I realised that losing that amount of weight drew a different type of attention to being *super morbidly obese*. Not sure why people can't leave each other alone, but hey ho! So now, I had a different set of problems caused by loose skin – not just aesthetically, but medically too!

So off I went to see Dr Goel again and she sent a letter to the CCG (Clinical Commissioning Group) to present my case for the removal of the skin on my stomach and thighs, arms and on each side of my lateral muscle, where all the loose skin problem areas were. The CCG board is responsible for making decisions on whether you meet the criteria required for funding.

Despite having a good case to have all my loose skin removed, I was only awarded funding for an abdominoplasty on the grounds that I had a hernia that was being dragged down by the weight of the skin – with supporting clinical evidence that the skin caused difficulties with daily activities and recurrent skin infection in the skin fold that failed to respond – despite appropriate medical therapy for at least six months.

Whilst this was granted, to my dismay everything else was refused – despite the same issues occurring in different parts of my body, on the ground of *How would I benefit more than anyone else in my cohort*, whatever that means. I shall leave it to you to decipher the meaning behind that because – to date – I am still lost for words.
I don't really understand this type of preposterous consideration, because there is no one else in '*my cohort*' that has done what I have done.

CHAPTER 16

Life Changing

A short time after the funding for the abdominoplasty was approved, I received a letter from the Plastic Surgery department at Broomfield Hospital, with an appointment to see a consultant plastic surgeon called Mr. Miles Banwell – who had loads of accolades after his name, meaning he was a big surgeon in big surgeon world. My appointment was on the 22nd April 2019 – the day after my mummy's birthday.

The 22nd April 2010 is also the day I picked up my second most beloved and beautiful car.

She was just over six months old when I picked her up. So far she has one lady owner, low mileage and full-service history (and I still have her but know sooner or later I will have to part with her).

That date, 22nd April 2019, is a date I will always remember for the rest of my life as it is one of the poignant days in my calendar and linked to other events – because had Mr. Banwell not done what he did to ensure I received the operation I so desperately needed, I most probably would not be here today. Unbeknownst to anyone of us, this time, I really was a *ticking time bomb!*

The letter arrived with an appointment date. Thinking about that day, I began to have some preconceived ideas in my head of what might happen and, of course, what Mr. Banwell might look like- – based on my calculations of reasoning and judgment of all the letters after the man's name.

Miles Banwell BSc, MB BS, FRCS, PhD, FRCS(plast), MSc(AesPlastSurg). Mate, I tell you, if I had all those letters after my name, I would be whipping out my licence every chance I got. It's impressive and it must have taken him years to get to where he is now.

So I expected him to be somewhat mature in age, somewhere around mid 60's, slight in stature, possibly short grey hair, donning perhaps a long white coat, who spoke beautifully, whilst peering over his glasses – without generalising here but they all do seem to wear glasses, don't they?

Anyway, my personal imagery and perception of what surgeons and doctors looked like were spawned from when I was a child back in the 70's from TV shows. Nonetheless, I had this preconceived image of who Mr. Banwell was and thought no more of it until we met.

On appointment day, I drove to Chelmsford silly early and awaited in the car park. One of my sons and his then girlfriend had also arranged to come for support and were due to arrive imminently, before which I made my way towards the huge white hospital building.

I walked through the revolving doors – into what looked more like an airport than a hospital. On arrival, I tried to use my internal sat nav for directions, but the place has some unique coding system – so in the end, I asked a couple of people for directions, who gladly obliged. Remember, this was pre-Covid days – so no masks, no social distancing, just normal everyday life.

I finally found the plastic surgery department, checked in with the receptionist, took a seat and waited. Soon after, my son arrived. As usual, I was in sports gear, covered from head to toe in Nike. Well, you want to look your best athlete, don't you? I must have looked like a right label idiot – even my own son looked me up and down and said, "You sponsored by Nike, love?"

Soon after, a nurse attempted to call my name, *Sarrrh, Sarraza*. I said, "Sarezah Lake?" She nodded. "That's me," I said, as I got up and moved towards her – but not before turning around to see my two little supporters who gave me a lovely smile to take with me.

As I got closer to the nurse, she asked, "How do you say your name?" "It's pronounced like Sir and Razor. Sir-razor."

The nurse directed me to another little waiting room from where I could hear this big booming voice in the next room which within moments said, "Bring her in, SAREZAH Lake," pronouncing my name quite beautifully, might I say. See, with a name like mine, you actually end up giving people marks for effort and pronunciation. She scurried back into my room, saying, "He's ready for you now."

Smiling like an idiot, I made my way to said voice's office. As

I walked in, I saw a strong, well-built man, with brown hair and greenish coloured eyes – not that I was looking but green eyes are actually very rare and green is the colour of my mother's eyes, so I am instantly drawn to them.

Anyway, these belonged to a very confident, relaxed, gallant and somewhat dashing man, who was sitting quite casually in his chair who – looking up at me – said in a very masculine authoritarian voice, "Hello, take a seat, I'm your consultant Miles Banwell."

You're who? *This* is Miles Banwell, I thought, as my eyes literally popped out of their sockets, thinking *You can't be, you don't look old enough to be a consultant, where's the long white coat and grey hair? Why aren't you peering over a pair of glasses with that judgmental look most people in authority have. And how come you are not 60-something!* The trouble with perceptions, hey.

Congratulating me on my weight loss, he said, "It is absolutely incredible what you have achieved, in a short six and a half years of dieting. It's just incredible, well done to you."

His eyes flicked between looking at me and my notes, trying to build a mental picture of me and what would be needed for my surgery. He then said, "Most people I see that have lost this amount of weight have usually had bariatric-type surgery – like a gastric band or a stomach by- pass. How you have achieved yours is remarkable."

I mean, he is very enchanting – so I found myself glowing from a little blush as I responded with a little bashful giggle, yes me! Brash Sarezah! Thankfully he didn't notice, seeing as I am a person of colour so bright red cheeks don't usually show.

I guess he was right, but I had never seen it as amazing, more that it was a necessity. But yes, I had worked really hard to get to where I was. It took sheer determination, consistency and, of course, a little stubbornness to get where I was. And whilst the skin was bad, I had seen much worse on social media where people had been left really disfigured due to the vast amounts of weight they had lost too quickly. Because I lost the weight gradually over time, my body had time to recover and tone from exercise.

I actually told Mr. Banwell that my doctors had referred me for a gastric band but it was refused on the same grounds as an operation for my hernia – which I had developed during my third pregnancy – as I was too big and they felt it wasn't safe to operate. This was explained in the letter from the surgeon to the GP which I was copied in on which actually said – excuse the pun – that *there is a massive risk to her life due to her size. We would have to administer a huge amount of anaesthetic which could end in death.* Oh look, that word *DEATH* again. Fantastic, hey?!

So had there been a choice I might have had a gastric band or whatever else was available, I was that desperate. But it wasn't and I didn't, even though I have even been accused of this on social media by people I know and don't know, assuming that I must have had some sort of help.

To them, I guess the concept of losing 19st-odd simply through diet and exercise is unfathomable, but I can assure you whilst it might be difficult to get your head around, it's not impossible. Others have made comments like, *Well, at least you didn't cheat* – as if finding a way of saving your life is cheating. I say, do what you need to lose the weight you need to, be it surgery or diet. Don't let idiots get you down as though they speak the truth. *Fuck them!*

During the consultation, Mr. B described my surgery procedure, saying he had to remove skin from the entire area as he can't just nibble away at the front of my abdomen, as your apron (the fold of skin) is circumferential, so it all needs to be removed.

He then stood up, saying, "The easiest way I can describe it is it's like pulling up your trousers and tightening your belt," as he mimicked the action. He said, "The operation is called a circumferential abdominoplasty – and it will take approximately 7 hours, including fixing the hernia. It's quite a dangerous procedure, so be aware."

Mr. Banwell went out if his way to ensure I had what I needed. Had he not, it is likely I would not be here. Mr. Banwell, in no uncertain terms, saved my life!

After a few more formalities, he finished with, "The only time we wouldn't operate is if you have a serious underlying condition, or cancer."

To which I responded, "Well, to my knowledge, I don't have

either."

We finished up and I looked at him and gave him a smile and thanked him very, very much.

Excitedly, I went to sit with my two faves who had eagerly been waiting for me. When Mr. B came out of his office and saw me sitting with my son, he said, "Oh, you must be the son." I mean, it's not hard to tell us apart as he is a carbon copy of his mama! After a few words were exchanged, Mr. Banwell left, looking straight at me, and gave me a little smile. That was the last time I saw Mr. B until the operation in October 2020.

Shortly after the initial consultation, I received a letter to attend a pre op for a medical assessment, to ensure my current state of health was fit for the operation. It seemed a bit early, I thought, as the waiting list was approximately one year. However, if there was a cancellation, I would be prepared. I wasn't in the least bit worried about it because I considered myself to be fit and healthy from all my weight I'd lost.

On arrival at the same hospital for the pre op, I found myself lost once again. I looked for lanyards on workers so I could ask for help. Sometime after, I approached a smart-looking man and said, "Excuse me, you look like you work here, could you help me please, I'm completely lost."

He took the sheet of paper with a *bothered me smile*, followed by a blunt, "What department are you looking for?" But before I could answer, he slightly raised an eyebrow and said, "Oh that's ironic, the department and person you are looking for is me, come on then, let's go." No way, I thought. What are the chances of that! Must be a good sign, I thought.

Off we trotted together towards his department, when he began asking what operation I was having. Of course I began, *well I, me blah blah blah*, then he interrupted quite suddenly and said, "Are you the patient that's lost over 19-odd stone."

"Oh yes, that's me," I replied, with a sickly *aren't I wonderful* grin.

"Ooooh that's you, I had a conversation with Mr. Banwell about you. You know, Mr.

Banwell is very impressed with your dedication to your weight loss." "Oh, is he?" I said, ever so slightly blushing.

Then the anaesthetist went on to say, "Well he is right to be impressed. It's very impressive." That's when he suddenly stopped and looked at me and said, "Tell me honestly, how did you do it?"

"Diet and exercise."

He looked at me with a little glint of disbelief in his eyes. I said, "Look, all my scans, X- rays and all my medical records are the proof that there are no signs of any type of bariatric surgery at all. I just got on with it and did the hard work myself! Besides it's not rocket science is it, eat less and move more!"

Sooner than I was expecting after the pre op, I received a call from the hospital. They told me the results indicated I had severe anaemia and that it was so bad, I had to have an emergency appointment with my doctor to investigate what the issue was and, additionally, the operation would be put on hold unless it drastically improved because, as it stood, I was not fit for the operation!

To say I was shocked is an understatement! I was absolutely gutted – and I mean gutted.

How can I have anaemia? I ate well. I was fit. *What the hell, man,* I thought. Every single damn time something good happens, something bad comes along to destroy it! *F' my life, just f' my pissing life.*

So, once again off I went to see Dr. Gaol who said that whilst my other counts were acceptable, my haemoglobin count was extremely low at 75, one of the lowest she'd seen – as seemingly a normal count for a lady is 115 plus. She indicated that the anaemia could possibly be because of my diet. I explained that I had a tendency not to consume much red meat, poultry, nor eggs because of their high fat content.

Plus I suffered from heavy periods, in fact very heavy periods, which I remembered from before when I was young, when I had a low red blood count. She said that was likely the cause. So she said, "I suggest you start to eat red meat and eggs and will prescribe some iron tablets as well as some iron infusions, recommend by the anaesthetist. And if after a period of time, there is no improvement then we will have to investigate further."

It was then I realised how I had radically cut my diet to the point where I was obsessed with not eating certain foods, after it was suggested by a trainer I was working with to go for a 'cut' style bodybuilder diet, where he advised me to cut out red meat, almost all sugars, and practically all fats.

I wasn't keen on doing this because I believe in balance, but he said this is the only way you will get results as you have plateaued, so I listened. It is likely that this style of dieting led to me having deficiencies, like iron. Because as soon as I began to eat meat again my iron went back up to over a 100 and the pre op team agreed to go ahead with the operation. I continued with the iron tablets and eating meat etc. I even felt better for it, but little did I know that this may have possibly triggered what was to transpire in the future.

During the waiting period for my operation, the Coronavirus Pandemic happened and in March 2020 the government announced that gyms were going to close due to this contagious virus. In fact, a worldwide lockdown programme began. And from that day onwards, many things changed for all of us.

The gyms closing down had a big impact on me because I literally had little to no weights or equipment at home. So with no equipment, I started to walk a lot more – along with doing HIIT, high-intensity interval training.

This did help in some ways as I began to notice a change in my physical appearance because I was no longer lifting weights, doing what is known as compound movements, which help burn stored fat quite effectively.

Frustratingly, I began to see all my hard work slip away, as the *supposedly* few weeks of lockdown, turned into months as the pandemic took the lives of many people as it swarmed through the world. Because of this, gym equipment had become sought after and therefore skyrocketed in price. So I had to beg, borrow and make my own equipment. This also meant all non-essential surgeries, like mine, had been placed on hold due to the overwhelming amount of people in hospitals with the virus.

Somewhat selfishly, I began to even wonder whether I would get my surgery. I feared it may be cancelled due to funding – as the NHS was on its knees due to the pandemic. Whilst I understood that, to me, so was my condition.

And yes, you can point the finger at me, I was living with a tragic amount of loose skin that caused infection and rashes from the constant rubbing and moisture under my stomach flap. But I also had a hernia that was being pulled down by the weight of that skin and unless I had that operation, the hernia could have strangulated, causing all sort of blasted problems. *Death* being one of them!

CHAPTER 17

Show Time

Finally, the long-awaited announcement came, and gyms reopened on the 25th July. Heaven! But unfortunately for me, damage was visibly apparent. I didn't let it deter me, so back to the grind I went to undo the harm done.

A few months later – and as if by magic – I received a call from my surgeon's office, informing me that there had been a cancellation, and asking if I would like my operation, which would be in a week's time.

I didn't even hesitate and screamed *yes!* Within a few days, I had a Coronavirus test and another pre op done, which included a full blood count, blood pressure, weight and an ECG to check my heart was fit for the operation. Nothing seemed out of the ordinary, bloods were perhaps on the low side of normal but deemed acceptable, I was fit for operation! Finally!

Nothing can go wrong I thought – well, not until after the operation!

Off I went on the 22nd October 2020 for my operation, two days before my lovely middle son Khaliq's birthday, which I planned to spend with him as I was only scheduled to stay in for one night – unless there were complications.

My youngest, Azim, came to stay that night as he was living and working in London. We stayed up all night talking, as I was really apprehensive about oversleeping and missing the operation. My son asked if I was nervous about the operation. Whilst I wasn't, there was, however, this little niggling feeling that I couldn't quite put my finger on.

In the end, I just put it down to pre op nerves and told myself not to worry. Besides, I was in the best possible hands – those of Mr. Miles Banwell. And I am of the opinion, when it's your time it's your time. So if I died on the operating table, then so be it.

First thing on arrival was my observation – my blood pressure was a little high, which they put down to nerves (amazing what anxiety can do to a very healthy body, isn't it?). I was then put in a room to await my surgeon. To my surprise Mr. B was not the first person to meet and greet me, it was his two junior surgeons Nick and Vic.

Whilst they had masks on, it was apparent that they were somewhat dishy, made apparent by the nurses behaving accordingly. I could see why. Nick looked and dressed like he stepped out of GQ Magazine, Vic fresh out of Bollywood. They introduced themselves. We spoke a bit about my weight loss journey, but I told them I was disappointed when the nurse said I gained weight in excess of 10 kilos (in English money, that's two stone) since my last pre op! Gutting.

They stepped out of the room, asking me to remove all my clothes down to my pants, then asked me to pop on the gown provided. Now, as it was a day where I needed a bit of good fortune, I wore my lucky pants. However, it would be fair to say they have seen better days. See, they were completely stretched and ill fitting, and saturated with holes. Oh, and they had one of the biggest holes at the front!

I looked a complete flipping mess – my hair looked like I'd been dragged through a hedge backwards, my face was looking drained and tired from having had no sleep. I was now in a horrible hospital gown that gaped at the back, under which everything was pointing south! And I've got black fluffy ankle boots on and tattoos everywhere. *How unsightly,* I thought!

Suddenly there was a knock on the outside door. "Come in," I said, before trying to hide my embarrassment over my appearance by making some quirky comment. "No judging. I look a mess, and I'm covered in tattoos, I used to be a metal guitarist you know!" (Well I was).

"Oh, just like me then," a voice quipped – and in walked Mr. Banwell, who peered from behind the curtains with the hugest of warm smiles, walking towards me with a Sharpie in his hand, closely followed by Nick and Vic and a female. I wasn't really sure who she was, well not until Mr. Banwell asked me to stand up and uttered the most mortifying words imaginable, "Can you pop your gown off please?"

"Erm, sorry, pop my what off?" I said. "Your gown," he said.

Mate, my mouth went dry – and my eyes opened with shock! As I just froze, staring at him, thinking *noooooo, they're all going to see me naked.*

"Well, I've got to take a look at you, haven't I," Mr. Banwell said, with a coaxing look in his eyes directing me to *Come on girl, slip it off.*

So, with a blank and vacant stare, I slipped my gown off, revealing all that my gym wear hid oh so beautifully. Revealing my hideous loose skin and augmented body shape.

I stood there in shame, bereft of life. Topped by the fact that, not only was my mutilated, misshaped Mr. Blobby body on full view, something worse was visible. *Worse?* I hear you all say. What could be worse than that?

Well my black, torn, mangled *lucky* pants, that's what – with everyone's horrified eyes in that blasted room landing directly on what I was conscious about. That being a fairly visible tear the size of a triangle right on where Mary, my lady parts, were. Beautifully peeping through the gap of my overhanging atrocity of skin and fat was my white menstrual sanitary towel – where the sticky part of that pad, the part gaping through the hole, had by now collected black lint from my leggings.

Bloody marvellous, I thought, whilst I rapidly blinked my eyes hoping the ground would just swallow me whole. *Just why? Oh, the humility!* And, yes, I know they've seen it all before and I understand that body dysmorphia is the tragic result and downfall of huge weight loss. But when you are standing there naked, it's crushing!

More humiliation followed when Mr. B took that Sharpie pen and began to draw lines all over my heinous gut. *A Sharpie*, you know, *a Sharpie*! A bright green Sharpie, mish (Turkish for mate)!

Oh, and if things could not get any pissing worse, Mr. B began hoisting up the excess skin on my gut and drawing some dot-to-dot business all around my body, informing me it is where he needed to cut it off. Mate, I didn't even look at him. Man, he didn't even flinch, you know. He just spoke all normal. Like this was in anyway normal!

What seemed like forever, Mr. Banwell walked towards the door to leave, then asked, "Have you gained a little weight since I last saw you?"

I nodded *yes*, and inside my heart truly sank. I felt like I'd let him down. Let alone myself.

Whilst I blamed Covid with no gym etc, which was partly true, I had also eaten some foods I shouldn't have, namely freshly baked Almond Tarts from Marks and Spencer bakery. Mate, they are another level! Them and Palmier. Woah!

Now, whilst I hold my hands up and take accountability for my actions, I grossly underestimated the calorific value, which I ate without an honest account. Remember, guesstimating included not weighing some of my food, and I added a spoonful here and there – which of course contributed to me gaining weight! (Additionally, a nurse in passing did say iron tablets can contribute to weight gain! *Not 10 kilos*, I said).

We all got ready to leave the room and get ready for the big surgery. It was showtime. I thought this would be a good time to make another stupid quirky comment.

"Oh I feel like I'm off to Savile Row."

Savile Row is situated in London and is well known for having the finest luxury and bespoke tailoring service and is possibly a place where Mr. B frequents because he immediately quipped back with, "Yes – and what stitches would you like?" then began reeling off loads of stitching names.

To which I didn't have a Danny, mate (Danny La Rue is cockney rhyming slang for clue).

So I said, "Oh you're the expert, you choose, chortle, chortle," as I was walked down to the anaesthetist's room with a nurse who was already waiting for me outside the door. That is when my heart started racing like the clappers with apprehension that it was all about to happen.

I entered another room and was met by a very bubbly anaesthetist – who could see I was anxious so tried to make me feel as comfortable as possible. She asked me to lay down on the bed and they began hooking me up to all these machines. By now I was really nervous!

She distracted me by asking me, "Where do your family come from, sweetheart?"

"My parents come from the island of Mauritius," I responded hesitantly, whilst transfixed by their military procedure.

"Oh that's lovely, sweetie," she said, in between talking to the others in a much lower voice as not to worry me, as if that helped, before she continued, "Sweetie, I want you think about sitting on the beach in Mauritius."

Following her instructions, I took a deep breath and closed my eyes and thought of my three boys running around the beach playing football with my boxer dog Mac – with the beautiful Mauritian warm sea gently lapping onto the white soft sand with the hazy sun shimmering in the background! That was the last thing I saw because, within a flash, it all faded to black.

Seven and a half hours later, to my delight, I opened my eyes. But I couldn't feel anything from my boobs down, it was just numb. The first person I saw was a male nurse then a female nurse. I went to sit up and immediately they ran over to me and said, "No, you can't do that," as they gently coaxed me back into a flat position.

I asked, "Am I alive or am I dreaming?"

The male nurse said, "No, you are in the ICU (intensive care unit), darling." "Oh I made it then, I didn't die!"

He let out a little laugh and said, "Yes, you are fine, darling."

He then asked if I wanted him to call any of my family to let them know I have come round. I asked him if he could ring my sons and husband. To be honest, I don't really remember much after that – other than a vague recollection of hearing him talk to one of my children or husband, saying the operation had been successful and that I was in recovery and would shortly be moved to a ward.

To say I felt groggy was an understatement. But, surprisingly, as Mr. Banwell explained prior to the operation, once the initial anaesthetic wears off you don't feel much in the way of pain. I suspect good ol' Oramorph helped with that too. I mean it does exactly what it says on the tin. But when you consider the type of invasive surgery I had, the hundreds of stitches from the inside out – where I had been sewn up simultaneously and left with huge scars which went horizontally and circumferentially around my bikini line – the pain was really not that bad!

I was soon taken from ICU and put on a ward with a few other women who had mostly undergone breast reconstruction surgery after cancer. I'd spoken to one lady who had surgery to remove several parts of her breast due to cancer. We became friendly, exchanging our stories of what brought us here. Hearing mine, she said, "You are so brave to have this kind of surgery."

I said, "What me? Brave? I'm not the brave one here, you are. I just lost weight, hun. You have cancer!"

CHAPTER 18

It Can't Be!

I slept most of the day after my surgery, waking up in between the nurses taking routine bloods, which seemed like every second (ok, slight exaggeration), but it was far more regularly than any other patients on the ward.

I really didn't think too much about it until day two came, when I was expecting to go home. But apparently, I couldn't because they wanted to keep me in for further observations as I was seemingly increasingly more susceptible to infection.

Fair enough, I thought. After all, it is a massive wound! I will most probably go home early doors tomorrow. Day three came and that didn't happen either, in fact there were no clear signs of when I would be leaving. The only thing that was apparent was all the strange eye contact and whispering between the various medical teams, whilst looking in my direction.

Something ain't right here, I thought! Especially since every request I made about going home was either ignored or I was fobbed off with an excuse! Day four arrived, and that is when the fun, if you can call it that, really did start. It began with a doctor coming in to see me who, on arrival, dramatically closed the curtains, bringing a chair very close to my bed.

He leant forward and began solemnly speaking, "I'm afraid a serious problem has developed, putting your life in jeopardy."

I looked visibly shocked, so he gave me a few moments to compose myself, then he continued, saying my haemoglobin levels were dangerously low, along with my other blood counts which, too, had plummeted to dangerously low levels and he suggested I had an immediate blood transfusion!

"Sorry, what? My who, my what? Danger, what do you mean?"

He didn't answer, he in fact hadn't finished what he was saying. "Sarezah, may I call you Sarezah?" I nodded yes. "If you do have a blood transfusion, your neutrophils are also extremely low. If you were to have a reaction, there would be a strong possibility it could end up in a fatality."

"Fatality?!!! What do you mean fatality? Look, I don't want to sound rude, but you can't just come in here, draw the curtains and drop *fatality* like that. I don't even understand what you're talking about. I wasn't good at biology. What on earth are these neutrophils business? What the hell is going on, I don't understand anything other than *plummeted* and *dangerously low* and *FATAL*, mate."

The doctor tried to console my anxiety. But what he just said sent my emotions into overdrive – to the point where I felt sick! *Pull yourself together,* I told myself, so I took a deep breath and said, "Let's recap so I know I've understood what you just said." He nodded an ok.

"I desperately need a blood transfusion, but if I do, there is a strong possibility I could react to the donor's blood, and if I react, I do not have enough 'neutra' something or other to fight the infection so I could end up dead?"

He nodded in agreement then looked away. *Well that's just pissing marvellous,* I thought, *bloody marvellous!*

"What's happened between my operation and now?" I asked. "At this stage, it's unclear!"

"For goodness' sake! In the name of all that's holy! How?"

He then asked if I had any religious beliefs that would prevent me from having a transfusion. Even though I answered no, in that very moment everything inside me said that under no circumstances, whatsoever, should I have this transfusion! As I trust my intuition one hundred percent I flatly refused.

At first, he argued that I must. But I still said no, on the grounds that if there is a chance I could react to the donor, then I would rather chance my own blood. He realised I wasn't going to budge, so he left, whilst I lay on that hospital bed, all alone, my head spinning, feeling something I haven't felt for decades – and that was a little bit scared!

That day rolled into another night in Broomfield Hospital. I tried to settle but, for some reason, I was breathless. It seemed no matter how deeply I tried to breathe I couldn't fill my lungs with air

– it was like I couldn't catch my breath, to the point where I felt a bit lightheaded.

Of course, I now know these are classic symptoms of not having enough haemoglobin cells which carry oxygen around the body – hence why I needed a transfusion. But, of course, I didn't then. Even though it got worse during that night, my intuition just said *don't have one*. Instead, I decided to haul myself out of the bed and stand next to the window for some fresh air that was seeping through a tiny gap, that I had secretly opened earlier in an attempt to refresh the stale hospital air.

That October cold breeze gave me some relief. Even so, I felt quite unsettled and somewhat apprehensive about everything that was going on. So, as usual in times of peril, I had that oh so very familiar conversation with the Lord! But this time, I was a bit cross!

So, in a whisper, I said angrily, "Look, what the hell is this? This isn't fair. I didn't starve myself for seven odd years just to die here in flipping Broomfield Hospital in Chelmsford. Why is everything always so shit for me, just why, why has everything nice got to be pissing overshadowed by some shit? Why don't you ever let me enjoy anything?"

Then I started really venting! "You know what, this ain't happening. This is a bloody injustice. I've done everything right. I've changed my lifestyle, given up chocolate since May 2016, I've had no fizzy drinks, no shit foods, no nothing! Just give me a pissing break will you!"

With that, I got back into bed, all angry, so I tried to do some breathing exercises to help calm myself down – and before I knew it was the next morning!

Ironically, I felt much better than I had done. At the time I thought perhaps it was anxiety that caused the breathlessness or maybe the iron tablets helped. Either way, I felt ok – but didn't want to get my hopes up just in case the blood test said otherwise! Although I did wonder if something out there heard my plight and thought *poor cow, she's right, let's give her a helping hand and let her breathe better.* Who knows, hey?

Later that morning, in came two of the doctors, one who I

named *green dress*. She was walking in my direction with a somewhat hoity-toity look on her face and said quite bluntly, "Look, you need to speak to the haematology team as your low blood count is extremely serious. The haematology team are very concerned that something is terribly wrong with you and want to do more tests."

Stunned, I asked, "Well what's wrong then?" "I can't answer that, I am not a haematologist."

"Look, I feel fine, I'm eating and drinking. I've gotten better and so has my blood count. I want to go home and deal with whatever needs to be dealt with out of here. Besides, I only have supplies for one day and I've been here for six already. Everyone at home is falling apart because one, I'm stuck in here and, two, they don't know why. My dog Mac hasn't eaten for four days and blah, blah, blah,"

But before I could finish, she blurted out, "Look, you could have CANCER!!!" "WHAT?" I said, gasping. "Isn't that rather presumptuous of you? Didn't you just tell me you were not a blood specialist? That's why you couldn't explain the results of my blood counts when I asked questions. But now, you are comfortable with blurting out on a ward full of other patients that the reason I need to see a blood specialist is because I now may have cancer, so now you are an oncologist, but not a blood specialist! Isn't that a bit insensitive, love? Not only am I recovering from major surgery, but this room is full of cancer patients. Surly there are better and more sensitive ways of explaining things, no?"

The other doctor shook her head in disbelief and apologised on her behalf and eventually *she* did apologise too. Truth is, whatever she said got my attention, because I agreed to see the haematology team – which, of course, was also enhanced by the fact that until I did, they would not release me from hospital as they had a duty of care.

From that moment on, everything felt like it had turned sour, because that word cancer was stuck in my head, leaving me with this dark harrowing feeling that something really wasn't right. No smoke without fire and all that, I thought. I hadn't even been able to enjoy what this surgery meant for me. How I wouldn't have to struggle any longer with the loose skin issues. All that I could focus on was that something was wrong. I felt so bloody sick of all things good overshadowed by some nonsense. *Surely things can't get worse*, I thought.

Before long Nick, the junior surgeon, arrived to check on me, and he spoke a bit about the palaver that was going on with my bloods. He said he would come back soon to re-dress my scars. So I took advantage of getting them a little wet, asking one of the nurses to help me get showered – as prior to this I wasn't able to shower properly, I was only permitted a strip wash until my catheter and drains were removed.

Mate, let me tell you, that was bloody painful! I had four drains attached to my body, two in the front and two in the back of my hips. Now, for those of you who have never had a drain, it's to collect fluid in a bottle, because after surgery the site collects fluid, for some reason, don't ask me why. Anyway, what is agony is when they pull them out, because it is blooming painful. It feels like barbed wire being stripped through your flesh, tearing through you. In fact, it is excruciating.

A lovely nurse helped me shower and I felt really fresh and clean. I hated that grubby feeling, seeing as I am a 'shower two to three times a day' girl – so several days not having one made me feel gross! This was not made any better by the encrusted and congealed blood all around my scar, along with iodine stains almost all over my torso, as they couldn't rub my skin.

The nurse did all she could to help me, including washing and conditioning my hair and making sure I didn't bend due to the nature of my stitches, and she helped me get my underwear on. She got them to my thighs and I said to her, "It's ok, I can take it from here." That was the point I had an absolute mirror moment, which will transpire a little later.

After my shower, for ease, I decided to put on a black woolly dress. Almost immediately after I got dressed, Nick the junior surgeon came in to re-dress my scars. But before he did, he paused and took a deep breath and said, "I have something to tell you before I take the dressing off."

"What's wrong now?" I said.

"Well, you know you had that hernia?" "Yes?" I replied with an enquiring tone.

"Well Mr. Banwell called in a general surgeon to come and take a look at it. And he was able to fix it."

"Oh, ok. Well that's good then, it's all fixed?"

"Well, sort of," Nick said very sheepishly, "but not quite, as there was a problem." My expression changed! "See, you don't have a belly button."

"Whatttttttttt?????????" I said.

"It was awful," he said, in his slight northern accent. "Your hernia was an umbilical hernia, which had been there so long (almost 23 years; remember, because of my size, surgeons were reluctant to operate on it) and because of the size of your tummy, it cut the blood supply off to that area, causing the skin around the hernia to die. We couldn't re-attach a dead skin belly button back on otherwise it would have rotted and dropped off, causing even more problems."

In response to that, I began laughing almost uncontrollably, as he stood above my bed looking at me with some bewilderment, and said, "Why are you laughing."

"I'm not sure, mate. I'm really not sure!" But in my heart, I was thinking *fuck my life, man!*

Eventually, the haematology team – together with green dress and a shit load of other doctors, along with Nick and Vic – entered and closed the curtains for privacy as the entourage gathered around my bedside, whilst I lay flat on the bed, with my neck all crooked as I strained to look at the lady who introduced herself as the lead haematologist.

She was quite a stern character who spoke in short abrupt sentences, in a strong African accent. "Firstly, congratulations are in order for your incredible weight loss achievement." I thanked her whilst mentally scanning the other 10,000 people standing there (well, maybe just ten or so), in my mind thinking *just cut to the chase please, why are you here!?*

After a few more well dones and pats on the back, I suspect in an attempt to relax me by massaging my ego, she then began to talk about this situation with my bloods, saying that my blood level results did not reflect my behaviour. Evidently my neutrophils – a type of white blood cell that protects us from infections – are the first to arrive on the scene when we get bacterial infections.

"Presently your count has plunged to 0.7 and has not returned to an acceptable level. In fact, the trend for all your blood counts post-surgery has fallen lower and lower, which is causing us some puzzlement, because by all accounts you should have a severe infection and should be in a back room, hooked up to a drip fighting against infection! But I am told by your surgical team you are healing extremely well and haven't spiked a temperature. So we just can't really understand why this is the case. And to add more confusion, you have a severe anaemia deficiency and a lack of B12!"

But before I could ask any questions, the curtain went back and Mr. Banwell appeared, smiling at me as he glanced over at the others, then he stood at the end of the bed.

There was an immediate tension in the room – and definitely some argy bargy between Mr. B and the haematologist – so I decided to intervene to help calm the situation. So I spoke to Mr. Banwell and said, "Is it ok if I say something to you?"

He turned his attention and with a warm smile said, "Of course it is."

"I am not usually an emotional person," I said, "but today, after I finally had a proper shower, I had a moment. The nurse helped me with my clothes until I got to a point when I said I can finish off. Whilst I was pulling my underwear up to where it normally goes, under the skin and fat of my belly, the underwear just kept coming up, because there was nothing there to stop it! Not sure what was going on, I immediately looked up and caught a glimpse of me in the mirror and saw my reflection, then just burst into tears, because for the first time ever, I did not have a big belly, instead I had a flat tummy."

My eyes began to well up again as I looked at Mr. Banwell. "That's because of you, that is," I said.

Mr. Banwell stood for a few moments, looking at me with a slightly tilted head and raised emotional eyebrows before saying, "Awwww! That's so sweet but no, it's not because of me, it's because of you. You did all the hard work. I just did what was needed."

"Mr. Banwell, you've changed my life and made me look like a completely different person to what I have known since I was a child and yes, maybe I did do all the hard work, but you put the icing on my 'weight loss' cake."

Mr. Banwell looked at me with the biggest smile, a smile that will last in my heart forever!

Soon after that, they all came to a conclusion and decided that I could go home on the premise that I continue to have several weekly blood tests, and liaise with my local haematology team at the hospital, who would take over my care.

Whilst the others left, I continued talking to Mr. Banwell, thanking him from the bottom of my heart as this man is a hero in my eyes. See, Mr. Banwell is one of those rare people who stands by his patients and provides them with what they need. He is a man who has deep integrity, who will unequivocally put himself on the front line for the good of his patient. And that is what he did for me.

However, little did any of us know at the time that without Mr. Banwell doing what he did, I would most probably be dead. Because unknown to any of us, I did have something terribly wrong with me. An underlying life-threatening condition that was ravaging through my newly sculpted body!

Whilst I will always stand by the fact that I never lost weight for the purposes of aesthetics and my weight loss was about being healthy – and even when I reached my goals after meeting Natalija who transformed my mindset – I kept wanting more for myself, so I never settled.

I pushed and pushed my diet and training and got the rewards for all my hard work and dedication. What more could I want, other than all that hideous skin removed. And I did. And even losing my bellybutton was a small sacrifice for the new me. I was elated at the results, absolutely elated. I even began planning my trips to the beach in a lovely new swimsuit, or even a little tankini or something. In all honesty, I was so happy. I absolutely loved my new body shape, I looked like Jlo – well, for about seven minutes anyway!

Soon after I got home from the surgery, I contacted Doctor Goel, explaining what they would be sending her in regard to my blood results and explained that until I had healed, and I was able to sit up – due to not being able to bend – I couldn't have the weekly appointments. She agreed, so for three weeks I didn't have a blood test. However one week later, I went to see Mr. Banwell at his after-surgery clinic and he was really delighted with the healing process – which, by all accounts, was healing incredibly well.

Because I was healing really well, I didn't think too much more about all that business with my blood counts – because if they were that bad, I wouldn't be getting better and stronger on a daily basis, right? With that in mind I decided to ring my doctor again and told her that, in my medical opinion – with no medical experience, of course – that as I was healing fast without any complications, I clearly don't have bad blood, so I don't really need to carry on with having tests.

But she almost insisted, explaining the necessity to carry on with these weekly blood tests – even if I am healing well. She explained that if the haematologist wants you to have the blood tests, then it's for a reason. "Let's just do them to be on the safe side, ok. It's best we know why your bloods are still low. We must investigate to ensure nothing is wrong."

I agreed to continue with the testing, even though I felt it wasn't necessary. Besides, going back and forth put a bit of a darkness over me being able to enjoy the new me and my new look! Because some nonsense blood test every five minutes was looming over my head, no doubt here to destroy my happiness – like life has a habit of doing. But, once again, I told myself not to let things run away and just wait and find out first – after all, it could just be nothing. Besides, that type of operation must put a huge strain on the body, so let's see.

But in my gut I had this terrible feeling that something was wrong, which I constantly tried pushing away, saying don't worry, everything will be fine. It has to be. I've done everything right, I lost all the weight, I've gotten fitter and I'm stronger than ever. It just can't be, so stop being silly and over thinking things, nothing will undo these seven long years of hard dieting, and nothing will take away your new dream body, so don't stress!

Besides, life can't really be that bloody cruel and nasty – and anyway, haven't I suffered enough?

CHAPTER 19

Investigations

After several more weeks of blood tests and appointments, a telephone consultation was made with a very pleasant consultant from the Colchester General Hospital haematology team to discuss the results. The consultant is a really lovely chap, very chirpy and informative.

He explained to me that a picture was beginning to build from the results from all the weeks I had been having tests – but before he could continue, I decided to give my 'expert' medical advice first (like I even had any), and I told him that I have always had bouts of anaemia on and off over the years, which was true. That anaemia was also relatively common within our cultural community, which affected many of my blood relatives. Once again, trying to bury my head in the golden sands of hope.

Even though I was what they call neutropenic, this too was not an uncommon cultural thing.

It is a well-known medical condition observed in individuals of African descent known as Benign Ethnic Neutropenia (BEN) which causes those from that background to have a low neutrophils count – like mine.

"So see, doctor," I said, "It must just be that, hey?"

The consultant listened both politely and carefully, but in the end, he simply said, "I'm just not satisfied that is the case." He said, "Your neutrophils have not raised above 1 since your operation. If your counts were around 1.5 and were stable around that figure, I would be more likely to accept that your low counts could possibly be due to your ethnicity. But something just isn't sitting right, even though you are well in yourself and there is no infection or indications of it being something else. I think I'd rather continue with further testing. In my opinion, your blood counts indicate that you may possibly have something called LGLL: Large Granular Lymphocytic Leukaemia."

"What?"

"It's not as bad as it sounds," he said. "It's completely manageable by tablets with no need for chemo. So try not to worry. To find out exactly what it is, I am going to send your bloods away to the lab in London for some extra tests. There, they will separate the bloods and blast cells blah, blah, blah."

As he talked, my mind just kept drifting back to what he had just said … *Leukaemia!*

Sensing this, as I was silent, he said, "I don't think it's anything to worry about – yet. We just need to be sure about things, ok? Please try not to worry."

But I did worry, who bloody wouldn't? He just said one of the worst things a person could hear!

My logical head came back and said *if the consultant isn't worried why are you? It's some low grade LGLL that can be controlled with tablets. Anyway, you only have to wait a week or so, that's not too bad, is it?*

Mate, that time went past agonisingly slow. I tried to keep busy and focus on the new me with my flat tummy and nice clothes I bought after Christmas in the January sales. Let's focus on that trip to Mauritius in late October where we will celebrate the ol' man's 60th, my birthday and renew our marriage vows, seeing as it's going to be 25 years!

CHAPTER 20

The Day That Changed Me Forever

26th February 2021 landed on a Friday which, for me, was a day for both cardio and a cheat meal – meaning a Costa coffee and my beloved Bunny Buns, which were freshly made iced buns or iced fingers from Sainsbury's bakery. Oh my days, these are the best things ever (but for some reason, despite popular demand, have now been discontinued, gutted).

So there I was, getting on with my cardio, minding my own business, thinking *What can I eat as a cheat meal tonight? Shall we have a roast dinner, or steak and chips with all the trimmings? Garlic mushrooms, fried onions, triple fried hand cut chips, with my own parmigiana cheese and lemon cream sauce? Mmm, yeah, we'll have that. I will prepare it all after coffee and buns.*

I was blissfully unaware until I was abruptly interrupted by a random phone call at around 09.30am. *Who on earth this*, I thought, as I looked down at my watch, to see a no caller ID displayed. I don't know who that is, probably some nonsense cold caller! For a split second I wasn't going to answer it. But something compelled me to take that call. Little did I know how a telephone call like that would change everything – forever!

"Hello! Mrs. Lake?" a very hesitant voice said. "Yes," I replied with a slight questioning tone.

"Hello, hi, yes, it's the doctor here from the Colchester haematology department. I, I, have the results of your blood test and, I'm so sorry, I'm afraid it's a lot worse than I originally diagnosed."

"Worse?! What do you mean worse?"

"Mrs. Lake, I am so, so sorry but you have Acute Myeloid Leukaemia!" "I HAVE WHAT? What the hell is that?"

"Mrs. Lake. It's, it's cancer. It's a blood cancer. And it's being accelerated by what is known as FLT3 and I'm sorry, but the cancer is quite advanced."

"A flit who?"

"Mrs. Lake, we need you in immediately to have a bone marrow biopsy. But it can't be done until Monday."

"What? Monday? Why are you telling me now then? Why not tell me Monday morning?' I yelled.

"I am so sorry, Mrs. Lake, I really am – especially to tell you like this. But your cancer is quite advanced, which means you have an extremely weakened immune system – and you need to collect antibiotics as soon as possible, because at this stage any infection could kill you!"

"'Could whatttttt!!! Kill me! What immune? What the hell are you talking about?"

Seconds later I felt this hot flush rush over my entire body, to the point I thought I was going to faint. The room began to spin, so I placed my hand onto the gym bench to stabilise my wobbling legs. I didn't want to collapse – especially as I was the only one at home. As I sat down my heart started racing and my ears went completely hollow and began ringing.

I was brought back to the moment when I heard the doctor's voice shouting out, "Mrs. Lake are you there, Mrs. Lake."

"Yes, yes I am here."

He continued to talk about some blast cells, about some percentages and some characteristics and chromosomes changes and CD33 and CD34. And FLT3 this and something else that. But for the life of me, I just couldn't process anything he was saying, as my concentration lapsed further and further, together with these waves of heat that raged over me, to the point where I began to sweat profusely.

My thoughts were invaded with, *five minutes ago I was fine, and now, I have some sort of critical condition! What the hell man?*

I sat trembling, gasping for air, with the only words I understood in that minefield of information – CANCER! It swirled repeatedly around my head. *CANCER. And how did I get bloody cancer? What the hell is even blood cancer? Oh my God, I've got CANCER, CANCER! I've got CANCER!*

I don't know if there are even any words to describe the emotions I felt in that moment. I went from feeling completely devastated, to feeling enraged by betrayal by the treachery of life – after all I had done to make myself healthy and fit. I thought, how can I ever trust in life again when it's so fucking cruel, how will I hope again? *What more could life pissing throw at me, what does it want from me? Jesus Christ, haven't I suffered enough?* I could not have ever imagined in a million years I would hear those words. And for the first time in my life, it really felt that my spirit was finally breaking!

Not for long though! Because Sarezah, in true Sarezah spirit, said *Nah, fuck this* – and grabbed hold of myself, internally shaking me to the core, screaming at myself within. *Pissing pull yourself together girl, it's shitty pissing cancer, don't give it power. It's nothing, anyway you've been through much worse in life. So you ain't fucking crumbling now!*

There and then I stopped and pulled myself together, telling myself we cannot afford to start falling apart! Returning back from within, I heard the doctor's voice frantically calling my name, "Mrs. Lake, Mrs. Lake, are you there?"

"Yes, I am, I'm sorry about that, it's just a lot to take in!" "Yes, it is, and I am really sorry to have to tell you like this."

"That's ok, doctor, thank you for calling and letting me know. What time do you want me to come in on Monday, and where do I collect these tablets you want me to take," I replied, in a serene, lost voice.

Only then did the doctor ask if I was alone. Apparently it's best I wasn't! "A little late for that," I said. I was home alone with Mac, my boxer dog! Poor boy, he was sitting with me in that cold summer house made into a gym for me as it was lockdown. He must have sensed something was wrong because he sat gazing up at me with big sad puppy eyes, whilst resting his chin on my lap.

Mate, I held onto that boy for dear life as I rocked backwards and forwards trying to find a small piece of comfort in that devastating moment – knowing sooner or later I would have to call my husband and three boys, who were still blissfully unaware, until they too received the call that will, in one heartbeat, change their lives, where we will be under a very dark cloud of uncertainty. Either I will or I won't survive. From now on it's all in the hands of fate!

The first person I rang was my husband, as it was almost his

10am break time, which is when historically we almost always call. He answered in the way he always does, "Hello love."

"Hello Guy," I said in a shaky voice. "The doctor called with my results. I have Acute Myeloid Leukaemia with some flit something."

The phone fell into a deathly silence. I almost felt the waves of his dizziness transport through the airwaves, until he eventually replied, "Oh no, shall I come home?" I think that must have been a rhetorical question, one said from complete shock.

Where do I even begin with my children, I thought! At that time, Rahim was 26, Khaliq 23 and Azim 22, and even though they were adult age, to mums – no matter what age children are – they will always be our babies. I delayed calling them as long as possible. Not just for them, but for me too. The thought of having to tell them destroyed me more than being told I have cancer. How will they cope with this news, their beloved mummy, the matriarch and rock of the family, has a life-threatening cancer!

Eventually I plucked up enough courage to make those fateful calls, in age order. I began with a *trying to be strong* voice. "Hey Rahim. It's mummy. Are you ok?"

"Yes mum, are you?"

"Yes, erm, I've heard from the doctor. I'm afraid it's not what he initially thought I had, mites. Rahim, I have something called Acute Myeloid Leukaemia."

The wretched silence spoke what he couldn't say. All I could feel was his sorrow. See, it's my belief that mummies and children still have an invisible connection through the umbilical cord that once attached us together in the womb and that link, I believe, lasts forever. Trying to keep strong, he said, "Oh, ok mama, I will come over and we can talk about it properly." And so I went onto the next call.

"Hey Khaliq," I said to my middle son. "Hello mummy, are you ok?"

"Yeah," I said in a croaky voice. "What's wrong Mama."

"I spoke to the doctor today, and I have my results."

"Oh yeah, mama. Is it good? Are you ok?" Ever the little optimist.

"I'm sorry, sweetheart. I have a blood cancer. It's a Leukaemia." I could feel his little legs weaken as he let out an emotional cry.

"Nooooo mama, no."

My eyes filled with tears as the impact of being diagnosed with cancer began to devastate my family.

Azim, my youngest, my baby, my little boy! Knowing he was at work I decided it best I sent a text first, which read … *It's mummy, can I call you?* (like he didn't know it was his mum).

"Yes, mummy, just give me a moment, I will go into another room." Within moments, he rang. "Hello mummy," he said.

"Hello mummy," I said back. (I call him mummy too, it's our little thing). Even though I tried to be as normal as I could, he knew something was wrong. Why would Mum ring if everything was ok and why is mum's voice like that?

"I've got my results. I have something called Acute Myeloid Leukaemia. It's a blood cancer."

After a short pause of silence, his tiny little voice said, "Oh ok, mummy. Can I come home to see you?"

"Yes please, darling, of course you can!" I muddled.

My dearest bestie Janey must have felt something as she messaged and asked had I heard anything from the doctors – to which I said yes. She immediately rang and I answered, "Oh Janey, I have Acute Myeloid Leukaemia, I have cancer of the blood."

My Jane and I were both emotional. But she said, "You'll get through this Suz, you will, you're a bloody fighter, you know you are, you're one of the strongest people I know! You will get through this. We will get through it together."

She will never know how much that melted my heart! That is why this lady is another one of my *ride or die* girls! And so I continued through the list of calling my closest friends. To be honest, that is one of the hardest parts about cancer. Telling those that love you and that you love that you have cancer. It's such an uncertain word. Cancer is so menacingly unpredictable. It's so tragic. But once you have it, you've just got to get on with it the best you can! There is nothing else you can do.

The next few days were a bit of a blur with many ups and downs. My mind was invaded with all sorts of thoughts and fears, with the photo slide of doom on constant loop – a show and tell story of my dark and grim reality, cruelly projecting every worst possible scenario as well as taunting me with the all-for-nothing crushing word.

Sarezah, look what's happened after all your hard work, all that dedication, the dieting, the relentless exercise regimens, the nights of tears due to hunger, a hunger you learnt to control and conquer from that traumatic upbringing, from looking like a monster to Jlo, all for what.

CANCER! Oh and you are going to lose all your cascading blonde goldie locks. Bye, bye. Cheerio! No more hair. No more beautiful pictures of your progress. No more motivational posts. No more anything. Except CANCERRRR!!!!!!!

Honestly, you couldn't write it, could you?

Then life's regrets started tormenting me, making me feel cheated – that once again, life has robbed me! My body was the best it had ever been, not that I was ever ashamed of being a big girl, because when I was a big girl, there was nothing to compare it to until I lost 19st plus. And now I was happy with what I had achieved, it wasn't just weight I'd lost – it was the determination and the driving force I had in me, the transformation from eating and existing in the way I did into something completely opposite.

My new look and the feeling of freedom of movement it gave me was such joy, especially when – from time to time – I caught a glimpse in the mirror at my new shape. For what? Bastard cancer to come and sneakily take it away. It was as if it was just waiting for the right moment to come and finish me off – once and for all. All that torment I managed to overcome and everything else that life threw at me but failed to break me and my spirit. So it thought *let's get that last trump card out.* Cancer! With that, my sadness quickly turned to feeling enraged.

But I soon realised there was no point feeling like that. It won't change the outcome, and I reminded myself that I had evolved from getting angry – especially at things that are out of my control. Telling myself how I feel is determined by the opinion I choose to give the situation. So no matter what the situation is, be it my final test in life, or just another hurdle, I had to do what I always did in any given situation, and that is to do my best to get myself through it!

One of the things I have learnt through my experience of having cancer is to be mindful about using certain words and phrases like *you will beat cancer* or *you have a positive mental attitude* (as it's one of my least favoured expressions).

See, in my opinion, it's not the strong that win and the weak that die. You don't really beat cancer, you either get through or you don't. I say that because, during my treatment, I saw many patients who fought relentlessly, and those that had nothing but a positive mental attitude, those who had faith and those that had hope – and they all still died.

It doesn't always matter what attitude you have or how strong you are – words, phrases and even actions won't always influence the outcome. Fate decides that from the moment you are diagnosed, fate will decide whether you will relapse or not, whether you achieve remission, or whatever else it may decide for you.

I understand it can be difficult to know what to say to a cancer patient – and I know most of what is said comes from a good place. But any cancer patient undergoing treatment will either be lucky enough to get through it – or not. It's as simple as that. Cancer really doesn't care who or how strong you are, it's just out to seek and destroy whoever it can. It does not discriminate, mate.

Which brings me nicely onto something that exists in the world today – and that is this self- righteous belief of what discrimination is. Some people think only Black Lives Matter. Some think only white lives matter. Some only think their life matters. Some believe in the bible. Some only believe in the Jedi! All believe their cause is of the greatest importance than the other.

But, you see, cancer now does not care one bit who you are or what you believe in. See, on a cancer ward, you will see that no lives actually matter, be it an old person, a youngster, someone fat or thin, black, white, Asian, Indian every nationality and or any other colour in this world.

You will see every gender, all sexual orientations, gay, straight, bi, you name them, they are there. Muslim, Christian, Hindu, Buddha, Jehovah, Ja Ja, Rasta, all faiths, all religions, mothers, fathers, brothers, sisters, children, aunts, uncles, every conceivable shape and form that a person can be. Cancer doesn't care!

And don't forget all those doctors and nurses who save your life as a cancer patient. They don't care, either, whether you are black or white, Chinese, Indian, straight, gay, they, them, he, she whatever. Not to mention if one of the medical team is one of those on the list of people you don't like but are helping to save your life. What are you going to say then? "No, stop. I hate you lot so don't save my life." Of course you're not. Surely life is worth more than ignorance, at the end of the day. We're all arseholes, no matter what religion, colour or creed you are. So here's a tip. BE LIKE CANCER, DON'T DISCRIMINATE.

CHAPTER 21

The Road Ahead

Many of us who receive a diagnosis similar to this can often find it all a bit overwhelming, especially at first. Whilst others seem to just get on with it and find some sort of coping mechanism to help them get through, others like to post on social media or join forums, and some – like me – are a little more private, only telling a very small circle of those around them.

Truthfully, there isn't a right or a wrong way on how to deal with a diagnosis or who to tell.

You do what is best for you. And if you are in a situation where your life is in some sort of jeopardy, remember that you really haven't got time to just crumble! Believe me, I know. Because this isn't my first time dealing with the threat of death.

It was during the first year of having my son Rahim. I was a single mum with no financial help (long story, that one). Anyway, I had to work two jobs to make ends meet. One of those was my day job on the railways, and the other was when I was a nightclub bouncer, a Westminster- licensed door supervisor in London.

Anyway, one cold night in 1996, I was sent to work in some seedy little club in Streatham, South London. During the course of that night's experience, I thought I'm gonna die here tonight, mate, talk about rough! Anyway, this Afro Caribbean British girl came up to me with some big-time attitude. She was vocalising because she had been refused entry into the club by a fellow door person for concealing drugs – but apparently we all disrespected her because we didn't know who she was, and we'd not let her in the club. Seeing most of us were of colour, there was no point using the race card in this situation. Anyway, she continued with her nonsense.

I reminded her, "It doesn't matter who you are, love! It's club policy not to allow anyone with drugs on their person into this establishment. So please, just go away!"

She responded rather aggressively and made all manner of *heard it all before* threats! I soon started to run out of patience, because trying to be reasonable clearly didn't work. So in the end I said, "Look love. You're being a c*nt now. Just f*ck off, yeah." (Sorry for swearing).

With that, she did 'F' off. Mouthing off something about "I'm not done here, you know, you wait. I'm gonna come back and finish you all, blah blah blah."

"Ok love. You crack on," I said, thinking that was the last of it, whilst rolling my eyes at my colleague, who had come close by in case it kicked off, or she pulled a knife or something. He shook his head and said, "Some people, man!" whilst he carried on about his business. It's a common occurrence so we were used to many empty threats.

Well, turns out we were all wrong. Cos my girl did come back, with a GUN. A gun you know! Because this girl had now gotten so seriously fucking offended at being stopped for entering a club that she went wherever to get a gun to teach me a lesson for the consequences of my actions!

To top it all, she had the absolute gall to stand in front of me and point that fucking gun at me. Mate, I was absolutely incensed by that reaction. For something as trivial as being turned away.

So, clearly not thinking straight, I walked straight up to her and snarled through gritted teeth, "You better f'ing use that, because if I get hold of that, I fucking will, and no one would have seen shit! Now f offfffffff, before it's too late." She stood there for a few moments, still pointing the gun at me, but I didn't flinch!

The nearby clubbers and some of my co bouncers froze, scared and shocked at what could happen next, whilst we all watched on and waited for her to make a move – but she didn't. She backed down. Because she knew she would have got absolutely fucked, one way or another. So Miss Thing kissed her gold capped tooth, turned around, cutting her eyes and stormed off. *Bye bye! Cheerio, Silly bitch!*

Without a doubt, I could have quite easily ended up with a bullet in my head – or anywhere else – depending on her aim, of course. Whilst I wasn't particularly afraid of dying, I wasn't keen on losing my life. That moment made me realise this work is not for me anymore. Even though it paid well, it's not worth my life. I have a son that I am responsible for. If something happened to me, my little Rahim would have no one. I reminded myself that time and time again. If you end up in a fight, doing your so-called job, and find yourself in hospital, prison or worse, the grave, there is no one to look after Rahim. Therefore, soon after, I left that job.

Anyway, a few days after that initial call, I felt I was beginning to come to terms with my diagnosis a little bit more. After all, what could I do about it? It's no good giving myself a hard time about nothing I can change. Besides, I had to make a few more calls to my closest of close friends – what I refer to as my extended family, who are more like family to me than my own family.

One of those is my 'good friend' Kader, Kad for short. He is the one who went to check on my mother's house to check she was ok. Kad is a brother to me, along with one of his actual brothers, Sash. Both of them call me by my family name *Sezah* or *Suz*, my childhood nickname.

I rang Kad first. Of course, it was heartbreaking, but during that conversation, he said something that has stuck with me ever since. "To be honest, Sezah, this is what you have been training for your whole life, isn't it?"

Kad had a point, my life had always been tougher than tough, so it was like my life tragedies were in training and preparation for this day. And – after all – if anyone knows what I've been through over the years, it's him. See, we've known each other since he was like 18 months old and I was like 11; now he's mid to late 40's, so it's fair to say he has witnessed mostly everything I have been through.

And in all honesty, not much can or has defeated me! I'm not even sure the SAS could even break me. Whilst I might not be as physically fit as them, I am – most certainly – mentally. They could scream at me all day, insult me or push me to the limit, and they would get nothing from me. Because since my childhood, in order to survive, I've had to become extremely tough – which led to me being extremely resilient!

Before I knew it, that Friday turned into Monday, and it was time for my first ever biopsy.

That was fun (more about that later), after which I had what was to become one of many consultations and appointments at the Collingwood Colchester cancer centre, to discuss the results and the plan of action with one of my consultants.

But before that, I had another hospital appointment with another consultant, my surgeon Mr. Banwell, as it was my three-month scar and tissue check-up. I was told I should delay going due to my low immune system issues and, of course, Covid. Nonetheless, I went, because I was not sure what was going to happen from now onwards. It's a good job I did, because after the first consultation at Colchester and then Barts, it seemed I may not get the chance to thank Mr. Banwell.

On the day of the appointment, I arrived and waited until my name was called. As soon as it was, I got up and walked towards the consultation rooms with a nurse. She directed me to a room and asked me to wait. In came a young lady, one I hadn't seen before; she introduced herself as a member of the team. Unbeknown to her what was going on, she went on to say – quite excitedly – how she had read my file and began telling me what an amazing weight-loss story I had.

I didn't look very impressed, not because of what she was saying, but because of that dark cloud looming over my head. So I kept quiet for a bit, before she went on to say she had read about my bloods in my file, saying the haematology team required me to have a series of further blood tests and was there an outcome to that?

"Yes, they did," I replied. "I have Acute Myeloid Leukaemia."

She stood there stunned, with sadness in her eyes, and said, "Oh no, that's rubbish." I shrugged my shoulders as if to say *What can you do*, then asked if Mr. Banwell was on duty and, if so, would it be possible see him.

She went off to find Mr. B and left me alone in the room with my thoughts, because she was the first person outside my small circle of family and friends that I had told about my diagnosis. Saying it aloud to someone that I have cancer made it feel far more real instead of surreal.

My thoughts were then broken by a gentle knock on the door. It was Mr. Banwell, who popped his head in to say hello, with a somewhat sorrowful look on his face, saying, "I've heard you've had some bad news."

I nodded. After telling him a little more about my diagnosis, I reminded him how well I healed really from all those stitches and didn't get one infection, to which he replied, "I know, incredible."

"But unfortunately," I continued, "unbeknown to any of us, I had an underlying serious illness – and with no symptoms whatsoever, none of us could known what was going on inside. What I do know, Mr. Banwell, is that had you not made that decision to do what you had to do, it more than likely would have gone undetected until it was too late. The haematologist doctor said I would likely be dead."

For a few moments, silence prevailed as no one really knew what to say, until Mr. B said, "So what happens from here."

"Intensive chemotherapy." I replied. "I will probably lose this as I grabbed onto my signature curly blonde ponytail with bits floating across my face."

"Well let's hope they have caught it in time! And look, you have overcome an awful lot already because you are an incredible person, and if anyone can pull through this, it's you."

I smiled at him, because Mr. B will never know how much his words meant to me. We said our goodbyes and I thanked him one more time, for everything he had done – and for saving my life!

CHAPTER 22

The First of Many

My first consultation came soon after my biopsy. My husband drove me and my son Khaliq (bless my Khaliq, he's literally been to almost all the appointments he's been permitted to attend, his little face has been everywhere) to the Collingwood Cancer Centre at Colchester Hospital.

I checked in and waited, alone, in the Covid area for a few minutes before being called in to have my consultation. After a few niceties, the consultant said words to the effect of, "You have AML – Acute Myeloid Leukaemia – a type of blood cancer. This means your bone marrow is making a large amount of abnormal blood cells. We do not have the facilities here to treat your Leukaemia, so you will be sent to our affiliated hospital, St Bartholomew's in London, nears St Paul's. Your protocol will be four cycles of one month block treatment. Meaning you will be an inpatient for at least a month at a time. There has already been an appointment made for you. A letter will arrive soon, detailing everything you need to know."

He gave me another load of tablets to take. At first I argued, saying I didn't need them as I was not sick in any way (stubborn as usual, not understanding how dire my situation was), but he insisted I take them, saying the tablets are for precautionary measures, to help prevent infections etc, saying that with my type of diagnosis, sepsis can happen very easily; it's therefore a prevention rather than cure of something that could lead to your death! Ooh that word again, I thought. So I took them!

It was really beginning to sink in that my once fit and strong healthy body – a body I had spent years dedicating myself from getting from 'fat to fit' (I'm being sarcastic because you should all know, by now, I hate that word *fat*) – has been invaded with an impossible to treat blood cancer! Fantastic.

Off we set to London, to the hospital that was going to be

my home for the next 8 months or longer. That train journey to St Bartholomew's was desperately quiet. I sat gazing out of the window, not looking at anything in particular, just focusing on the reality of my dilemma, cancer! A word that is shrouded in uncertainty.

Then, occasionally, I would glance back at my husband, who looked so lost. At times our eyes would cross paths, looking for some kind of solace. There were no smiles, no words, just the sorrow cancer brings. I sat watching the familiar landmarks go by, remembering much happier days when I travelled to and from London countless times, without anything quite as heavy a burden as this resting on my shoulders and hurting my heart.

Soon enough we arrived at London Liverpool Street, where we decided to walk from the tube station to the hospital, even though it was late February/early March, and cold and drizzly – another one of my husband's bright ideas. (Rolling of the eyes!). This man loves walking!

"It's not far," he said, but I'm getting wet. "I'm not supposed to get ill, am I?"

"It's just here, it won't take five minutes," he said. "You said that five minutes, ten minutes ago!"

Eventually and flipping finally, we arrived at the hospital! We ended up walking through the back entrance rather than the main one. As we walked through the big Victorian-looking iron gates into the courtyard, I was surprised at how beautiful this place was. Little did I know it was to become my little escape, and a secret route to the French bakery, *Paul*.

Oh my days, what a place! As we walked through this incredible courtyard into the main hospital, I saw the most beautiful fountain which was the focal point in the middle of the square. For a few moments, I almost forgot I was here for an appointment to see the blood oncologist. It looked too nice just to be a hospital, indeed it was truly an impressive piece of historical architecture.

Suddenly my sightseeing was brutally interrupted with my husband's voice. "It's over there, love," pointing at the west wing of the building – he loves a bit of map, right up his street and all that. I'm not like that. If I can't find something, I ask. So off we went into the building. I felt my heart beating a bit, together with a little rush of anticipation that came over me. It all just felt like a horrible dream.

After I booked in, we were informed that due to Covid rules we would have to sit apart, meaning I am once again left alone. Funny that, especially since what came to light, where some of those rule makers openly flouted the Covid rules that they forced us to follow – whilst they broke them with no recourse whatsoever. These leaders enjoyed their Christmas and birthday parties telling us we have to follow the rules or we get a £10k fine. These bare-faced liars did whatever the f they liked, whilst all us little mugs obeyed the rules – including us cancer patients, which meant we had to sit alone and die alone! Disgraceful.

Being in that waiting room was really tough. All I did was sit helplessly watching each second tick away on the wall-mounted clock, in an attempt to distract myself from the apprehension I felt inside. The only comfort I had was the knowledge that all the other people in there – who all ranged in age, colour, sex, and size – were there for the same reason, too. Every one of them had the same expression on their faces – sadness, disbelief and devastation!

Eventually, the consultant called my name, quite beautifully I might add. I texted my husband and, together, we went into Dr Smith's office, with both our hearts beating a little faster than usual. He muffled a *Hello* through his mask and asked us to take a seat and pointed at some chairs.

He began to explain my illness in a little more detail, and then onto the different stages of treatment. At first I zoned out a bit, but pulled myself back because, after all, this was to help save my life from cancer. He continued to say that treatment largely depended on whether you were fit enough to have intensive chemotherapy.

"In your case, you are definitely fit enough. You will initially have two induction stages then two consolidation where a high dose of chemotherapy will be administered to kill the cancerous cells. The goal is to clear the blood of Leukaemia cells (blasts) and reduce the number of blasts in the bone marrow to normal. The induction treatments will consist of the standard chemotherapy drugs that are used to treat Acute Myeloid Leukaemia, this will be during the first two cycles.

The chemotherapy is called Daunorubicin and Cytarabine; both will be intravenous, then – depending on your second cycle results – all being well, you will go onto the two consolidation treatments, where we will run Cytarabine for the last two cycles. You also qualify for a trial called AML 19, which is under our professor here. It consists of an immunotherapy called Mylotarg, and you have been randomly selected to have one out of two possible shots."

And boy, oh boy, did I find out later on how powerful a treatment Mylotarg is.

"The treatment will be carried out for approximately a week during your stay in hospital.

It's short and intensive. After which, you will need close medical monitoring and nursing supervision. You will be able to go home in between, once your blood cells begin to recover. During your stay you will have to have daily blood tests to determine when you need blood transfusions because your bloods will not contain enough healthy blood cells as all cells are destroyed in the process.

"This is also a time where you will be vulnerable to infection, so it's extremely important you are in a clean and stable environment, where your health can be monitored for any infection, which you can have quickly assessed and treated. One of the most important factors about getting any type of infection during treatment is it can very quickly turn into sepsis, which can kill you."

All I could think was *this is just getting better and better.*

"The chemotherapy will be administered through a blood vessel in your arm via a PICC line. After cycle two, we will do a test called an MRD, minimal residual test, which I believe now is coined as measurable instead of minimal, in layman's terms. This means it measures the presence of Leukaemia cells at a deeper level, this stands for minimal residual disease. This refers to cancer cells that are still remaining in the body that can't be detected by standard testing. These cells have the potential to come back and cause a relapse."

In fact, I was told later during the course of my treatment that this type of test is so effective that it can find one cancer cell among 1 million normal cells.

The doctor went on to explain that the test will be carried out via a bone marrow aspiration, which I have already had, so no surprises. The best outcome would be an MRD negative result, meaning no disease is detected after treatment; an MRD positive test would mean the chemotherapy has not worked as hoped. Therefore we would need to find a suitable stem cell donor.

He said, "We have two options for obtaining a suitable donor. One is from a family member – a sibling is preferable as this will have a better outcome if the donor has the same tissue type as the person receiving the donation, otherwise it will be a suitable donor from our database.

"Whilst we have a worldwide extensive database, we don't have much of a database for ethnic minorities. Being of Mauritian descent means it won't be easy to find you a suitable match if we cannot find one within your close family that is sufficiently matched and medically fit. We will firstly look at your brother, who is likely to be a 75-100% match. Your three children will be around 50%."

I informed him that my children are fit but my brother has some medical conditions. The consultant, with a concerned face, replied that he may not be a suitable donor.

It's at this point that I would like to make a sincere request to any of you who are of mixed ethnicity, be it minority or a majority, black, white, anything: Please, please go on the register to donate your stem cells. You could be saving someone's life. If you want to learn more please go to the www.anthonynolan.org website. It's simple and very easy. They have an expert team that will guide you through each stage. There's no pressure and you don't have to, but you could be saving someone's life. Or, one day, you may know someone who may need it.

The consultant talked me through the admission process, saying I would be assigned a cancer clinical nurse specialist (a CNS). Her name is Sam. "In fact I don't know where she is, she should be in here, she must have got caught up with a patient or something."

Within seconds of him saying that, there was a knock on the door and a sweet happy voice spoke, as Sam entered the room.

"Hello, sorry, sorry I'm late, giggle giggle!"

We all turned to face the door as this beautiful angel that steals the hearts of her patients stood before us – soon to become my lovely friend 'Sammy'. A true beauty, a beauty that is just not physical, but a beauty that radiates from the inside out who, much like a flower, exudes a perfume that fills the air with an invisible scent, giving joy to all around. Well that's Sammy.

Sam stood there with her little giggle and her long brown hair that was tied up. With her big doughy blue eyes, and the warmest of smiles that shone through a Covid mask! Immediately I felt her kind warm heart, and from that moment, I knew I was going to be alright.

The consultation concluded with dates for admission with me thinking it would be in a week or two, until he said, "We are hoping to get you into hospital in a few days."

I was like, "What??? Friday!!! I haven't even got a suitcase, or wash things, to go into hospital for a month or longer. I don't even have any night clothes. I need more time."

He responded with, "But your cancer, it's quite advanced, it's very serious. We need to start treatment straight away."

I looked directly at him, and pleaded, "I don't feel ill, please give me till at least next week. I promise I will be careful and shield. Just let me sort out my life. Please."

He looked over at Sammy, then agreed. Thank goodness, as I was able to sort out all the things I needed to, from making sure the food shopping got delivered to all the finances. That was a crazy busy week. And, to be honest, I had so much to do that I didn't even have time to think about having cancer.

"Before you go with Sam to finalise the admission procedures." he said, then placed his pen on the desk and turned to look straight at me, "Mrs. Lake, I can't promise the treatment will work or that you will even see the end of the year. But we will do all we can for you to get through it, as best we can. And I would rather treat someone like you who is strong, as well as fit and healthy. At least you have a fighting chance."

Well that's just bloody marvellous, I thought. *Can't guarantee you'll see the rest of the year or the treatment will work. Bloody fantastic!*

That's when I turned to look at my husband, for a can't believe it 'eye roll'. But as I did, my man didn't look so good. In fact, he was whiter than usual, which is quite difficult as he's already pure white.

Listen, there is as white as a sheet, then Casper, then my husband! And this man now looked like he was about to faint!

"Are you ok, love?" I said. "Do you need some water or something?"

That's when Sam stood up and rushed over to him. Rushed, you know, saying, "Oooh, sweetheart, are you ok dear? Do you need some air? Shall I open the door?"

"What a drama queen," I thought, as I looked at him with a slightly crunched up questioning expression that said *what are you doing*, shaking my head in disbelief! But then I saw that he was having some sort of panic attack and was having a bit of trouble breathing. So me now, trying to lighten up the situation, started cracking one of those in-house husband and wives' jokes, and said, "God, you've always got to make it about you haven't you? I'm the one with the cancer, you know!"

And yes, he did laugh, whilst dramatically sipping some water the lovely nurse Sam gave to him. *Crikey*, I thought, *the man needs to pull himself together, he can't start falling apart before I've even started treatment.* Truthfully, though, he was in shock and we all deal with things differently. Think about it, all of a sudden your wife of over 25 years may die from a disease that just popped up into our lives out of nowhere!

Besides, whilst I am used to tragedy, my husband isn't. In fact, this is one of the first times something of this magnitude has happened to him. Fortunately for him, the man's not had much of a tough or tragic life. I mean the only real tragedy he has had is watching his football team, season after season, losing! (I am teasing, but even by his own admission he would say he has had very different life experiences to me and indeed others).

The journey back home was a little different to the journey up, because I bumped into a gym buddy, so the chit chat helped take my mind off things – even though in the background the cogs were whirring around, mentally getting things in order of what I had to get done before I headed off into hospital. Whilst I was sort of ok, I could see my husband was really struggling.

Even though he was pretty silent, I could see in his eyes he was heartbroken! See, my husband, like many others, isn't very good at dealing with anything that involves emotions or trauma. His response is to withdraw and stay silent. On the rare occasion he does try to communicate in these types of situations, it usually comes out wrong, or he ends up angry and frustrated, namely at himself for his inability to deal with or communicate what he wants or even should. Then I get cross and it ends up in a row, especially when I explain to him this is not the way to deal with what's going on.

An example of this is when my mother died. A situation arose on the day I buried my mother. I told him after the funeral this was the only time I really need him to stand in and take over for me, because I was vulnerable due to the trauma and the aggressive behaviour targeted towards me by my father who was getting involved where he shouldn't have. In fact my father behaved quite badly.

But my husband didn't – despite seeing how vile the situation was, he remained silent. It was at home in the evening that I told him there are times you have to do the right thing, especially by the person that you say you love. And not do what is right for you.

That comment led to us having a monumental argument, where he said something that to me was quite unforgivable and, in my opinion, wicked – after which it had a big impact on our relationship for many, many years. It doesn't help that I am not forgiving, but things said, no matter what the situation is, can't be unsaid. It taught me a valuable lesson. Without any exceptions, don't show any vulnerability but – most of all – don't be disappointed with the ones you think will put you first, in the same way you would put them first!

But over the years, I have understood that he does what he can to contribute in the best way he can. And he does go to work, working as hard as he can to help provide financially. At the end of the day we might have differences but we do get on and still have a laugh.

For a few days it felt like I was in an emotional whirlwind. I went from feeling ok about having cancer to worrying about my family, to fuming at the injustice of having flaming cancer altogether! And with each thought the influx of every worst possible scenario that could happen during treatment, like what if I died, or what if I had a serious side effect. Not that this is a new concept. I am well known for assuming the worst possible outcome. My husband and I joked about it and gave it a nickname WPS… *worst possible scenarios*. It's something that definitely stemmed from my childhood, I assume the worst because, for me, the worst did happen.

And for me, it's from having those 'WPS' moments that I learnt how to cope with the trauma I have experienced throughout life. It's where survival mode would always kick in, making me *just get on with it*. Besides, I'm really not the sort to just crumple. And anyway, even if I did want to crumple, I didn't have time for that, because I had a tonne of stuff to sort out – from things at home to preparing for at least one month in hospital, as the darkness of St Barts was looming and fast approaching.

CHAPTER 23

Cycle One

17th March 2021 was the date set for my first cycle. I waited for transport to arrive because I was not allowed to take public transport as I was medically vulnerable. I was immunosuppressed, where if I were to pick up any type of infection it could be fatal as my immune defence system was severely reduced.

Transport was booked for a specific time but could come up to two hours after. So I sent hubby out to get some coffees for us and thought it would be a good idea to make a quick curry for hubby and Khaliq and some for me to take as I'd been pre warned that hospital food is awful.

It turns out it was much, much worse than just awful. And little did I know, patients don't have much in the way of accessibility to things like a microwave, or even a toaster. In fact, not much was available for us patients, something that I was about to find out.

Anyway, the curry was bubbling nicely and just before I was about to put the rice on, the flipping driver pulled up on the drive of my beloved home. I looked at my husband and said, "He's flipping here."

My husband said, "Don't muck about."

I said, "I'm not," so he looked out of the window to see the driver approaching my front door, which I opened saying, "Hello mate. Could you just give me a few mins. I wasn't expecting you to come just yet. Hahahahaha." You know, that silly embarrassed laugh to let yourself off for not being ready when you should be.

"Oh that's ok, love," letting out a little chuckle himself. "Don't worry, love, you're not the first patient that's said that."

Patient????? That word hit hard. That is what I am, a bloody patient. I'm a cancer patient.

He looked at my husband who was standing just behind me and did that little bloke to bloke nod and asked if he should start to take some of the things to the car. As he stepped in, he saw all the things I had, and said, "Oh my word, that's a lot of stuff."

I looked at him and cracked a joke, saying, "I know, it's like I'm coming to hospital like I'm a celebrity or something!"

He laughed. They began to take stuff to the car. Poor Mac, my beautiful boxer dog, watched everything and somehow knew something was going on. This was going to be the first time I was apart from him since the day I brought him home in the late summer of 2012. To be honest, he had really bad separation anxiety and, for each cycle after that, as soon as he saw the suitcases he would become withdrawn and stop eating, so I did my best to hide it from him until the last moment I was leaving.

Once the car was packed, my husband called me saying, "It's all ready."

I finally tore myself away from Mac after squeezing and hugging him and said, "Mummy loves you, Maccy."

Outside, I took a last look at my lovely car. Not ever knowing if I would ever come home again, or if we would ever take a drive again, with the hood down, living the dream. I leant over and gave my car a kiss goodbye. Yes, I kissed my car. Then I turned to my husband, who looked broken.

So that we both didn't fall apart, I started to be my usual bossy self and began giving him instructions on what to do with the rest of the curry. After a few moments of silence, I said, "I better go."

He nodded. I grabbed hold of him. I could feel the tears filling both our eyes. We clung onto each other tightly, for as long as we possibly could. See, for us, this is first time in over 25 years we have spent more than a night away from each other. I got into the car, trying to be strong for us both but inside I was like *What the hell man, just a few short weeks ago everything was normal and now I have cancer, and I have to go to hospital for at least one month, for intensive chemotherapy treatment, to save my life. My life, you know, my life!*

I gazed out of the open window of the car for those last few moments before we had to go, wondering if I would ever come home again. I closed my eyes, filling my body with as much village air as I possibly could, savouring the beginnings of spring, thinking how fragile life can be. One minute we are going about our business then, in an instant, we are in the face of some adversity. And now, somehow, you have to try to find the strength to deal with what is presented before you, and that might mean fight for survival.

I reopened my eyes, took a breath and did my final check to ensure I had all I needed in my sports cross-body bag. Money, cards and keys, check. I let out a big sigh and looked at my husband's sombre face and leant out of the window to give him a kiss goodbye.

"Take care," I said.

"You too, love," he said in a shaky, saddened voice.

I paused and looked straight into his eyes then said, "Guy, if anything happens, you look after my children please, they are my everything! Take care of yourself and my Mac. Make sure you both eat ok!"

I held his trembling hand through the window. My heart sank to the pit of my stomach, I really didn't want to let go of his hand. Instantly my throat swelled with heartache as I watched both our eyes fill with great desolation as we prepared for me to leave, followed closely by tears. With no more words left to say, not knowing if this will be the last moment we may ever have, until the voice of the ambulance driver broke the silence by saying "Ready love." "Ready," I said. "Ready."

The driver began to move the vehicle slowly off the drive onto the main road, whilst Guy and I continued holding our little entwined fingers together until we had no choice but to let go. I spun round to catch the last glimpse of my husband out of the back window of the car, before distance separated us. I watch him standing helplessly in the middle of the road waving goodbye, as we faded away.

I felt the warm tears from my eyes rolling down my face, and began thinking about all the time we had wasted arguing over stupid things that we thought were so important. As I watched him standing helplessly in the middle of the road, I suddenly thought, *The bloody idiot better have keys in his pocket, he better not lock himself out like he has done a flip load of times! Ffs!* Then I chuckled to myself, because even in times of despair, that bloody wife inside never leaves!

The driver interrupted my thoughts by saying "Are you ok, love?"

bringing me back into the moment.

"Yes, mate," I said. Then I thought, no good dwelling, time to pick myself up, dust myself off and straighten up and get back to the reality of the situation. I knew I had to shake off the emotions of goodbyes. And I continued saying, "Yes mate, I'm gonna be ok. Thank you." And in my head my thoughts turned to one thing, War! One between me and Cancer!

The first part of the journey consisted of small talk with the driver, in-between texts/phone calls with my children, husband and a very small circle of friends. Occasionally I would look out of the car window, recognising certain landmarks that had been etched into my memory since a child, especially when we approached the outskirts of East London. This is also where I met my husband, who lived in East Ham. We would drive to and from each other's houses, freely, might I add, as there was none of this daylight robbery nonsense regarding emissions called 'Ulez'.

Back then we were all able to freely pollute. But now it is only a luxury afforded to the wealthy!

Mate, that London traffic was relentless and boringly long. I occasionally rested my head on the headrest, tilting it to the side so I could gaze out of the car window and watch the world go by, immersed within my own thoughts as my mind contemplated my fate, whilst weaving in and out of my lifetime of memories.

Trying my hardest to distract myself from plummeting into the dark abyss of what might happen, I focused my attention on the faces of the many people going about their lives, then began wondering if they'd had a tragedy that struck their lives. Are any of them dealing with someone who is sick? Are they sick themselves? Have they lost someone to Covid? Has their marriage or relationship fallen apart for the many reasons relationships fail? Was it from isolation, did they realise they actually had nothing in common, whatever that means? What happened to opposites attract? Or do they think there is something better than what they already have? Just to realise it's all the same shit.

Getting through London took forever – to the point where every five minutes I kept asking the driver how long it would be before we would arrive. Poor bloke, he must have been fed up with it. But after about the 1000th time, he actually said, "Only about 10 to 15 minutes now, love."

Hearing that made my stomach flip. It dawned on me that it wasn't that I was eager to arrive at my destination but because I wanted to stay as far away from the place that was filled with an uncertain outcome as much as I could.

We turned into a road and came across the Old Bailey, where my heart sank a little bit more as my thoughts transported me back to a time when I was a youth, when I dreamed I would one day be a barrister. There was even the slightest little glimmer of hope of achieving that. This came soon after my disastrous conclusion that I will never play in a band. So I decided to do an Open University Law Degree back in 2009-ish. Thinking, if I can pick up a guitar and write an album without being able to read or write music let alone know the notes on the fretboard of the guitar, how hard could it be to do a law degree.

Well, needless to say, it was tougher than I thought. Even though I gave it my absolute all, the truth is I was just not good enough. My basic education was so low and I only had a handful of CSEs. I didn't even have any 'O' levels (that's what my generation of exams were called).

Whilst I managed to scrape through five very long years, and when I say scrape, I mean scrape, eventually my low-grade education caught up with me and I failed my last year.

And unfortunately a number of reasons prevented me from continuing, namely my home life. It was extremely difficult trying to do an independent degree with three teenage kids, and a *don't want to get involved in all their drama* dad/husband; it was what it was, nothing I could do. At least I've got a diploma in English Law. And, of course, it helped me with my dictation – otherwise how could I write this (half full and not half empty and all that)?

Sadly, as I have mentioned before, my lack of education stems from an early age due to my father's cultural backward ideology that as a daughter I was just going to get married off. So he didn't, and wouldn't, invest in my education, proclaiming it would be a waste of money and time. Which he reinforced when I turned the tender age of 16 when, to my disbelief, he tried to arrange a marriage for me. But that didn't work because, fortunately for me, I was too 'fat' and way too headstrong and from a common, low-class family, as seemingly this particular family wanted a subservient girl. Poor thing!

Thank God for my big fat common mouth and matching body, hey. It saved me from being pushed from the frying pan into the fire! But it didn't save me from a bash (although by that age I was completely desensitised to pain as I'd become quite hardened). Apparently, it was all my fault that my father had been humiliated by such feedback, and it was all my fault because I was fat and rough and common.

But, secretly, I knew what really got to him. It was the opinion that the father of that family had of him, that he was a low-class man, with a low-class family. Of course, blaming me was easier, like it aways is and always has been throughout my entire life, than admitting – like anyone else who is in the wrong – that he is not the man he thought he was to the outside world, and that's what the bottom of a bottle of whisky will do to you… lie!

To be honest, it wasn't just me that was doomed. See, it wasn't fantastic for most of us girls growing up in the 80's – even though it was the beginning of power women. As young girls leaving school, the reality was that most of the girls I knew weren't wealthy, nor were we born into status.

Therefore, for girls like us, we were limited work-wise to the likes of care work, nursing or working in a shop. Some went to typing school to learn shorthand, for secretarial or clerk positions. For others, their option was to get married, settle down and have a kid. Or be a single mum to get a flat. Thankfully it's changed enormously, and better opportunities are available, but there is still some work to be done.

It's funny what thoughts drift in and out of your head in times like these, memories that feel so vivid. Which made me think, maybe this could be my final destination. Only time will tell.

The silence was broken once again with the driver announcing our arrival, as he pointed to big iron gates at the back entrance of the hospital, with a sign saying *St Bartholomew's Hospital.* Oh wow. We're here! This is it. From now on, my fate is in the hands of this place and all that's in it.

He found a place to park, and we began to take out my luggage. I did a few quick visual sweeps of the car to make sure I didn't leave anything behind, then said, "We have to go to ward 5C," which he was already familiar with.

As we walked to the transport entrance lounge, a few things started to look familiar from my first visit. We walked towards the lifts on the ground floor of the KGV building, King George V, when all of a sudden, I could smell coffee. I looked to where the coffee machine noises were coming from and saw it was in the basement. I thought, *that's a good sign.* It wasn't Costa or Nero, it was called Fontana. I'd never even heard of it before. But it turned out to be really nice coffee. And more than that, over those monthly treatment cycles, I got to know the lovely people that worked there, who would truly take care of me – almost every single day.

After a few short moments, it was our turn for the lift. We amassed all my stuff and after a little tussle and a battle of wills, the driver was quite adamant he was going to carry all the heavy stuff, so I just let him. He pressed floor 5 and the doors closed.

The first floor we stopped at was floor 2, where the staff and visitor restaurant was located. We then arrived at what was to become very familiar surroundings, on floor 5. Looking around, trying to familiarise myself, I thought to myself how pristine and clinical it was. We got to ward 5C, a holding ward, where I would stay until all my infection tests came back negative, so as not to spread infection to other vulnerable patients. All being well, I would then be moved to a more permanent ward. I had been semi promised ward 5D as it was a place that had a small physio gym, with an exercise bike, which would be just enough to keep myself going.

The ambulance driver had a lanyard with a security strip that opened the doors of the hospital. Otherwise, we would have had to press the buzzer, like the many times I did after, to confirm who we were via a video speaker to the staff on duty, when we walked in and were greeted by friendly new faces who would soon become familiar!

The ward looked very different to what I had seen before. Like most of us, we were familiar with wards that have big communal rooms with four to six beds in one bay. This ward was nothing like that. It was a long corridor of separate rooms on one side that are next to each other. The rooms had two door entrances, one in the corridor that led to a small room with a basin and a wall-mounted glove and apron holder, which nurses would religiously use before entering your room, to control and limit infection. The second door led to the actual patient room.

The nurses greeted us, and the ambulance driver said: "I have a new patient for you." "What is your name," the ward sister asked.

"Hello, I'm Sarezah Lake."

She said, "Ah yes, we spoke on the phone. You are in room 1, all the way down the corridor on your right."

All the bags were in. The driver said his goodbyes and I sat on the bed, thinking, *Right this is it. I am at St Bartholomew's Hospital, room 1 ward 5C, it's the 17th March 2021, approximately 14.42, to receive treatment for Acute Myeloid Leukaemia. So let's get on with it and give our best shot! It's me versus cancer. A battle that could easily be to the death. Either way, one of us is going to win, so let's go.*

We do not have time for complacency or wallowing in any self-pity. We know what we've got, an amount of cancer cells packed out in my bone marrow accelerating at a rate of knots, together with some mutated genetic gene called FLT3, which is way above my head – only made more understandable by my cousin Uzma who researched it all for me and explained it as best she could.

But it was way too many big words for an Essex Girl like me. All I know is it's not great. This gene turns me against myself or something! It's like cancer won the toss of the coin in a game of football and had the advantage. *Fan-fucking-tastic* (sorry, the Essex came out again. You know what they say. You can take the girl out of Essex, but you can't take Essex out of the girl).

My conversation with myself was halted by a knock at the door and in entered a nurse to take some swabs for my Covid test and other tests, like MRSA etc. Mate, as if the Covid test isn't bad enough. But there was another test, the last one, horrifying to say the least, as the nurse directed me as to what to do. Off I trotted to the bathroom, pulled down my Nike leggings. The first one wasn't too bad. I followed the instructions and swabbed my groin area, broke off the stick, then popped it in the test tube with the solution.

And the final one. "Put it in your anus." "Sorry, Pardon??? Anus? How?"

"Yes, your anus, as we need to do a rectal swab."

So she guided me as to what to do. Oh, mate, I had to put that stick in my a*rsehole, you know. Then swirl it around, break it off and pop it in the tube, mate. Where's the dignity?

After washing myself and my hands – thoroughly, might I add – I handed over the swabs back to her. Whilst it was all new to me, I suspect it was a daily routine for her, cos off she went, like nothing, telling me, "The doctor will be in soon to talk to you. Do you want anything to eat or drink?"

"No I'm OK, thanks."

"You will be able to order food from the out of hours menu."

Ooooh, I thought. Bit hotel-like this. What could go wrong? Well for a start the food mate, Jesus Joseph and Mary! It was nothing short of vile!

Within a few moments, there was a knock on the door and a "Hello. I'm your doctor, Jasmine. So you've had your swabs done. They should be back within 24 hours. Once they're back – and hopefully it all comes back normal – you will be taken to another department to have a PICC line inserted. This will be a permanent line in your arm where it will easier access for bloods, chemo and, of course, transfusions. After your results are back, we will start your chemo. Hopefully, by tomorrow, a bed will become free on one of the permanent green wards as 5C is an amber ward, meaning some infections are on an amber ward whereas a green ward is infection free. So if you have Covid you will have to stay here, otherwise you will be transferred to 5D where we have been advised of your fitness regimes by our Cancer Specialist Nurse, Sam, so we will do our best to get you on 5D."

In fact, on every treatment cycle, the med team went above and beyond to ensure I had a gym, even when I couldn't get to it. (More about that later.)

"Any questions," she said.

"Yes, how do they get the PICC line in my arm and which one of my arms is it going in?" Not because I was stupid – well not that stupid – but I didn't know!

She replied, "It's a small process." This is a term I very quickly learned medics say so as not to cause any anxiety.

Just before she was about to leave, I said, "Oh, one more thing. It's really cold in here." In fact, cold was an understatement, it was pissing Baltic and still is in those wards. You want to know why? I tell you why, the faulty designed air conditioning system, that's why. An air conditioning system that is designed to chuck out cold air right onto the patient all day, every day. I really couldn't acclimatise to the temperature as I'm used to my house or car being the same temperature, and not under 8 degrees, mate. I do admit, I like it at a nice 22 plus degrees, all year long. However, this system is flawed and, believe it or not, I'm still fighting for it to be changed. But hey ho, that's another bloody story.

Despite it being cold, I tried to settle into my new environment. The bathroom was very clean and functional, but extremely clinical. There was nothing very homely about it. It was like a public loo with a shower in. The room didn't have anything cosy. It was just there ready to save your life and get you through the symptoms of chemo. A stark reminder of where you are. A hospital!

I decided to open my bag to get some clothing bits out. As I did, I saw that my husband had secretly put the cherries I'd bought for him in my case. That made me feel both happy and sad. I took those little cherries, with their smiley faces and put them on the hospital table next to my jug of rank hospital water. Now, just so you know, for the past 35-odd years I have only drunk Evian bottled water.

I started drinking mineral water when I was a young professional, when I was working in my role as a union representative for the TSSA Union. One of the girls from the union based in the London office asked me if I wanted to go out for a drink after work, seeing as it's POETS day.

"POETS day, what's that," I asked? "Piss off early, tomorrow is

Saturday."

After a little laugh, I told her, "Thank you, but I don't drink." Besides, my dad wouldn't let me go out in London and he was expecting me back at a certain time. Unbeknownst to her, I would get into a big pile of doo doo if I didn't go back when I was expected. I feared that I would lose my job as my father had already threatened me that if I didn't put the money in his account he would ring up my office and make a false complaint, so I would lose my job.

Seeing it was the only positive thing I had in my life at that time and a massive way of escaping the volatile home life I was trapped in with no way out, I did whatever I could to keep the peace and make him happy. I knew that giving him my money was a good peacekeeping exercise. So I negotiated. I explained I could give him most of it. But I would have to keep some for travel and food, or he would have to come and take me to work and pick me up. As he was a drunk, he agreed. I told him I earned less than what I did. Thankfully, he never investigated it further. I guess he relied on the fact that I was too afraid of him to lie.

I hated the control but – at the time – my father's clutches were strong. I just had no choice.

It's not like I could just walk out like most western kids. The community wasn't like that back then and there was no support like there is now. They just had a hold over us, especially over the girls. Thankfully, now I know better. But at the time, I was powerless and very young, just a 19- year-old.

Anyway she was like, "Well just tell him you have to work late." I was like, "He won't believe me."

So she said, "Give me his number and I will call him and say I'm your boss's secretary." I was like, "No. He will know."

"No, he won't. I'm very convincing."

She called him. I was a bloody nervous wreck. Who am I kidding? I thought he will know. I shit myself because I knew the consequences of being found out could range from a beating to me losing my job.

She signalled me to come closer so we could both hear my dad's voice. That woman answered. The step thing. "Hello, could I speak to

Mr. Dookhith, it's Sarezah's office here in London. I am the secretary." My father got on the phone. "Hello, it's Melissa. I am the secretary of Sarezah's boss; he has asked me to contact you because the meeting they are in is going to overrun and she won't be able to get away till about 7-7.30pm. So by the time she travels back on the tubes and train, we are looking at her getting home past 10pm. If she is lucky. Of course we will ensure that she gets back to Liverpool Street safely, and then she will get a taxi back home, which will all be reimbursed when she claims expenses."

He had to agree. He couldn't act savagely, not to her anyway. "Yes dear," he said. "Thank you for letting me know. We will be waiting for her."

I had mixed feelings and was definitely paranoid about it. But he sounded OK with it. So I just rolled with it. She put the phone down and gave me an expression of *yessssss*. So off we went to the city for drinks. Something I had never ever dreamed of doing. And here I was. Little 'ol me from Colchester. Drinking in the city with the big girls.

OMG the first wine bar we went into was absolutely nothing like I had seen before. It was so fancy and sparkly clean. Some sort of jazzy funk music was playing in the background. It felt fantastic walking in with a group of girls from my London office, who were all gorgeous and sophisticated. I guess from all the attention I got within moments of being in there, that included me too. I was a stunning buxom young lady, with long dark curly hair, and huge brown/green eyes and red glossy lips, with an all year round bronze tan, a colour that my husband says everyone wants to be. If you could bottle that up and sell it you'd be a millionaire. (I think that's his attempt at being complimentary).

But I wasn't interested in that kind of attention – that wasn't and isn't what makes me feel all razzmatazz, especially on that day. See, what made me feel elated in that moment was my first true taste of freedom from the prison of life I had been used to so I relished in my new found liberty, which became the catalyst to drive me to escape the place I was living in.

So at the bar, one of the girls asked me what would I like to drink? "Errr, I don't know. I don't drink alcohol."

Then one of the girls said, "Get her a Perrier sparkling water with a twist of lemon." I nodded and said, "I will have one of those, thank you."

Oh my days, it arrived in a tall glass tumbler with ice and lemon and a cocktail stirrer; it certainly looked more glamorous than just water. Then I took the first sip, and it sizzled in my mouth and felt sensational! It completely changed my life and from that day to this I began drinking mineral water.

Like I said, it's funny how historical events pop into your head when you have time to sit and think and reflect – something that happened a lot during my hospital stay. I guess water came to the forefront of my mind because for the first time in over three decades, I was told in hospital I wasn't allowed to have bottled water due to certain minerals, so I had to drink tap water. Tap water, you know. Tap! That was not the only thing forbidden either. There was a host of other foods, like salads, soft cheese, and in particular deli meats, due to the bacteria risk. These can cause infections when our cells drop to neutropenic flat.

CHAPTER 24

Don't Fade Away!

My first day in hospital soon turned into my first night. So I got myself ready for bed with a not so nice lukewarm shower. At least I smelt nice as I'd bought my home bathing rituals with me which included some travel size Molton Brown shower gels, face wash, face creams, body butter and some perfume. I even brought make up with me. I mean why not? You want to feel nice, don't you?

I said all my good nights to those I love, then tried to settle as much as possible. I'd placed the nurses' call button on the side of my bed, as instructed, then attached my cross-body Nike bag to a handle. Next to me, on a 'swirling' hospital table, I put my lip salve and my little cherries that I had been holding for a while for a bit of comfort, close to the rank jug of hospital water.

The curtains were drawn and taped down with medical supplies in an attempt to block the outside gleaming night lights of the hospital. I then turned the lights off, using the genius, multi- purpose nurse buzzer controls – which of course I explored to the maximum, pressing every button to see what they would do. Finally, I pulled the blanket over me, that my dear bestie Jane bought me to take with me. Thank goodness, really, because I used it to shield myself from the freezing cold air that was pumping directly onto me.

I took a few deep breaths as I lay in the semi dark room, surrounded by little lights flashing, and thought, *Fucking hell, man. How did we get here, aye girl? This is laughable. Seven and a half years of hard dieting and exercise, no chocolate since 21st May 2016 (and to date still none), no bread for four and a half years, no fizzy drinks, no booze. No nothing. Then I finally had that unsightly and troublesome skin removed, where I looked like Jlo for 7 minutes, only to have shitting, pissing, bastard, fuck face cancer that is coursing through my wanking veins trying to finish me off. Oh, and to add to it all, my lovely flat tummy won't even see a fucking beach this year or perhaps any other fucking, pissing, bastard year, cos my man – Mr. blood cancer consultant – can't guarantee the treatment will work, or that I will see the end of the fucking year! Fan-fucking-tastic!* I felt cheated, once again, like life had betrayed me.

In all honesty, despite my attempts to stay positive, that first night was overwhelming. To the point that I felt like getting out of that clinical bed and running away, to where, God knows. Maybe on the streets of London, or maybe I could even somehow find my way back home. I felt myself mentally slipping away and, with nowhere to run, the tears of uncertainty began filling my eyes – which eventually overspilled and ran down my cold cheeks onto the cold pillow as I lay in that cold bed, in that cold room, into that cold reality of my cancerous hell.

Then I said to myself, *Come on darling, let's stop! I'm here for you, it's just you and me!* So I held out my hand wand for the 1000th time, and dragged myself out of those rocky emotional waters, as I didn't want to drown in that *no hope left* moment. So I gave myself a pep talk and said we can't start crumbling now, let's pull ourselves together. *We ain't got time to cry, we've only got to fight it. We've got to fight it, Sarezah. Don't let it taunt you! It doesn't know what will happen and nor do you. Let's just watch and wait, so until we know, we don't know. But never let our fears and thoughts torture us!*

I had no sooner dozed off when I was startled by the door opening, as the healthcare assistant came to do my 10pm observation. In fact the same thing happened at blooming 2am, then again at 6am, making it really hard to adjust to those first few nights, together with the constant flashing aircraft landing strip lights, to the point I was actually expecting a jumbo jet to land in my room any second.

With the relentless ward noises, the nurse calls constantly beeping, the running around commotions and squeaky trolleys, the crash team in and out trying to save lives, all the talking, honestly, it was a long night. It didn't help, either, that I came from a leafy quiet village. But I told myself, push through big girl, this is not forever!

That first morning, just before 06.00am and every morning after that, I was awoken by one of those infamous hospital squeaky trolleys, followed by a knock on my hospital room door.

“Good morning,” a cheery nurse’s voice would always greet me, “It’s time for bloods and observations.” Then she would start doing her thing! She went on to say that I would be having a PICC line put in later that day to which I responded that they told me that yesterday.

With that, she left and I got up and did a few morning standing stretches, then had a toilet and shower, brush teeth etc. I called my husband and replied to a few texts and waited for my breakfast, or should I say gruel, to arrive. I will tell you why – you see, my breakfast every morning until then was porridge. Knowing it was on the menu, I thought *cool*!

Now, I know it’s not the Hilton and I wasn’t even expecting that. But I was expecting something edible. Mate, it was so bad that even Oliver Twist would not eat it, let alone ask for another bowl. But I knew I had to eat something, so I ate what I could stomach and tried not to be negative. But as you all well know by now, to me food is life, and no matter how much positivity I had, it didn’t impact the quality of our hospital food which – take my word for it – is nothing short of appalling, inedible muck.

It’s definitely not ideal when you are in a hospital, fighting for your life. Food is not all you have to look forward to, but food is the very fuel and nutrition that is needed in order to recover. To be honest, I was really cross at myself for being completely ignorant and underestimating how the food would be, thinking patient care came before outsourced profit! *Wrong.* To make things worse, I was not at all prepared as I didn’t have much in the way of snacks, as my normal diet consisted of freshly prepared food.

I did manage to tell the chief executive of the hospital during an executive committee meeting (when I was asked to give a talk after being invited and later appointed as a patient representative) that the food quality was almost diabolical. In fact, it was so bad that when I bit into an apple it was rotten, and I had to spit it out! Disgusting! I even told the committee when I did that talk that I’d wondered if it had come off a skip, because it was way past any sell by date. I always got the usual response of, “We’ll look into that,” which normally means the NHS executives will pass it on to a delegated committee that can sit and talk about the subject that will be headed “Rotten apples" (oh the pun!), then pass that to a sub-committee, then to another, and in the meantime nothing gets done as it all gets washed away and lost in translation!

Even now, three years plus has passed, and they've done little-to-nothing to change much – despite me battling with them. And it's not just about food that is failing the NHS, it's almost everything. But all they did when I raised any type of concern was to give me the run around.

Numerous times I have been pushed from pillar to post. In the end, no one is actually held accountable, and no one is available to make a change, because new people are appointed to do nothing more than the last appointee. Unfortunately, this is why the NHS is on its knees: poor administration, poor management and lack of leadership from people who tend to make poor decisions and cuts to patient care and not where it should be.

To date, my biggest gripe about being in hospital wasn't the medical care but the poor standards provided for patients. There is little to no mental health support. There is no

entertainment in the wards. Nothing! The food is revolting. Some of the other patients told me they had to order from Uber Eats and Deliveroo to get something half decent to eat, but I'm not a takeaway girl. I have mostly only cooked and eaten my own food. That is one of the reasons I also created healthy versions of meals that I loved to eat.

And, besides, eating out wasn't advised by the hospital med team, saying once my cells drop to zero, neutropenic flat, no fast foods are permitted, in case the area where the food is prepared is unhygienic and could lead to food poisoning – which for us patients with no immune system could lead to sepsis and death. Wonderful, I thought. Just wonderful! So defo no takeaways for me. So I had to eat what I could to survive!

And that was the beginning of yet another very long and difficult battle with my weight, partly because I had to compromise on what I was eating, by having to return to certain foods that I had closed the door on many years ago – like bread, cakes and biscuits.

"Course you did," I hear a few say, "Don't you mean you used the opportunity." Nope! It was eat, or don't eat, and don't recover – then die. No brainer really! Hey ho!

Fantastic! Couldn't write it! But in the words of my dear friend Rob, my son's ex boxing coach from the East End, I mustn't grumble!

However it did teach me one thing, that at times you have no choice but to adapt in any given situation and get on with what you have to do to, especially if it is to survive. Hence that's why *Paul*, the French patisserie nearby, became a firm favourite of mine. Much like many French foods.

Food wasn't the only thing I had to adapt either. I had to make changes to the way I trained and curb the intensity due to the chemo and low blood counts. So I could only do a light workout, without too much of anything and no upper body as soon as the PICC line was eventually inserted. I was permitted to walk, so that's what I did, I got my steps in.

During quarantine, I used to do 5k steps in that tiny cell of a hospital room. Round and round and round and round I would walk, with headphones into one of the beloved mixes my son did for me. As the music was pumping, I built up a sweat whilst stomping around and around that tiny little room. Then when I was clear, I was able to go out for my daily walks.

The time soon arrived for me to have my PICC line fitted. That was fun! A nurse guided me into the line department and then into a small room, where I had to fill in some papers, including a disclaimer. They asked me to take my top clothes off, including bra, and pop the gown on. That immediately transported me straight back to Mr. Banwell, where I had to take my gown off. Thankfully it never came off, it was only to get to my arm more easily.

I lay on the bed as the PICC line man took out all kind of incision tools, whilst the female nurse chatted away, I suspect to distract me – which wasn't really working because I couldn't take my eyes off what he was doing. Anyway, the male nurse began to get the ultrasound machine in position, as well as me.

He sanitised the wire and the end of the head of the machine. He took a long, sterile plastic sleeve and covered it, so nothing touched my skin. Then he poured clean gel on and began looking for a suitable vein in my left arm. As he began to scan my arm, I tried to crack a joke saying, "Oooh, I hope you don't find a baby in there. All stupid things happen to me, ha, ha, ha." To which he responded with a sort of a huffing sound; reading between the lines it meant *sssh, I'm trying to concentrate.*

Of course, I didn't sssh. Ever the curious me, I kept asking questions. *Ooh, what does this do? And where is that going? It looks a bit grey ant egg-ish hazy, doesn't it? I'm glad you know what you're doing.* To be honest, he was alright with me and all my annoying comments. He even got me involved by turning the monitor around to show me what he was doing. He pointed on the screen and said this is what we call a Micky Mouse, referring to it, and said this is the common femoral artery. Saying stuff that was a bit too technical for me, but it meant something to him.

A few moments later, he said, "Sharp scratch" followed by him injecting local anaesthetic in different parts of my arms. Which made me start to think, is this going to be as painful as bone marrow aspirate? Several injections later, he said, "Do you feel anything?" as he tapped a few different places in my arm.

"No. Not really."

"Ok, good." His eyes fixed on that snowy grey screen as I, too, was once again fixated on him and what he was doing.

I lay there for almost 45 mins, enduring a strange kind of discomfort and sensation. It could be likened to something crawling up and scratching your skin from the inside. Quite bizarre!

Nonetheless, it all seemed to be going well, until we got to this certain point in my arm where he began to look a little flustered, together with asking me to turn my head this way and that way.

Some moments later, he turned to his assistant and said: "It's stuck in an area on her neck and won't budge any further," then stopped rather abruptly and pulled the line out. "I'm so sorry, we will have to try another time. If that doesn't work then perhaps we will have to look at an alternative, like a Hickman line (a central line that is placed on your chest)."

"Oh gosh," I said, then went back to my ward, with no PICC line! Back on the wards, lunch was being served. Seeing I didn't eat much for breakfast I was quite hungry, something I wasn't used to. Breakfast was a meal that set me up for the day.

So I told myself that the next meal I chose had to be a safe bet. Therefore I had pre ordered a jacket potato, thinking nothing could be worse than the sloppy porridge. Well it was. In fact, it was nothing short of foul! Honestly, it was barely edible.

The potato was not in the least fresh, it was rock bottom quality, dare I even suggest close to perishing, if not actually off. The beans, if that's you can call them, were tasteless and every other one was hard and crunchy. Whilst I wasn't expecting Heinz, I was expecting something edible! And to top it all, the cheese was bloody rubbery.

Oh, I thought to myself, the joys of outsourcing to private companies, hey! Profit margins come before quality of produce and patient care. Of course, they will say different and deny when challenged about the freshness or quality of their produce. They always will.

Shortly after that appalling lunch a nurse came in with some good news, saying all my tests had come back negative – so I was going to be moved to 5D, meaning I get to use the gym. And I was going to have my own room, but it wasn't quite ready, so I would have to wait in another room.

I was told to pack up and gather my things as the nurse would arrive soon to transfer me on to ward 5D. And finally I was told the med team had given the green light to start my first dose of chemo and was just waiting for pharmacy to dispatch it and then go through rigorous checks. For some reason I was all excited at the news, it was almost like I wasn't in a hospital fighting cancer.

I looked at my watch and thought *you may as well go for a quick wee and a freshen up, it's unlikely she will come now, mate.* No sooner than I was in the toilet, hovering over the pan, she was there. I say hovering as I don't sit on any toilet except mine, mate. And when I say mine only, I mean mine only because I don't even use the toilet downstairs at home. Since I became a bit more mobile, I don't have to endure the family toilet.

With boys, no matter how clean it was kept, it was always a little bit grubby. And since I could, I loved being able to leap up and down those stairs just to take a pee in my clean bathroom. I never took it for granted that I could as there were many things I couldn't do during those terribly long years of being super morbidly obese, which led me to being immobile, needing help with almost everything, including the toilet. I've had many, many years of living in a house full of boys who, for some unknown reason, piss everywhere except in the toilet bowl. Filth.

So anyhow, here I am hovering over the loo, when I hear the flipping door open, coupled together with this big booming jolly Nigerian voice that said: "Hello, it's your nurse. I'm taking you to ward 5D."

"Oh hello, sorry," I said. "I'm just doing a wee wee."

"Take your time honey. No rush. Oh my lord, is this all your stuff? My goodness, you came prepared."

I laughed and opened the door with my dripping hand to see my very beautiful Nigerian nurse standing before me.

As soon as she saw me, she was like: "Whaaaatttttt. Look at you. You are so beautiful.

Mmmm. Let me see you. Turn around. Show me yourself. Girrrl you're so fit. You look strong."

I mean I giggled. Suddenly, big tough me went all bashful and shy. I know, right? Loud mouth, brazen Sarezah, blushing!

"Well it's a long story," I said as we gathered my things together. She said: "You can tell me all about it as we walk, my dear."

So I began to tell her my weight loss story. I, me, blah, blah, blah lost 19st then ending with Mr. Banwell, not only made me look like Jlo, even though it was only for seven minutes, but ended up saving my life. And here I am in hospital, with a terminal illness, battling for my life, in a room with you, my nurse – who indeed was filling me with gratuitous praise for looking fit. Honestly, you couldn't make it up!

But despite the dark humour, the truth is I have a very serious blood cancer where at any time during treatment I could die. But in that moment – and many moments to follow – she, and all those other nurses, made me feel really good, and it all began to feel like I wasn't even in hospital.

In truth, no one in hospital ever made me feel like I had a serious illness, it was quite the contrary. The entire med team – be it nurses, doctors, registrars, consultants and professors – cared for and supported my needs, together with all the other staff, from cleaners to the food service.

They helped me get through absolutely everything, from sitting with me, laughing with me to consoling me when I got ill and even helped me sip water when I was sick. They are by your side and comfort you throughout the day and throughout the night. They rooted for me, no matter what time of day it was they came. Most of them don't always have their breaks. They work extremely long and debilitating hours – just to make sure they are there to wipe away your tears and anything and everything else.

We chatted whilst we walked down the hospital corridor towards ward D. On arrival we went through to the reception desk where I saw Sister Jess. "Hello, we are just going to pop you in a room with another lady until your room is ready. It won't be long."

I spoke briefly to the lady in the room. Mate, she was a seasoned pro in-patient by the looks of things. She had everything in her room, herbal tea and coffee, biscuits, blankets and all sorts of things. I felt like a total novice, as I really didn't have much in the way of anything. Let alone food.

Without too much of a wait, a nurse arrived and took me to Room 7. *Oooh, that's a good sign because it's my lucky number,* I thought! Although I'm not entirely sure it is lucky. I guess it's known as a lucky number, just like number 13 is unlucky. How we've developed as a society to discriminate due to superstition against numbers is beyond me but, hey ho, mustn't grumble, besides I don't make the rules. However, to me the number 7 is meaningful. Firstly, my birthday is on the 7th of November. And my hero, Eric Cantona, played number 7 for my beloved football team Manchester United. And now, my middle son Khaliq has a number 7 tattoo on his forearm, that he had done during his visit to Thailand, in honour of me, so I will always be with him.

Once I settled down, I sat next to the window in my new home for the next month or so, looking out at the beautiful London skyline.

I saw several planes ferrying people around the world, thinking, *If only that was me.* Then I thought of home, and felt my little heart sink a bit, seeing it was a Friday.

I thought I would be having my little *cheat meal* now. But instead I'm in a cancer hospital covered in uncertainty! How on earth can everything be ok one minute and in a flick of a switch, not?! Life can really be fragile, things can truly change instantly and, until it does, we continue to just plod along, blissfully unaware, like me, until one day we are in the face of some adversity.

Which actually brings me nicely to another point, or should I say gripe. It's something I have thought about once or twice, especially whilst I was in hospital (Lord knows I had time). And that's the concept of a *cheat meal.* Mate, it's beyond me that some people even debate that and try to tell you why you should or shouldn't do something, who have opinions on flipping everything. These revellers of self-righteousness start telling you why you shouldn't call it a *cheat meal,* because *cheat* has negative connotations to it.

I'm like, "For goodness sakes, it's just a meal, stop hanging on every single word and making it something it isn't."

Forever labelling everything in a way that is derogatory is unjustified, in my opinion! But hey ho, we are all of course entitled to whatever opinion we like and if it works for them, then fine. I say focus on what's important to you and what works for you, not what others want you to think.

In spite of feeling unsettled that evening, I reminded myself that this was only a temporary situation, nothing lasts forever! Besides, we have a job to do. So let's just get on with it, there's nothing you can do, let's just go with the flow.

From then on, I did my best to do just that. Whatever came up I tackled it best I could. And if anything got too much, I told myself you can always have a good ol' moan, and moaning gets it all off the chest. Trust me I love a moan, in fact I can moan for England, and to anyone or anything that will listen! But, like everything, you do have to limit it, can't be moaning all day long, cos that ain't healthy either.

Conversely, you can't bottle it up, it's not healthy! You've got to find an outlet for all the stress and strains of life that won't cause you damage. Moaning is way better than turning to the many varieties of addictive substances out there as well as booze and food! But also try to remember stress can cause many underlying health issues. There are many theories that stress contributes to low immunity which, in turn, can lead people to develop cancer. Of course, both can be caused by lifestyle which, to me, makes absolute sense because – take it from me – having a family is bloody stressful at the best of times.

Stress can fester inside of you, causing damage. Realising this, I found better ways to channel my stress and – in turn – the frustration it brings. I found a way to convert stress into strength, so I would either go and smash the gym or do some cardio, or even walk, or cook and clean. Cleaning is my least favourite thing in life, but it's got to be done. The point was to find anything that helped clear my mind and stay focused.

Being in hospital was no different really. I had to channel my focus and energies into something. And seeing I was going to be here for the foreseeable future, I decided to make the place look a bit more homely, and definitely warmer (thank the Lord I had a heater otherwise, believe me, I would have f'd off home mate; that place was, and still is, Baltic!). I faffed around trying to make the room look a bit cosier. Soon after, my first evening in room 7 was coming to a close so, just like I would at home, I decided to have a shower and get myself ready for bed.

No sooner than I started to gather my nightwear and take my trainers off, there was a knock on the door. It was sister Jess saying they have a slight problem because they couldn't get a PICC line in; they needed to insert a cannula in my hand instead, so they can administer my chemo.

"Chemo?! What chemo? Are you giving me chemo tonight? Isn't it a bit late for that sister?" "Oh no," she said. "We start the chemo treatment as soon as it's available from pharmacy.

We don't wait until the morning. Even if it came in the middle of the night, we'd administer it then."

"Oh," I said, "It's not a 9-5 thing then?"

"No," she said, "not unless it's high risk, like Mylotarg, then we do start then to make sure crash teams are available."

"Wait a minute. I'm having that Mylotarg."

"Yes." she said calmly, "in a few days," as she looked at my record.

Facckkkkk, I thought, everything is becoming real, real quick.

Mate, the task of trying to insert the cannula was fun – despite sister Jess and several other nurses trying to get that blasted cannula in just about every vein possible, with no luck whatsoever – to the extent that my venous system deciding this ain't happening, you've already pissed me right off with what happened today with that PICC line. So I'm playing hard ball and now I am literally giving everyone the middle finger – because each time someone tried to insert a cannula, my veins collapsed.

"It won't work, love. Besides it's also blooming freezing in here so my veins are not pumped." At which point I had a lightbulb moment, and said to sister Jess, "I know a way to pump my veins up, and that's to get in the gym and do a cycle to get the blood pumping into my veins!" She looked at me for a moment and I said, "Well if anyone knows their body, it's me."

So I did just that. I stuck my headphones in, put a bit of Rammstein on. Son, Du Hast followed by a bit of Slipknot, cycled my little legs away, until 20 minutes and 9 kilometres later, I had big fat juicy hand veins. And, needless to say, finally a needle found its way successfully into my hand, albeit it was bloody uncomfortable, so chemo could be administered in the morning – or so I thought.

CHAPTER 25

The First Dose

At 11pm, the chemotherapy arrived, and I was told it would be administered shortly which, of course, was way past my bedtime. Thankfully I was already showered; that was fun and games trying to keep the cannula dry. Sister Jess did her best to wrap it up and make it waterproof, but I still ended up getting it a bit wet, despite showering with one hand up in the air like I was Freddy Mercury!

After waiting in anticipation, two nurses came in a little after 11pm. They were quite energetic, bright and breezy. I wondered if they would still be like that after their 14hr night shift.

"Chemo time," one of them said.

This was it, I thought – the first step to hopefully making me better.

They conducted a thorough procedure, checking my name, date of birth and hospital number. The nurses checked and checked again. They matched all the numbers and the prescribed chemo, to make sure it was definitely for me, as there is no room for error, the wrong medication could be potentially fatal.

Finally one of the nurses began the treatment, explaining the procedure as she went along. "First, we will use a saline solution to flush the line (a medical procedure of clearing the intravenous line of any other medication or anything else to keep the entry line clean and sterile). Then we will do what is known as drawing back the flush to make sure the line is open."

As I watched, a rush of blood came through, followed by her pushing the flush forward again, until it was all finished… trippy, I thought. She then picked up my first ever bolus of chemotherapy, a single dose of a drug called Daunorubicin; she screwed it into my cannula ready to start the procedure. She looked at me and nodded as if to say 'ok'. I nodded back after a brief wave of apprehension and pushing aside the *what if I react to the chemo*, before nodding back and so it began, chemotherapy!

I watched, mesmerised by this huge syringe filled with a luminous bright red, toxic-looking liquid, which was screwed into the end of my cannula, then she began to gradually administer minuscule amounts of that substance, slowly into my body.

"It's a bit of a funny colour, isn't it?" I said, trying to crack jokes. "It looks a bit like Cherryade, the cheap one, with all the E numbers."

The nurse laughed, but not enough to break her intense concentration. Slowly, slowly, she continued. I was absolutely transfixed watching her. She did try to talk me through each stage, in layman's terms, of course. She said we have to go slowly, so we don't overload your system, as this is a very toxic chemical. *Great,* I thought. *Very toxic. That's the stuff,* I thought, as I continued to witness this bright red mixture getting pumped into my veins, mil by mil, putting all my hope and trust that this mixture will save my life.

Minutes later, and somewhat alarmingly, I'd noticed my veins had changed to a deep cherry red, literally the same colour as the chemo. "Gosh," I said, in a mild panic. "What's happening?"

"Don't worry," she said. "Some patients experience colour changes in their veins." Mate, *some* I thought, my poor hand looks like a road traffic map on the ol' sat nav.

Anyway, soon enough, the bolus was almost empty, and only had a few mils left. I continued watching until the very last devil red drop entered my body.

Immediately after, she administered the second part of the treatment, Cytarabine, which took seconds as it was only a couple of millilitres. "All done," she said, doing another flush. And that was that, my first dose of standard chemotherapy treatment done and dusted – all within 30 odd minutes from start to finish, happy days!

Wasn't that bad, was it, I told myself. But little did I know, hey, what was waiting around the corner for Sarezah!

Sometime after treatment, I began to feel a little strange. I can't explain what or why, I wasn't sure. Besides, I am not sure if it was physiological or if I could sense something alien running through my veins. See, up until that moment I'd never had any type of infusion other than an iron shot, when I had the pre op and my iron was low.

And the seven years before that, the most I had medicine-wise was the odd antibiotic, and a couple of days of taking Feminax during my monthly cycle to get me through the dreadful pain of what is known as *lady tummy* or *mummy tummy* in my household – which, for me at times, is nothing short of dreadful (and please, before you judge, unless you've had a period and know what it feels like for a girl, keep your mouth shut, you won't be thanked for it).

I broke away from my thoughts as I needed to go for a wee wee, so off I trotted. I did my business as usual, then turned around to put the toilet tissue in the loo to flush away. As I did I was shocked. My eyes widened because I saw what looked like bright red blood in the toilet. I thought *Shit, I'm dying,* so I immediately pressed the buzzer.

The nurse came in and had a look at my wee, then reassured me it was just the chemo.

Evidently it turns everything red. Including wee. *Much like beetroot does*, she said. I was like woah! Thank goodness! Honestly, the relief! Besides, we still had the next six days to get through, I thought I can't start dying now. I finally got into bed, and mentally ticked off day 1, we've now got day 3 then day 5 to go. But so far so good.

Saturday 20th March saw take two of the PICC line insertion attempt, by the person I'm told is the expert in this field. On arrival, the consultant anaesthetist burst into the room somewhat theatrically after I'd said, "Come in."

"Right," he said, "I'm here to do this PICC line they couldn't fit."

"Oh hi," I said, then continued, "Yes, they did have quite a bit of trouble getting it in, apparently my veins are wonky or something."

"Oh well, I'm not them!" he said, with a slight smirk. *Alrighty then Mr. Confident,* my face said what my thought, thought!

He gowned up, with a little assistance from my good self, which just meant tying his gown into a bow to prevent it from slipping down. I must say, with what I could see, the consultant was a rather handsome chap! Anyway, he began with the same process as before, sharp scratch, local anaesthetic, moments later that area was numb.

His eyes fixated on the screen of fuzzy ants' egg nest, as he continuously pressed the transducer (a small hand-held device that resembles a microphone) inside the crease of my elbow, from time to time reapplying a big dollop of that gloopy gel, to help glide over my skin to seek and find those useable, big 'fat' juicy veins.

Of course, I tried to crack some jokes, but he wasn't having it and just carried on looking at the screen, making an occasional oomph noise of acknowledgment, but reading between the lines it meant shut up. He asked me to turn my head, and one second later he said, "There, it's done!"

"Pardon?" I said, "What do you mean it's in?"

"You have a fully functional PICC line."

I said, "That took like three minutes." (He laughed at that one).

He went on to flush both ports! Flush, flush. Blood, blood. Two ports. "Beautiful," he said.

And like a gust of wind, he departed as quickly as he arrived.

He left me staring at these two dangling alien port things hanging out of my skin in the crease of my elbow, a line fed into my vein inside me that led close to my heart, so it could pump the chemo all around my body. They clanged together each time I made the slightest of movements in that arm. Mate, it was weird. It was like a monster's inside episode, I thought.

How will I shower, I thought? *What happens if I end up pulling it out when I'm in bed or asleep? How will I sleep, even? Oh my days, what clothes will I wear?* All these questions, I thought. But I tell you, you soon adapted, I mean you just have to, what else can you do?

CHAPTER 26

If It's My Time, It's My Time

The morning of my trial chemo arrived, and I was greeted in my usual way by Patricia, one of my amazing nurses. I asked her how was her Night Shift? She said "It went well, Mama Lake," (that's my chef name as I did a few cooking events as a guest chef pre-Covid days and it's sort of stuck with me, where I am affectionately known by many as Mama Lake, and was adopted by my beloved nurses).

"You are going to have your trial chemo today, Mylotarg," Patricia said. I nodded and smiled as she began the everyday process of taking my morning routine bloods. "Mama Lake, you are almost halfway to chemo graduation day." (Graduation day is a term used by our nurses at Barts to express the day we completed our intensive chemotherapy treatment).

Patricia began to raise the bed to hip height so she could take bloods from my arm. She was cleaning my PICC line area when I told her it was still a bit sore and visibly swollen, which apparently is normal and will soon settle down. (Normal!!! A phrase I heard a lot during my treatment).

"Can I do my exercise and walk before the chemo arrives, Patricia?"

"Yes, of course, Mama Lake. You will get your normal chemotherapy mid-morning. Then the Mylotarg in the afternoon. It will run for two hours. It must be done before 5pm, really, to ensure that there are the maximum number of staff available on site in the event you have a reaction to the Mylotarg."

Evidently it is *normal* with this type of inhibitor treatment that each person may have a different reaction, and the effects won't affect you until you have it. These effects range from having a heart attack, seizure, or stroke, to something else that is sinister, or you just die! DIE!!!

Gosh, I thought. *Die! Be positive, Mama Lake,* I told myself to be positive. Deep breaths. Make the ball then push it away (evidently something to relieve stress). Don't let the word *die* negate that positive outlook! Flowers and light and all that! *Bloody marvellous, hey,* I thought. *Bloody marvellous!*

Soon after, I had yet another morning of breakfast gruel (even though it was gruel, Josh – the regular food man – made it *'thick and creamy, the way you like it'* – in an attempt to make the best he could with what he had for us patients. He made that food with the kindness of his heart, he did, God bless him)!

Anyway, after I ate what I could I went off to train in the gym, and did both my walks by lunchtime, just to get it over and done with, in time for the ol' Mylotarg. I knew how potent this drug was as it had been spoken about throughout my consultations where I was told it was an effective drug because it literally destroyed everything that moved. Even my dear cousin Uzma, the immunologist, researched Mylotarg and said it had a high success rate. So I was informed and fairly prepared.

It only really hit how serious it all was when the med team came into my room and sat with me. During that consultation I had to sign a disclaimer form. And at various points it all became quite intense, especially when they began explaining the survival rate percentages, which were 50-50.

"Of course," I jokingly said, "That's a bit black or white isn't it? I mean I'll take 52-48%." But no-one laughed. I was left out on my own on that one. Trying to stifle out a laugh, I cleared my throat to very serious solemn faces. I suppose it's not really a laughing matter, is it?

But thankfully the consultant went on to correct me and said, "It is only a 50% chance of survival with this immunotherapy, but that is 50% more of a chance than not having it. See, if you don't have this treatment, the cancer cells will 100% kill you!"

Bloody marvellous, I thought, as I grinned. Yet another reminder of just how seriously sick I really was.

We were all set to go after my nurses did my 1400hrs observations. They did the usual check points. Sarezah Lake, date of birth, please. 7/11/68. Hospital number, blah, blah blah. Checked and signed. Ready. Line cleaned and flushed, making sure no air bubbles are present. Thread the line through the drip machine and hook it in the end of the bag of colourless Mylotarg that's hanging at the top of the machine. Screw it into my PICC line, ready to rock and roll for at least the next two hours.

This was my first ever chemo I had on a drip. It was completely mesmerising. I sat there watching it for ages, as it drip, drip, dripped into my arm through my bloodstream, to my heart, where the heart will pump it around to reach the rest of my body.

Wow, the science of it all, I thought. *How clever.* The machine, super sensitive, would sound a horrendous alarm if there was a position, bend or crease it didn't like, whilst flashing a countdown timer.

Time passed by very slowly watching each and every drip. It seemed like an eternity.

Finally it did end, and I pressed the nurse buzzer soon as the infusion alarm went off. Whilst I waited I took a mental note of the time, which was just around 4pm on Monday the 19th of March 2021. The nurse came in, did her thing and observations, all normal, then asked if I felt ok. I nodded.

"Call me if you need anything," she said, and off she went to attend other patients. I was gazing out of the window when I heard a knock on the door.

"Come in!"

"Hello sweetheart," said Sammy, in her normal cheerful happy voice. "How do you feel?" "I'm ok, Sammy," I said, because – on the whole – I did feel ok, perhaps a little strange, maybe an inexplicable tingling inside, which truthfully felt rather nice. It was like a warm sort of rush! I mean I expected to feel something, after all, there was an alien substance flooding my body, killing everything in sight.

For a moment or two, I wondered if what I felt was similar to having a placebo effect, you know, when you are told you have had something that can affect you, so subconsciously, you start having symptoms and feelings in and around your thoughts.

Anyhow, Sammy continued, saying I must immediately say if I felt unwell. I smiled and nodded at her as she turned round and blew me a kiss, saying she will come back later to check. *Best go for a wee and a freshen up,* I thought, seeing it was around 1630hrs and tea is usually around 1700hrs!

But when I got up off the chair, I was like *woah*, as a rush of blood went straight to my head, making me feel all woozy. Of course I tried to steady myself, but found it really difficult, and even though the toilet wasn't far, I really had to focus my attention on what I was doing as well as hold onto nearby things to help steady my body.

Seconds later, I really began to feel very unusual, and I seemed to have developed this mild sort of chill, that was coming over me in waves. I shrugged it off and put it down to the blooming rooms being constantly freezing, and that I may be dizzy because I got up too quickly after sitting for a long while. Go and lie down for a bit, I told myself!

Almost instantly when I lay on the bed, those chills got worse, to the point I began to shiver. Then that got worse, then bloody worse, then worse again, to the point that shivering gravitated to every part of my body and before I knew it, I was shaking violently from head to toe, to the point I felt myself almost convulsing.

Shit, I thought! *What the fuck is happening?* I looked for the nurse buzzer to call, only to realise I had left it flipping hanging above the bed and couldn't reach it. *Fucking fuck my life,* I thought. I'm going to somehow have to get it, but when I tried to get it, I couldn't bloody co-ordinate my movements, because by now, they had become totally involuntary. My brain was telling me to move my arm, but my body was like *nope!*

Shout out, I thought, but when I tried to shout, to my absolute shock, nothing came out. I couldn't move nor make a sound, I could only think, *Shit,* I thought, *Shit, what the hell am I going to do, it's not like I can use the force* (Star Wars fans will understand) *and think someone to pissing come!*

But, as if by magic – miraculously even – my nurse Sammy came in to my room, and when she saw me convulsing like that she immediately rushed to my bedside and pulled the emergency cord, then she dropped to her knees, by my side so she could hold me down in my bed.

"Sweetheart," she said. "Sweetheart! Look at me. Look at me. Stay with me sweetheart!"

Stay with me, what the heck does that mean. *Stay with me,* I thought.

Before I knew it, my breathing began to shorten and very quickly it became laboured! My ears began to ring, as the sound of the code red siren bellowed through the air. That is when I began to panic knowing, this time, that siren was for me – because now my situation was truly grave.

Then my eyes began to roll back into my head and a spiking pain began to consume my entire being. Sam's voice tried to distract me from the situation. "Look at me, sweetheart, focus on me, SWEETHEART!!!!" The fear and panic in her voice said everything. All I could do was just lay there, watching myself from the inside out just slipping away, further into something I did not know.

Literally seconds later, the crash team smashed into my hospital room, with all sorts of bleeping machines bombarding the room, together with as many available life savers as possible. I heard Sam screaming at them, by the sounds of things something medical, whilst still desperately trying to hold me down.

Whilst I struggled to gasp for air, my eyes rolling even further back into its sockets, my hearing had become completely muffled, where I felt I'd been submerged into water and was drowning within myself.

"Can you hear me, sweetheart? Look at me!" Sam's voice continued in the background.

Everyone in that room was manically scrambling around, tearing off aprons, shouting commands at one another. Soon after, I felt myself begin to drift, and before I knew it, I began to fall in and out of consciousness!

I desperately tried to hang on for dear life to what vague awareness I could – in between the panic and chaos of the code red crisis thick in the air. I felt I was helplessly heading towards the road to doom. The crash team were doing all they could, racing against time, ready to revive or resuscitate or do whatever else had to be done in order to save the life of yet another complete stranger. I tell you what, the conduct of the medical staff was completely military.

They began plunging injection after injection into my stomach, God knows what and God knows why. I guess they were hoping something would work! Hope, that's all you've got in those moments, that and a prayer!

Meanwhile, all I could do was spectate this nothing short of a bedlam scene, knowing that with each precious second ticking by, it could end in either a tragedy or victory. And as the time passed, I began shutting down, further and further, plummeting rapidly into the dark abyss of the unknown, with my life in their hands. *Is this it?* I thought. *Am I going to die?*

That is when I turned to the left of me, trying desperately to focus my eyes on Sammy, who by now was screaming at the others to do this, and do that. I looked at her lovely face through that mask and said, "Tell my boys I love them."

It was that moment when I thought of them that my eyes filled with tears, wondering whether I would ever see their little faces again. She looked at me and screamed, "No! No. You listen to me, NOOOO!"

Whilst I couldn't control my body, I still had control of my thoughts. So I told myself, we must keep fighting against this relentless attack from Mylotarg, that is trying to smash the life out of my organs. And even though I helplessly felt myself fading away, I just kept fighting to stop myself plunging into darkness. I looked over at Sam again and saw terror in her eyes, her voice hiding what her eyes couldn't. Truth be known, no matter how well trained a nurse is, when it comes to critical situations like this, they don't know what the outcome will be, you will either make it or you won't. It's as simple as that.

Finally I closed my eyes, because I was struggling to keep them open. I spoke softly to myself and said, *Sarezah, if it's our time, it's our time!*

I looked back at Sam and said, "I think I'm going to die, Sam."

"No!!! No!!!" she said. "You look at me! You are not going to die, sweetheart! You are not going to die."

I turned to look at her, and everything went hollow. *This is it,* I thought. *I'm going to die.* Then I felt Sammy shaking me! "Nooooo! Sweetheart. It's just your body tricking you." And somehow, I managed to find enough energy, fuelled by always having to have the last word – and managed to muster just enough strength to say, "Well it's doing a fucking good job!!!" (Sam let out a little panicked laugh at that one).

Suddenly, I felt an absolute stillness, a calmness that had almost a sense of serenity – and I felt something calling me, almost inviting me. So I turned my head to the right, in the direction of what was calling. Mate, when I saw what I saw, I shit myself, because right in front of me stood a huge brown ornate door that appeared to be slightly ajar, and that had a bright fantastic creamy white light shimmering through that gap!

At first, I thought, *Is this a dream or is it something for real! Maybe I'm hallucinating from whatever the hell they have given me,* desperately trying to rationalise what was there right before my eyes, quickly realising if I had enough consciousness to think that I am off my nut then perhaps I wasn't, so I looked back to the left to see if Sam was still there, and she was.

Then I looked frantically to the right again. Shit, that flaming shimmering door is still there.

Then, it started to make some sort of rumbling noise! I was like *What the hell is this man!*

And that flipping rumbling got louder and louder, but not only did it get louder, to my horror it seemed like the door was starting to open and immediately I felt some sort of strange magnetic force begin to pull me towards that shimmering light. I was like, *What the hell is this man? Is this it? I am going to die!*

That is when good old Sarezah's survival instinct kicked in, so I dug deep, remembering the words of my mentor Natalija Dolgova! Thinking *Last round, Sarezah, give it your max,* finding whatever strength I could find in my body, I pulled myself away from it.

Mate, as soon as I pulled, this flipping force pulled me back, so I pulled a bit harder, then it pulled a bit harder, like we were in some tug of *give me your soul* war. I was like, fuck that man! I'm not pissing dying here – at St. Barts hospital!

Almost immediately after, my attention was momentarily taken away from that anomaly, as I became aware of my body, which was truly hanging on for dear life! I lay there almost helplessly listening to the echo of each thudding heartbeat in my ears! *Thud... Thud... Thud!* my poor heart sounded, as it desperately struggled to keep us alive!

So with what little hope I had left, I rolled my head to the centre of my sweat-soaked pillow, and awaited my fate. I briefly looked up towards the hospital ceiling and closed my eyes and thought of my three little boys, whilst the muffled sounds in the background gradually faded away, drowned out by the sound of my heart pounding!

I desperately clutched on to the bed sheets, fighting to grab some air into my suffocating lungs when – out of the blue – something popped into my head. *Is this how my mama felt when she took her last breaths before she killed herself? Was my mummy gasping for air like I am,* I thought. *Oh my Mama, why did you do that? Maybe I will die too, mummy* – after all, this is the closest to mortality I had ever felt!

Then, all of a sudden, everything went completely still. There were no sounds, it was totally silent, it felt like nothing, just complete emptiness. It was as though time just stopped – and in that timeless moment, I thought, *Shit I'm dead.*

Look at the door, I thought, *look at the door.* So I gingerly turned my gaze to the right to see if it was still there or had I slipped through, to whatever lay behind that distinctive brown ornate door?

And there it still was, calmly flickering away its mesmerising bright creamy light. My eyes were transfixed on the tranquility of that gleam. Then I felt something near me, and it eerily whispered something in my ear. I did not know the language, but I understood it was telling me, *Just let go! Let go and cross over that threshold.*

To date, I don't know what it was. All I can say is it felt like some sort of telepathic communication or an energy calling and gently inviting me towards the light, conveying some sort of message that nothing hurts here, slip over and watch all the pain you have felt melt away.

I tell you what, just for a few moments I contemplated going. *Just slip away from this place,* I thought. *Let it take me away to what it was offering. We've suffered enough, just slip through that door, come on darling, let's just go!*

Then it began to gently pull me towards it again. I felt almost paralysed, as I helplessly watched myself drawing closer and closer to that door!

But for some reason something inside me wouldn't let me go. So I fought against it and I screamed! *NAH NOT TODAY MATE, NOT TODAY!* And with that, I summoned every single bit of what I had left inside me, and I pulled myself away from it!

That is when the battle started again! The force resumed its power and rumbling, then tugging me even harder towards it as I pulled myself away. Immediately my ears unhollowed and the sound rushed back into the panic of the room. I heard voices screaming at one another, then one voice bellowed, "WE'RE LOSING HER… CLEAR" – followed by the high pitch sound of the defibrillator filling the air! That was the last thing I heard before everything went BLACK!

CHAPTER 27

Am I Dead?

Hello, I said to myself and thought, *Woah, why does my voice sound all echoey inside my head? Am I dead? Is this what dead sounds like?*

To me, it felt like I was in a lucid dream! See, ever since I was a child I was able to experience being physically and consciously present in my unconscious mind, usually within a dream. It's something I researched when I was an adult to put a name to this feeling and concluded it must be lucid dreaming.

I know, to some, it might sound a bit airy fairy, but certain things do exist and sometimes are inexplicable. But it was within my dreams that I actually found some solace in the tragedy of my mother's death, and where I have battled a few other things that, again, are inexplicable! But that is another story!

I continued looking around my mind, still wondering if I was dead. I mean, I don't feel dead. But how would I know? I don't know what dead feels like, do I? So in my dream-like state I tried to move my body around. As I wiggled my body in my mind, I felt my eyes physically open, but my vision was quite blurred, so I still wasn't sure where I was. It didn't seem I was somewhere devil red or heavenly white. Not that I know what hell or heaven look like, but there you go.

Anyway, am I dead or alive, I thought. Then I felt I was able to lift my head and as I did, I realised it still looks like I'm in the hospital room. I then looked for familiar things, firstly my watch and saw 21:21. I was like, *Woah, I can see my watch! I must be alive!* thinking, surely your Apple watch doesn't come with you if you die? Of course not, I must be alive, because I can feel that rotten cold air cascade down onto my face from that bloody majorly flawed design of that air conditioning unit that was above my bed. I then lifted my head a bit higher to see that all my things were still in the corner of my room where I left it.

I am alive, I thought, in room 7, on ward 5D and not in some parallel universe, or ICU (intensive care unit).

I shuffled my body around then heard my dear nurse say, "Oh hello, Mama Lake. You're awake? Would you like some water?" She then handed me the plastic tumbler that had a straw in it. I nodded. That nurse held the tumbler and guided the straw to my mouth. I took a sip and even though it was stale and lukewarm, it felt like it was the best water I have ever tasted, because it was given to me by a kind and caring nurse with all the love of an angel!

The nurse sat with me for some time, doing several observations, then went off to get the doctor to come and check me over. Before she left, she handed me the buzzer! Then it dawned on me that it had been a long time since I had spoken to my children and husband. What if they tried to call or text and couldn't get through? They would be worried. I better check my phone.

I unclipped my cross-body bag that was attached to the bed. But as I reached around I realised I was still pretty shaky, and my body ached like hell – I felt like I'd been hit by a ten-ton truck. But I managed to get the phone out and as I touched the screen the light came on and I could see several texts from Rahim, my eldest, and a few from my middle and youngest – to which I replied saying, "Sorry, I was sleepy from the drugs," so as to not alarm them.

But to my surprise there were no texts or missed calls from my husband – which I thought was a bit strange because it was now around six hours since we last spoke to each other. I began to feel a little anxious, thinking the worst, like what if he has had an accident or – worse – locked himself out of the house, whilst taking the bins out or something, I mean it would be the first time he's done that. So I rang him.

"Hello," he answered with a slight question in his voice of *'Who is this ringing the home line at this hour.'*

"Guy," I said in a dry, croaky voice, with my chattering teeth, "It's me, it's Sarezah."

His response was somewhat surprised. "Oh!" he said, "Are you ok?" realising my voice didn't sound quite right!

"No I'm not ok love! But first, are you ok? Because I haven't heard from you for like six hours!"

"Yes, I was watching a film then had some food and a shower and that," he said.

"Oh good. I got worried, I didn't see a call or text from you. Anyway, look I have had a reaction to the Mylotarg. It all happened very quickly. I will explain more when I have some energy. But I think the crash team saved my life."

"Oh no," he said.

"Look," I continued, "I'm not sure I'm going to make it through the night you know. I've felt something I never felt before and that was my body shutting down, it was so scary."

"Crikey," he said.

"Look love," I said. "Look, if I don't make it through the night, please, please take care of my boys. Please. I know it will be hard for you because you're not good at emotional stuff. But they won't have anyone if I die. Please, please promise me you will take care of them! I'm begging you Guy, please!"

The silence after that was quite deafening, so I broke it and asked him: "Why did you leave it so long to call me? You knew I was having Mylotarg today and there was a risk that I could have reacted to it. So instead of calling, you watched what?" I said.

"Lord of the Rings," he replied.

But before I could respond, my Khaliq came home after his shift in the restaurant kitchen. I said, "Let me speak to him."

As he took the phone, I just started rambling, because I wanted to say so much to him in case I die, even if it came out incoherent – but because of the trauma my teeth were still chattering so I couldn't speak properly.

The most tragic part came to light a few days later when he told me that phone call was the moment it hit him that I was really sick, because he said, "You did not sound like my mama," and went on to say after that call he went to his room and broke down. Hearing that hurt my heart, man. That poor kid. All alone in his room with the cold hard reality that his mum is fighting cancer.

And then, later that evening, one of the ward staff told me they did try to contact my husband to inform him of what had happened, but there was no answer on his mobile or home number. I was like *Wow man! Really? Man knows where I am, and what I'm going through! I'm miles away from home, alone, in a hospital, isolated, on some first cycle, having life threatening treatment! And you, you are absorbed by some film, or whatever else you are doing, whilst I am having some sort of life-or-death reaction to a drug you fucking well know all about! Wow! Just wow,* I thought.

I'm not gonna lie, my heart sank a bit, I felt a little disheartened. I know we all act differently in certain situations, and yes I get that he was perhaps just trying to find some normality. Or maybe he even thought, she's tough, she'll be ok. After all, I am the strong one!

But you know what, even the strong one in the family sometimes needs a helping hand, especially when they are on their knees! But at the end of the day, what can you do if he doesn't. Nothing! He is who he is and despite how much I've tried to guide him to do things out of his comfort zone, it doesn't always work.

Besides my husband has always said: "You lead and I follow!" Most of the time I understand. But this is one of very few times I really needed to him to be the strong one – ironically not for me, but for the children. To be honest, for many years it bothered me. I just thought man is making excuses and dumping all the responsibility on me and lets me handle everything for an easy life.

Maybe he did a bit of that or maybe, like I came to realise, he just can't do anything other than what he can do. And no matter how much we have had disagreements over everything, no matter how hard he tries to change, he just can't, and what he can change is only temporary. But, at the end of the day, there really isn't anything you can do, if someone doesn't or can't do certain things! So in the words of my dear friend, the colonel Tony, *Say your piece and move on!*

I am sure many of you can relate to this – whether it's a husband, wife, boyfriend or girlfriend. If you are in a similar situation, you have one of two choices: you can either put up with it or not put up with it. You have to weigh the pros and cons and abide by the decision you make until you can't.

If, like me, you finally understand that someone like a husband might not be able to do some of the things needed in life – but he is able to do things that many other people would have a massive problem doing – you have to have acceptance and some form of communication between you and learn to appreciate who you are and who they are in the relationship.

Besides, I have come to realise that when you find yourself as the matriarch of the family, everything is pretty much left to you to run – be it the house, the bills, the shopping, Christmas, birthdays, whatever. Over the years I looked after everyone's needs and ensured the welfare of all parties. I had to be the strong one in any given situation. I totally understood, I was the foundation and scaffolding that held up the family and kept us together.

Even through my treatment, I did my best to be there for them. I would cook for the boys in- between cycles and make sure my husband had everything he could possibly need to make it easy for him whilst I was away. Now, some of you may think that is a bit of piss take but, in all honesty, I came to realise that it was so hard to understand that my life was so fragile – because in their eyes, I was unbreakable, I am tougher than steel. *She can pull through anything, she always has, she has to, she's all we've got.* And that was at the time of the biggest driving forces that pushed me. Well, mostly. The other was my inability to give up and let something get the better of me.

Anyhow, later that night I tried to ask the nurse a few questions about my reaction to the Mylotarg, like, "How long have I been out? Had I had a stroke? Did I have a heart attack?

Because the last thing I heard was the defibrillator going off," I said. "So what happened to me?"

She just looked at me with a warm pleasant smile and said: "Not now, Mama Lake, you rest. We can talk about it in the morning."

Do you know, to this day, I don't know what happened. Even though I asked many times. I was just met with a nod and a smile, followed by "We can talk about it later." But later almost never comes in a hospital. There is just now. I guess it's a way of protecting us from not knowing what we don't need to know and only feeding us on a need-to-know basis. They don't want to make us worry unnecessarily, because Lord knows, we need all our strength to fight the cancer and the chemo. So our nurses and the medical teams protect and serve you in the best way they can.

Even though I was feeling quite drained and tired from that awful Mylotarg reaction, I couldn't settle, because in my heart, I was a little afraid to fall asleep. So I lay there in my hospital bed, trying to think of random things to keep me from drifting off to sleep, which was a feat in itself because I was already feeling a bit high and floaty from all the Oramorph that was given to me to help ease the pain caused by the shaking and seizures where my muscles had tensed so hard. Mate, Oramorph, that's some lovely stuff that. (Oral morphine is a strong pain killer that treats severe pain).

Whilst lying there I thought about how close I had come to dying. And that door with its creamy bright luminous light, wondering what an earth was that all about, and what the hell sort of force was that pulling me like that. *Was it even real* I thought *or was I hallucinating, who knows?*

Only I do, as I know I could see that door on one side and knew enough to recognise that Sam was on the other side. I thought about the children during that desolate time. Even though I tried so hard to remain awake, eventually fatigue and exhaustion set in and slowly, slowly, I felt myself my eyes getting heavier as each blink lasted longer, and I felt myself begin drifting away!

But in one of my hands was the nurse buzzer. I wasn't going to ever get caught out like that again! Finally I felt myself slip away as the blanket of darkness set over me with a final thought, *Will I wake or will I die in my sleep tonight,* as I drifted into a deep sleep.

Just before night turned into day, I felt enough movement in my body to realise I am still alive. I gently opened my eyes, to see dawn breaking through the sky, feeling relieved that I made it through the night. I took a few deep breaths and looked for familiar things like my Nike cross body bag that had all my important belongings in. I had developed the habit of keeping those things right next to me as it had my purse and phone etc in it. I'd clipped it to the side of my bed so it didn't fall. And, ever the distrustful type, I knew it would make it more difficult for someone to swipe it away, of course, in the most extremely unlikely event. Better safe than not.

CHAPTER 28

Have a Word

I heard the nurse coming with her dodgy squeaky trolley – another confirmation that I had not died. Knock knock.

"Morning, Mama Lake." It was my lovely nurse, Patricia.
"Morning."

"Are you better this morning."

"Yes, thank you, just a bit groggy, but ok."

Patricia did my bloods and left me to do what was to become my daily hospital routine. I'm not gonna lie, I felt like crap. My body felt like a truck had hit it. My head was banging and I was still wobbly. I gently lifted myself out of the bed, as I was still a bit sore and achy from those horrific seizures during that reaction.

Plus, I was still trying to get used to that blooming PICC line in my blasted left arm. It literally banged and clanged dramatically, with every single flipping movement. Honestly, that bloody PICC line, Jesus Christ. I literally couldn't do very much. All it did was just dangle around.

In fact, my family started to give the PICC line different names. My eldest, Rahim, called it my *audio in and out jack.* I was like *cheers mate*. My middle son Khaliq – in his true Mauritian tongue-in-cheek smutty sense of humour (just like my mother, who has clearly reincarnated in him) – said they look like *two little willies hanging down your arm!* Azim was like, *Mum what's that in your arm. It looks horrifying, like some kind of Saw film business!*

Even though I felt rubbish, due to staff shortages I had to take my shower alone, but I made sure I was stable enough and put things nearby like the shower chair – just in case. I took it nice and easy, and when I was done showering I slowly dried myself then came out of the bathroom wrapped in a towel and sat on the bed, to take a little rest before getting dressed. I began thinking about how my body reacted to that immunotherapy drug Mylotarg and thought how close I came to dying. And I thought, *We just can't die now, not at the first hurdle. We just can't. We've been through so much in our lives just for it to end like this. No!*

With that, and for some reason, I began to speak to myself – aloud. Don't ask me why, I just did. I felt I needed to tell my body we can't give up. So I said, *Look, if you give up on us now, we're dead! Gone! Finished! Look, I'm in this one hundred percent. So is my mind, my heart and my soul, we are all in it, but we can't do this without you. We all have to work as one. Mind, body, soul and spirit – or we will die. We cannot be weak physically or mentally, we have to be strong and stand together, because if we don't, this bastard cancer will find the chink in our armour and destroy us from the inside out and kill us. Let's not let it, let's fight together!*

The next day, I was in the gym!

All I can say is whatever I said to my body it must have heard because the next morning I was not the same person I was the day before. In fact, I learnt something very valuable – the power of the self. The power we all have and the will to survive has to overpower the fear of dying. Not to say that, at times, the battle is just too much. I am aware that, at some point, terminally sick patients will have to – or even want to – concede. But for me, it was not my time, yet!

Before I made my way to the gym, I forced some of that gruel down my neck, telling myself, *We've got to eat girl, we've got to do what my Aunty Rashida said, pinch your nose and down it.* Mate, it was nothing short of revolting. I know it ain't no Hilton and, yes, I should be grateful I've got food. But look, when you are a cancer patient fighting for your life, food is one of the most important factors for a recovering patient. Then why is hospital food not – in any way shape or form – nutritional? It beggars' belief that those who are in charge think it is acceptable to allow us to eat this kind of quality of reheated reconstituted food, that is nuked to death and void of anything worth eating!

After managing to eat something, I trotted to the gym, knowing that will help raise my endorphins and get my serotonin levels back up, so I would feel a bit happier about things. I left my room 7 to go to physio room 18. One of the nurses at the station said, "Excuse me, where are you going?"

"The gym," I said, pointing in the direction I was headed. She paused for a few moments, then nodded and said, "Ok, make sure you don't do anything too strenuous."

I opened the door of the gym, switched the lights on and proceeded to walk towards the huge windows to open the curtains – pausing for a few moments to look at the beautiful view of London, leaning on the window ledge, watching the world pass by. My thoughts drifted to what if I'd died. I wouldn't be able to look out of the window. *Well, you didn't,* I said. *You're alive, so stop dilly dallying around thinking of what might have happened – and get on with what we came here to do... work!!*

See, I say *work* and not *workout* because, for a very long time, I have always treated my workouts as though I am getting up and going to work. In fact I treated weight loss as a job. So I knew every day I had to get up and do it! Just like those who get up to earn your pounds stirling. I get up, go to the gym and work hard to lose my pounds!

Besides, at this point, I had no choice – my body is used to a certain level of activity.

Reducing it would have had a catastrophic effect on what I have already achieved. So, in order to keep going, I developed my own little ethos, and that is, once I reach a goal, I don't stop there. I move the goal. So I keep going and never stop. I've done this for so long that it has become a way of life now.

I began my workout with a 20-minute cycle, followed by some light hypertrophy body exercises. Like I mentioned previously, the gym is only a physiotherapy gym, therefore limited with no actual gym equipment. So I did what I could and adapted my training like I did in lockdown, where I had to make do with little to no weights. Although during lockdown, I did manage to scrounge a few bits, from my *bolt on nephew* (meaning family without the blood ties) Joshy – who is Rahim's very close friend. Joshy has been part of our family since 2012. So until Joshy helped, I had to make do with 10 litre paint cans filled with sand and water to make it heavier.

I also did a lot of HIIT workouts, but my biggest saving grace during that time was I bought a spin bike – albeit not a fantastic one, but it did the job. So since lockdown, I did workouts that – at the very least – would maintain most of what I had worked for.

Actually, one memory I have of hospital is when I was on the holding ward, there was a bike at the end of the corridor near a small window. When I cycled, I would look out of the window which faced the street and opposite was a Pure Gym. I longed to go in there and train – but obviously I couldn't.

Anyhow, I was coming to the end of my workout. Normally I finished a sesh (session) with a few ab exercises, and a good stretch – and today was no different. I took a physio mat in the room, rolled it out and cleaned it – just like I would in the gym, as always listening to music on my headphones. The music I play depends on my mood I am in. But during my hospital stay, I mostly listened to house mixes that my son Rahim did for me.

I descended down onto the mat and got into a plank position with my head facing away from the door. I was lost in concentration – and blissfully unaware of what was going on behind me – until I finished and turned around to lay on my back, in order to do a few crunches.

As I did, my eyes opened wide because the room was filled with my med team! They were standing there – staring at me. The prof, short for professor, was saying something, but I couldn't hear a word he was saying – until I took a headphone out, and said, "Sorry, I can't hear you, I've got headphones in."

There was an awkward moment of silence, as they all started glancing at one another with questionable eyes. The prof broke the silence and said, "What are you doing?"

"Errr, a plank!" I replied.

"Well yes, I can see that. But you had a reaction to Mylotarg two days ago. We were expecting to see you in your room – in bed, recovering!"

"Oh yeah," I said. "That was Monday. I'm ok now, thanks!"

"Oh right then," he said, as he looked at the others, baffled – as if to say *What on earth in St Barts' name is going on here then! Miss reaction over here isn't behaving like we thought she would.*

Just to confirm, the prof then asked a few questions. "So you feel ok then?" "Yes, thank you."

"You don't feel ill or sick?" "No."

"You are going to the toilet ok?" "Yes."

I began to notice a few of them scribbling some notes down, whilst looking at me somewhat mystified.

"Ok. Well, carry on then, but take it easy," said the prof.

I nodded – and off he trotted with the rest of the med team into the merry sunset. However one of those members gave me a little wink with her big blue *smising* eyes (*smising* is apparently smiling with your eyes) and that is the first moment I saw her- – my registrar, Sarah.

Mate, she is one of the most beautiful girls in the world. This lovely lady, Sarah – along with Sammy – both became my absolute rock in hospital. They have been amazing in every single way, from start to finish. It's the medical team who get you through it all.

In fact, all of those that work in the health profession have helped me one way or another.

From the professors to cleaners, to the kitchen staff, the security team, to all the guys in the coffee shop. They get you through it. Well they did me – so a massive thank you to each and every one of you.

Anyway, shortly after the med team left, I went back to my room 7. There I sat down trying to relax before observation time (I didn't want my blood pressure to be too high, because of all the extra exertion). I started to think about what the professor said and thought about their reaction to seeing me train and that wink.

In my mind, it must have meant a good thing. So I started to feel a bit euphoric – in the sense that I stood my ground against the cancer and came back from a drug that will either cure or kill you. And for the first time in my treatment, I saw cancer has weaknesses too.

So I spoke to that too and said to the cancer in my body, *I know what you are. You prey on anyone you can. You don't discriminate, do you? You don't care who your host is? Your objective is to decimate whoever you invade. You will engage in battle with all the drugs they use to fight you! You don't care, as long as you win and add another name to your long list of victories.*

Well, maleficent cancer that is coursing around my veins, you had a good ol' go at me, didn't you? but you failed, mate, See, it's not the first time that I have stared down the barrel of death – and no doubt it won't be the last. So let's see hey. Let's see what we both have! And let's see what happens!"

CHAPTER 29

Graduation Day

Monday 29th March, my first Graduation Day from chemo. Round one done! And to be honest with you, I felt ok, maybe a bit tired, which I was told was because my blood count dropped and therefore needed what was to be my first of a fair few blood transfusions. And as soon as I had the blood transfusion (which took blooming two hours), I felt much better – so a massive thank you to those that donate blood, your kindness went to save my life and many others.

The next day my platelets dropped very low, in fact under 10. Bear in mind a normal platelet range is around 150. This meant I was in dire need of a platelet transfusion. Now I didn't know much about platelets (of course I do now). So when the platelets came in a drip bag and I saw what it looked like, I was like, *What the hell is this?*

Unlike blood red, it was like Tropicana – the fruit juice! I was like, *Ewe, this looks off, you know!* The nurse laughed then explained that is the colour of platelets! It was bright orange. She also went on to say that it is actually called a pool of platelets, because it doesn't just come from one person – like blood does. In the case of platelets, there are multiple donors!

And for me, it turns out I was allergic to one of the donors because, after my transfusion, I ended up having a reaction. Luckily it was only skin hives, which meant it was topical, so none of the ol' anaphylactic shock business! In order to help ease the symptoms, I was given their version of Piriton intravenously via my PICC line. After a while I began to feel quite nice. And before I knew it I was like, *Woah, this is lovely!!!* Especially when it was combined with Oramorph pain relief. Happy days! It's a nice, nice feeling!

Please don't think I am promoting getting high or glamorising getting off your head – or whatever else you want to call it. If you take drugs for recreational purposes, that's your business. Likewise if you drink alcohol, great. But I don't because it's just not for me. I've dabbled in a bit of weed and – when I was younger – a bit of powder, but drugs just wasn't my thing. Not because I wanted to be in control or anything. Just because I didn't like it.

I don't drink alcohol because, to me, it tastes like shit, so why bother? In fact, I haven't drunk alcohol since my fortieth birthday, where I drank champagne almost all day. So by the time the party got going, I was absolutely paralytic, to the point I was sick, sick and sick, both ends mish – and, without being too graphic, my poor friend Serita, Sarah, cleaned it up for me.

I completely humiliated myself and thought, *this is shameful, not fun.* I felt rotten after drinking and bloody miserable, so that ain't happening no more. And from that day to this I haven't had any – not to say I won't one day. But it's unlikely!

Anyway, back to low blood count! Now having a low count means your immune system is compromised. Therefore any little normal bacteria in my body that would ordinarily be ok to a person with a normal count, for us cancer patients, that could now potentially cause great harm, or lead to sepsis negative. Hence why we have to stay for one month until we recover.

During the time when my counts were low, I developed some minor issues, so I was given Oramorph to ease the pain on things like my eye lid, which had developed some sort of sore on the eyelash area. There was also a blood blister type mouth ulcer that was on the left side of my cheek, that literally got bigger by the second – which, apparently, was an effect of having a low platelet count.

After I knew that information, a few pennies began to drop, as I cast my memory back to when I had a few of these type of mouth blood blisters before my diagnosis. Maybe it was my body trying to tell me something but, like most things, we often tend to brush them aside.

Like fatigue symptoms. Many of us have some form of fatigue, so when I was tired, it was more like I was sick and tired because of having three kids. a husband and a dog! I mean, I wake up tired and go to bed tired. So, you brush it off and end up adapting to those symptom. I guess, on reflection, there were a few signs my body was trying to communicate to me, but I just ended up rolling them into the rest of the problems of life.

To be honest, being in hospital wasn't really that bad. I was away from my day-to-day environment, my so-called *normal* life, so being here was a rare break from having to be a wife and mother, and the all-rounder – even though I had to run the home from my devices in hospital.

I found time to reflect deeply into my thoughts that were not invaded by a *mummmmm* or *Lovvvvvvve,* or a snoring dog or even husband. In fact, it was beautifully peaceful – other than the constant beeping and hospital noise. But I guess that noise was better than all the grown-up children drama they bring.

To be honest, I saw being in hospital as a bit of a holiday – seeing as the last time I went abroad was 2003, and that was only to Paris, followed by several short family trips and a disastrous family holiday to Newquay in 2008 which led to never going on holiday again!

Lost and forgotten memories popped into my thoughts. Some made me cringe, some laugh, some even made me shed a little tear. Having time on my hands also gave me the opportunity to take a little look deeper at me, and who I was from childhood to now. It began to look like there was a certain pattern in my life, where if I experienced something good it was somehow counteracted by something bad and at times fairly tragic.

But then I thought, that is life – good things will happen, and bad things will happen. Some may be coincidental, and others may not. But, either way, you have to deal with it. Or, as my dear friend Tony (the retired colonel) would say, "You can only deal with what's in front of you." or my favourite, "Suck it up, cupcake, and just get on with it!!!"

However, in this type of isolated environment, you can easily find yourself slip into a world of self-pity. Like, *why me? It's not fair!* I know, at times, I did. But instead of letting things eat away at me, I reminded myself had I not gone through what I had, I would not be the person I am today. Because, from tragedy I grew stronger, from physical pain I became more resilient, from abuse and turmoil I became more valiant!

So I will deal with having cancer according to who and how I am. And I accept that any time I might die – after all, when it's your time it's your time and there is nothing you can do. You just have to embrace death and accept your destiny! And when that happens, nothing will ever be the same for those who love you, but this is life. Nothing ever stays the same forever!

CHAPTER 30

Nothing is Forever

By the 31st of March, the effects from the chemo were really beginning to take their toll. That massive mouth blood blister got worse, and with no immunity it wasn't healing. It just kept bursting blood in my mouth (I know, gross, right?) – which meant I had to have Difflam mouthwash to keep it from getting infected.

Simple spots turned to massive sores, I had some severe bruising where the PICC line was inserted and in a few other places too; I had swollen and sore eyes, a blooming chemo rash. I ain't gonna lie, I was starting to feel fed up.

So most nights I went to bed early. On the morning of 1st April, I woke up thinking, *oh I've made another day,* and you know what they say, every day above the ground is a good day, even if it does fall on April Fool's Day.

And, in all honestly, it felt like April Fool's Day every day in hospital because we'd been fooled by the powers that be – because, for some reason, they don't think it is necessary for patients to have access to anything that make may make their long stay a little easier.

For one thing, there is no entertainment in the rooms, no TVs and no radios. Even those with devices couldn't get a great data signal and the Wi-Fi connection was terrible. There is no access to a microwave to heat up food that may be brought for us, in fact there is no nothing or nowhere to reheat anything. Or even make some toast. There was always some nonsense excuse as to why these things were unavailable. Believe me, I have brought all this to the attention of those in position – to no avail. But I'm still fighting!

Sunday 4th April 2021 – more or less two weeks after my first lot of chemo. I was still feeling a bit raw, so I was almost grateful that it was a Sunday because I could rest as there was no training that day. To be honest, considering what I was going through, I still looked fairly well. Even my hair was still looking great, still blonde and curly although maybe a little drier than usual; my body still looked strong and curvy, despite not having done a proper heavy weight workout since I came to the hospital.

Anyhow, a Sunday meant it was hair wash day and a little pamper day. You know, wash hair, condition, waiting to rinse it off means a nice body scrub exfoliator and so forth.

So I slid the band from the top of my pony tail to the end to let out my hair. I felt a sort of strange sensation from my scalp and a bit of a strange sound but carried on until I caught a glimpse of the hair band, and to my horror there was a clump of my golden curly hair attached to it.

For a few moments I was like *what's going on?* Then my heart sank as reality set in and I realised my hair was falling out. I felt a bit frantic, to be honest with you – but I told myself not to worry, it will all be ok. For those precious few moments, I was in denial. I then started to loosen my locks and run my hands through my hair, like I always do – but as I did, more and more hair came out in between my fingers.

I stood there, helpless, with these clumps of dry, brittle, lifeless hairs, stranded in my hands – and felt nothing like I'd felt before… powerless. Powerless to stop the effects of cancer, powerless to stop these side effects. So I just stood there, powerless, as I felt my little eyes well up with tears and roll down my cheeks. I felt absolutely devastated. Once again, feeling cheated by life, watching it slowly take away a bit more of me – this time my signature shoulder length blonde curls.

With that, together with the feeling of malaise, I began to feel myself slipping into a downward spiral. So, time to have another sit down and have a chat with myself again.

Look darling, I told myself, *we've just got to dig deep and bounce back. You can't let this have a significant impact on you mentally or allow it to drag you down into some kind of a depression. It's hard, girl, but we've got to push through.*

I sat back down on the bed, with a clump of my blonde locks in my hand, crunching it together to see how the chemo had killed the hair cells at the root. And just like a rose that is dying from its bloom, so too was my hair, as I watched it drop out like petals towards the floor.

The next morning as I lay down onto the bed I said to myself, *Sarezah, we have a terrible disease, it's going to have an effect on us. What can you do girl – nothing! Besides, it's just hair, come on darling! And anyway, so what if Cancer is 1-0 up in the first half of the game. We're just gonna have to play with a bit of an injury, ok.* Then shouted out in my head *United* (short for Manchester United, my team).

With that, I took a big sigh and said *Well fuck it then, let's shave it off! I'm not hanging around waiting for it to fall out with patches here, there and everywhere.* So that's exactly what I did, with the help of the ward manager finding me some clippers, together with the trusted assistance of the ward clerk doing the honours.

I told her to cut it off first then shave the rest off. I can tell you sitting in the chair listening to the snipping away of my hair was weird. Soon after, she leant over and said "ready?"

"Ready," I said, as I closed my eyes. The buzzing of the clippers erupted as she turned them on, *shit!* I could hear her sniffing a little cry. So I reached over my shoulder and took her other hand, "Come on darling, don't cry," I said. Cancer is truly savage to everyone involved.

Mate, when I felt the cold metal of those clippers running over my head I felt sad, man. So sad I couldn't even cry – what's the point, crying won't change anything. Chemotherapy treatment, on one hand, aims to saves your life for something in return. It's a give and take situation. Your hair for your life. *Crikey!* I thought.

"It's all done," she said.

"Thank you, darling," I replied. I then got up off the chair and walked towards the full- length mirror on the bathroom door. Mate, when I saw myself, my little heart sank, you know. My head was completely bald. The Sarezah I once knew had totally gone.

So I walked right up to the mirror to have a closer look at myself and, after a closer inspection I thought, *actually it's not that bad.* Then I looked closer at my face and thought, *bloody hell girl, you really are beautiful aren't you? Look at your eyes. They're huge. No wonder you've always got a shit load of free things over the years. Woah they are just beautiful.*

Actually, it was the first time I saw my face first, and not my big hair. I studied my features and realised everything was just perfectly aligned on my face and, to my delight, my bald head enhanced what was already there! Put that together with my tattoos and my nose ring, I thought, *Girl you got style, kind of sexy and edgy.* And of course, being my biggest fan and all that, I wasn't upset with not having hair anymore.

In fact I actually felt quite happy, because not only did I feel even more beautiful, but it was also absolutely liberating. My head felt so free – not just physically but mentally. It felt like a massive release from the limits of thoughts and conditioning behaviour, that hair is our everything, it's our crowning glory, be it man or woman. Like being slim is the only way you will ever be attractive. Or anything else the media demand what beauty is or isn't. As I say, as far as I am concerned, beauty radiates from the inside out.

Having said that, it did take a little while to get used to not having hair – especially when I looked in the mirror. I would be like, *Sheshhhhh. What the hell,* realising it was me. But what can you do? Nothing, you've just got to roll with what you've got.

Like I said, I really loved my new edgy look. So did everyone else. I recall when Sister Jess first saw me she was like, "Oh my God, you look so beautiful." Then said, "Of course you would, only you could pull it off." Bless her she named me, *Chemo chic*. And I was like I take that. *Chemo chic*. Gosh, I even started to look in any mirror even more, just to admire me. Any mirror was fine, be it on the way to the gym to smash my workout, or for my walk, any reflection in the door or window. I was like *ooooh, sexy.*

But no matter how wonderful I felt, Cancer still got that first goal into the back of the net, so 1-0 to Cancer – but after a few days had passed I noticed something quite remarkable, because whilst I lost hair absolutely everywhere else as well as my head, there were two places I didn't lose any hair whatsoever. It couldn't take my eyebrows or eyelashes. That's right, it completely bypassed them. Cancer scored – but on the counter attack, I got a goal in too, so now it was 1-1.

I tell you, I started to feel all empowered and goddess-like. Well

I did until I spiked a little temperature for a day or two. Then a bit of belly ache. Then another sore on my eyes. Then a rash. Then stomach cramps. More mouth blood blisters and ulcers from hell. Then a bloody bit fed up with it all, no more *Chemo chic.* More like *chemo is making me sick, mate*. But I reminded myself, *keep strong girl. Keep going forward* – and before I knew it, I'd bounced back, straight to the gym and for my daily 10k steps.

Chemo done. Hair gone. A day rest in between drugs. It was now time for the second part of my treatment, which aims to target that FT3 mutation – an oral multi targeted kinase inhibitor called Midostaurin. Yeah, about that, it's pretty rancid. Why? Because not only did it smell like cat piss, yup, cat piss, the most common side effect is Rapid Weight Gain! Yes I said rapid. I mean no one wants to see rapid anything, let alone rapid weight gain. I was like *fuck my life.*

Other effects include sickness, heart issues, and a list of other stuff.

This is a strong drug. Without getting all technical, which I'm not qualified to do, it's aim is improve your survival rate which, of course, is a good thing. And whilst one of the main effects is weight gain – and, boy oh boy did I find out the hard way of how that 'rapid weight gain' would affect me – when I complained about it to the consultant during my long maintenance programme (a year after my cycles), he replied, "Well, you're alive."

CHAPTER 31

One Down

13th April 2021. This was the last day of cycle one. I was going to go home today. I waited all day, fearful of every single observation just in case I spiked a temperature. Remember, I wasn't fully recovered, I only had 0.9 of one neutrophil. The normal range is 2.5 and above. Thankfully, I didn't spike, otherwise I wouldn't be going anywhere. Although the time passed fairly quickly, it was a long month. And it was the first time ever I'd been separated from my home.

Finally, the transport arrived, way past tea time. I got in the ambulance transport, before hugging a few nurses and saying, "See you next cycle." All strapped in, quick visual check again, to make sure I had everything – and off we went. The usual chit chat, with some quiet moments to think and reflect on what just happened for the past few months and how much I'd changed in those four weeks. Not just aesthetically, but mentally too. In between, I was feeling happy I was going home to see my boxer dog Maccy – oh, and of course, the others.

Driving through the back country roads leading up to my home in the town of Colchester felt kind of strange as it seemed like such a long time since I'd been here. Everything looked a bit different, familiar roads seemed unfamiliar, like time had changed things.

Even when we came into Layer-de-la-Haye it seemed peculiar – especially since it was a road I have loved since I passed my driving test back in 1989, at the tender young age of 19, and bought my first car, when I wanted to explore beyond a bus ride into town or the shops.

So, music on, wind blowing through the windows, off I went to explore. I'd end up on many long country drives – one of them being through the village of Layer-de-la-Haye. I used to dream about living here. I wanted a house in the country with a beautiful garden and a convertible car. And I got it.

Pulling up outside my house was even more strange. Whilst it looked the same, it looked different since it was so long since I'd seen my little house. Sounds weird I know, but I felt a little disconnected from all that used to be familiar. Maybe it was the treatment and what I had gone through. Maybe I had changed, who knows. Anyway, as the ambulance pulled up to my house, the first person I saw was my husband, who was smiling as he approached the vehicle.

My hubby and the driver got all the bags out of the car. Even though things seemed strange I was still happy to be home. And that I'd made it back and didn't die on cycle one. As I was speaking, with my very obvious voice (think deep husky and Essex, bloke-ish at that) Mac – on hearing my big, booming dulcet tone – began whining and whimpering.

He was so desperate to see me that the poor boy began scratching the dining room wooden door, where my husband left him, in case he ran out. Of course he would never normally do that, he's been taught since a puppy what he can and can't do, but for obvious reasons I understood why he did scratch the door. So I secured myself in the house and made sure he couldn't run out, as I didn't want to chance it.

Mate, when I opened the door and saw his dear little face, my heart man! He just couldn't believe I was home. His little ears were so flat against his head and his eyes so mixed with joy and sadness as he looked to see if it was really me. His belly was almost touching the ground as he began crawling towards me in disbelief.

"Hello Maccy," I said. "Hello, it's mummy." He then gently – and I mean gently – lifted his body up using his back legs and landed softly on my torso to give me a hug. Now, you have to understand, Mac is not allowed to jump on anyone. He's a big strong dog and could easily knock someone over, so I've taught him not to jump, nor to lick anyone. Not everyone likes that, including me.

My Mac looked straight at me. I tell you, I grabbed that dog and squeezed him tightly as he let out a little dog grumble as if to say *mummy, you're back.* I just kept saying, *hello mummy* (another one I call mummy. See, I don't have a mummy anymore so when I love something endlessly, I call them mummy or mites).

Bless him, he stood eye to eye with me, ears still pinned as far back as he could, and I swear I saw tears in his eyes, just like he could see tears in mine. It's so true what they say about dogs. They are the only thing that will love you more than they love themselves.

I looked up for a moment and could see from the dining room through the lounge into my beautiful garden. Whilst I was away my husband had been busy cutting back trees and tidying up, in an attempt to make my garden more beautiful for when I came home. I went out into the garden to have a look, closely followed by Mac then my husband, who I hadn't really had much time to look at or even say hello properly.

So I turned to look at him and my face changed and unfortunately, I said aloud what I thought, "Gosh, you look awful, love."

"Oh, haha," he said, "do I?"

I immediately apologised, but I was shocked. He looked somewhat dishevelled and skinny, I mean he didn't look like that when I left. So I said, "What's happened to you, love? You've lost so much weight. You look so pale. Do you feel ok, you look kind of peaky?"

He laughed at all the questions and said, "You don't, you look great, considering what you've been through."

Well, of course I do. I've not had to cook, clean, wash clothes, deal with stress, no kids, no noise, no drama, no nothing.

Concerned, I told my youngest son that his dad didn't look so well and had become really quite thin. He said, "Well that's because you haven't been home feeding him 10,000 calories a day! He's lived on nothing as you weren't there doing everything for him, including cooking."

I do cook for him every day. Curry, roast, steak and chips with everything else, pasta, beef, sausage bangers and mash, home made everything you could imagine, so I guess my youngest son Azim had a point. My husband isn't the type to look after himself very well – even when there is a choice.

See, even when I was in hospital, I still did almost everything – from paying bills to getting food delivered for him. I guess I've done it so long for him. It's just the way it is now. We do what we do and it works sometimes and doesn't others.

After settling in and catching up with the few who knew I was in hospital, I had something light to eat, then went to my own shower. Oh my gosh. That fresh Layer-de-la-Haye water straight from the reservoir to the water treatment centre up the road, straight through to my tap. Beautiful, fresh, clean tasting – although I don't drink it, I'm told it tastes good. Like I said, I have only drank Evian water for the past 30 odd years. Why, because I do, so mind your business.

Finally, I could control the temperature from lukewarm, so 'apparently' we didn't burn ourselves, bullshit. *Got to cut our budget somewhere, so let's take it from the staff or patient budget, not from those who sit on their bums doing useless irrelevant stuff.* Anyway rant over.

It was a luxury to be home in my vibrant pink and gold coloured bathroom. The water felt so much fresher and cleaner than in the hospital. With no hair to worry about getting wet, I stood under the shower and let the water fall on my head, absorbing myself into the moment and reminded myself, mate, we made it home. One down, three to go.

I got into bed alone that night, after I already asked my husband if I could just have a few nights of sleeping by myself to get some peace and quiet, with no nurse bleeping, no hospital sounds, no talking, no observations – and definitely no snoring, the one thing I didn't miss in hospital. The final thing I did before bed was to give my immune system a little boost, so I injected myself with a drug they gave me, called G-CSF, a cell booster.

I got into bed quite early, around 20.45. Before drifting off, I lay thinking about a few things and reflected on what had happened over the past month, including that near death experience, my hair loss, which prompted me to rub my little bald shaved head for a bit of self-comfort, my little Buddha head as I endearingly called it!

Truthfully, I felt quite triumphant, *one done and three to go* I thought as I drifted away to the familiar sound of the owls twit twooing that live in the nearby trees behind the open fields at the back of my garden of my beautiful country home. My eyes got heavier, and I drifted further and further away into a peaceful sleep, thinking, *I made it back. I made it home. I made it.*

Well, until bang on 2am, when my eyes miraculously opened wide ready for my nighttime observation. I was even disoriented for a few moments thinking I was still in hospital only to quickly realised I was home. Softly, I drifted myself back to sleep, just to be woken up again when I nearly fell out of the flipping bed, a bed that I had slept in for over a decade.

But I had suddenly become spatially unaware of how high my bed actually was compared to the hospital bed which was a lot lower, I guess to prevent injury to patients. So I thought perhaps its best that I slept in the middle of the bed for a while until I get my bearings back, seeing that my bed had suddenly become the same size as *The Princess and the Pea* story (for those that don't know, her bed was really high).

A while later, after my aspirate results came back, I had a telephone consultation where I was told I achieved my first remission test dated the 22nd April 2021 – a date that ironically has special meanings to me: one, it's the day after my mother's birthday; two, it's the day I picked up my beloved car in 2010, and lastly, it's the day I met Mr. Miles Banwell, who's actions subsequently saved my life and now a new birthday that offers hope – so that day is definitely a good day.

Thankfully, my bloods recovered fairly quickly and before I knew it I was booked ready to go on cycle 2: May 2nd – which is actually the date of our wedding anniversary. So I asked Sammy if we could delay it by a day or two – which she agreed, bless her.

We celebrated with a special Chinese meal from my favourite restaurant, the Noodle Bar in Colchester. My dear friend Ting, one of the owners, gave me my meal on the house. This man really is kind to his customers, let alone his regulars. He always looked after me and my family. Whenever we've gone, something is always on the house. He makes his customers feel special and often goes out of his way to ensure we have absolutely anything we need. I am one of those who has had the honour of sharing many deep and philosophical conversations with this incredible man.

CHAPTER 32

Cycle Two

So on the 3rd May 2021, off I went to Barts for cycle two. The journey wasn't as strange or as long. Traffic was moderate, although the driver on this occasion didn't stop talking. He went on and on and on and on. *Jesussssss.* He didn't even come up for air.

We got to Barts late afternoon. I wasn't about to eat from the out of hours menu, if that's what you can call it. I mean there is a lot to choose from on an extensive menu – of inedible mush. And knowing that, for this cycle – and those thereafter – I came well prepared. And that day when I left home, I took with me one of those lovely homemade Sangers – steak and onion with my own homemade garlic mayo, all stuffed in half a loaf of all fired up bread, with the insides scooped out, buttered and layered with all the above.

Cycle 2 was literally a breeze. I was in and out in less than a month. No temperature spikes. Not one. All I had was a bit of jippy tummy, diarrhoea, which turned out to be something called C. Diff – Clostridium Difficile – where bacteria begins spilling from the colon into your abdominal cavity, which can quickly progress to being a fatal disease if not treated promptly. Yeah, not ideal that!

Now, the worse thing about having that was that it meant I had to blooming stay confined to my room until it all cleared up as it is highly contagious – and on a cancer ward where everyone's immune-suppressed, that's a big no. Which of course I completely understand.

However, what that also meant was no gym! I was like, *no gym, what do you mean by that, no gym,* with an intense blank stare combined with a fairly angry expression that was apparent on my face, together with my eyes now fixated on my poor consultant Dr Jamie, who had the task of having to break that news to me.

He went on to explain a bit more about what I had, all the time apologising to me because he knew what my training meant to me, saying, "I am so sorry, but you are now in quarantine."

I was gutted that I couldn't leave my room – at all. Not even an outdoor walk around the square – until it was approved by my wonderful Professor Gribbin, who understood that I needed to continue with my exercises and outside walks, saying he fully trusted I would look after myself and keep clear of anyone – which I did.

I double gloved, masked up and stayed 20 metres away from anyone, let alone 2 metres. I got it. It was a hostile environment for the most and I had to respect that. Even the nurses that came in after that were covered head to toe.

Besides, I didn't want to be responsible for the tears and sobbing of someone in their room because they are so ill, or rolling around in agony from the infections they develop from this evil disease, and yes, I have heard it all mate. Crying, coughing, screaming in agony, puking from the absolute bottom of their stomach. Honestly it's beyond tragic what a Cancer patient has to go through.

But that wasn't the worst of it. I can tell you the absolute worst thing I ever heard. It was a young girl in her early 20's who was in the room next to me; she was ill for days, and I mean sick. One night I heard her sobbing her heart out and calling out for her mummy. *I want my mummy,* that poor girl cried throughout the whole night, terrified she was going to die. That fucking broke me, that did! Absolutely heartbreaking.

I just wanted to go into her room and hold her and make all her fears go away and tell her it will be ok, *don't be sad your mummy will be here soon,* but I couldn't as she was quarantined.

That made me hate this disease even more. It's just callous and cruel.

Later on, I asked the then ward manager, Angus, if it was possible to have a couple of weights and a kettle bell just so I could do a few bits in my room, and he replied with *let me see what I can do.* Mate, within minutes he came back with a bike he scrounged from somewhere else and a load of weights from the physio gym just for me to use. I could have cried, I was so touched that my training needs were so important that my ward manager went out of his way to ensure, at the very least, I had some kind of ability to keep training.

Seeing as I was confined to my room, I thought I would make

the most of it and ended up doing something I never do at home – and that's binge watch a couple of series. The reason I didn't like watching the television much was because it had bad memories attached to it.

See, when I was huge with little to no mobility, I was hopelessly stuck in front of that mindless, brainwashing droning of that television. So as soon as I started my weight loss journey, I vowed I would never sit on that sofa and watch TV again. And I don't. Of course there are exceptions, I will watch it if there is a great game of football. Or now a Netflix series, but in my office on my laptop. I can't bring myself to watch the television!

However, my husband loves to vegetate in front of the box. Man can watch any ol' mind numbing nonsense. So when he is in that phase, I'm like, *you crack on with that and sit there and be a cushion, I'm off out mate. I will go and reach my goals.* So off to the gym I would go! Plus the gym isn't my husband's thing as he has bouts of social anxiety; often, in crowded places, he will feel uncomfortable. As I am not, this is something I have had to understand and where I can I help him, so we don't go anywhere where he may feel anxious.

There are many ups and downs in a marriage and the longer the relationship, the more compounded those problems become! Marriage certainly isn't the Disney fairy tale that we are led to believe it is. In fact, quite often, there is no happy ever after, as the divorce statistics will tell you.

In my opinion, for a marriage to survive, it takes an awful lot of tolerance and acceptance from both parties. And, as the years go by, the love you have for one another will change. What you once had at the beginning – all sweetness and giggles – will either fade away or develop into something different, maybe it will deepen into a companionship or likewise.

And at times it can be bloody tough; you either push through or it ends. But ultimately, if you still have each other, and if you still have a love for one another, then it's worth holding onto. And I guess that is our story, through all the trials and tribulations – it is the love that has glued and bonded us together for nearly 30 years.

I can tell you one thing for sure. If there is a reincarnation after death, I will not come back in the next life as a wife. Oh no, not me, in the next life I am coming back as the Mistress! Mate, they get everything, and they don't have to do anything. Mistresses don't have to wash, cook or clean the house. Nor do they have to do the dinner the way the husband wants.

They don't have to constantly remind them, *have you done this* or *have you done that,* or *have you put the bins out.* Nor do they have to deal with organising every single event including your own birthday party – yes, I even had to do that for my 40th, and the cake and everything!

I remember telling my husband one Christmas that, "you think Santa has flipping been," because I'd done everything, from buying all the presents, wrapping them up, to buying all the food.

So yeah, I am coming back as the Mistress. And if I ever write another book I will call it,

I'm coming back as the mistress, followed by *The monumental failings of men.*

Anyway, a few days later the med team, on their daily routine, came in all smiles, informing me I was completely clear from the infection and my blood cells were recovering – and because of that it's likely I would be going home soon. I was delighted to say the least.

We continued chatty chatting, when my beautiful registrar Sarah said, "Tell the prof the funny story about Natalija," and of course, always happy to hear the sound of my own voice together with my love for telling a good story, began with a "Well, Natalija, who is previously my pro-Russian Baltic Boxing Champ personal trainer," (the expressions on their faces said it all), "had this new client. The client was an ex top military someone or other who stupidly said to Natalija, 'Look, don't go easy on me, I'm used to hard training.'

"When Natalija told me this, she looked directly at me with her menacing eyes and a sinister laugh – as I shook my head in disbelief because I knew what would happen to anyone saying something like that to someone like her – and said, 'Sarezajjjjjjj, I took him outside the grounds to train him and did what he said. Guess what?! He was sick in corner. I destroyed him!" And of course, after delivering that punchline, my entire med team erupted with laughter.

After we settled down, Professor Gribbin – another lifesaving true hero – took the floor and said, "I could listen to you all day. You are such an inspiration to us all. You are such an uplifting person, and you just keep pushing. I love coming to see you, in fact I save you till the end of my session because I always end the day on a high note. Maybe, I should come in at the beginning of the day instead, so it sets me up for the rest of the day."

Honestly, I was really moved by what Professor Gribbin said. I was so taken aback that this genius of a man who is held in such high esteem, due to his contributions and achievements – a person who has worked tirelessly, in a career spanning over several decades, a person who is undeniably at the top of his game – is so humble to say something as sweet as he did. It's moments like these that got me through the tough days, as well as knowing I had a team behind me that would do all they could to ensure I get through this treatment.

With that, I was sent home after three and a half weeks from start to finish. But coming home from this cycle was very different and, dare I say, a rather difficult experience compared to my first cycle. Whilst I was excited to come back home, in record time I'm told, my husband and middle son – who was staying at home at that time – were clearly not expecting me back so soon.

Not that I blame my middle son, he literally worked and still works all day as a chef (and now work in Michelin Star restaurant), so he more or less only came home to sleep, then was up and literally out again.

My husband on the other hand didn't work all day and all night and had weekends off but chose to let things slide into a bit of a shit hole. Which, of course, was a bit easier for him because there was no one breathing down his neck or nagging at him. So as soon as I walked through that door, I was hit by the smell of chip pan oil as well as a greasy residue on the walls in the kitchen. To be honest, I was furious and confronted my husband, who defended himself saying, "I didn't think you were coming back so soon!"

I was a little shocked at that response and replied, "Oh right then, no *well done you're home early because you smashed it!* If that was you in hospital," I said, "you would never come home to this."

This led to a full-blown argument where suddenly I was no longer a cancer patient coming home to recover, I was just the moaning wife because something wasn't good enough. I told him, "Just because I am away in hospital doesn't mean you can let things slide and live like a single man with no wife breathing down your neck to tidy up after you. So you took advantage of the opportunity and allowed the house to fester for over three weeks then would give it a quick once over when I was due back!" Not ideal, let alone not a good way to live.

Anyway, soon after that, I decided to go for a shower and go to bed. But not before I hugged and played with my best friend Mac, who didn't leave my side and followed me around.

I didn't eat much that night either, just a few shortbread biscuits, because my husband hadn't got the food on the list I had sent him, and now it was too late because he didn't think I would be back this early!!! I just blankly looked at him, thinking *good grief mate!* But some people just don't think about what should be done!

Some of you may think I am talking quite frankly, or perhaps over sharing a bit or even offloading, but I want to be honest about my experiences and not paint a picture that was untrue or pretend to the outside world that it was all plain sailing – so that if anyone else had or is going through something similar, they don't have to feel alone.

And besides, throughout my life I have learnt that just because you are experiencing some kind of hardship, life still goes on, be it your home or work life, and sometimes sympathy only lasts for so long and only stretches so far.

During my time in hospital I met other cancer patients who didn't have an easy journey through their treatment either; some of the cancer patients did not have the emotional and mental support at home or even in the hospital. At home is a different thing but, in a hospital, you expect some kind of help.

I mean, there are glossy posters offering support to us patients, but when you look further than the advert there isn't anything currently or in the near future that is available for cancer patients due to all the cuts having to be made by those in position.

Trust me, since I have been a cancer patient representative, I have tried to make a difference, but despite how hard I have tried, very little has changed. See, at the beginning they say, *oh yes we know about that and of course we will look into it,* or *we will have to pass it to the relevant department.*

But what that really means is the so-called directors will pass it around and around from committee to committee, who never deal with it, and it ends up getting lost in translation somewhere along the line, and we end up getting nothing. What is even more infuriating is when biased reports come back – and they say otherwise. Take it from the patients mouth. We still suffer, in varying degrees, by those who are evidently supposed to have our best interests at heart.

Then there is the financial struggle; terminally ill cancer patients are not able to work during their treatment. Some patients told me they had to turn to Macmillan on many occasions because they were not eligible to claim from the state unless they only had six months to live, and if they could claim it was taking months to process payments.

Whatever happened to the duty of care that we are supposed to receive from our so-called elected government? They all say one thing and do another. Let me help explain that a little further.

It would seem that whilst there are differences in the names of political parties – Conservative, Labour and Liberal Democrats, their well marketed manifestos highlight all the changes they would do once we vote them in. But once in power, all that flies out of the window and everything remains the same, if not worse. Political parties are like a potato. You can have chipped, mashed and boiled, but at the end of the day, it will always just be a potato! Therefore, no matter which party is in power, it will aways be the same.

Which brings me on nicely to the word *greed,* which can be described as the desire to have more of something, one of them being the greed of food, another is money. And those who have control of money leads to the greed of something that isn't always fair. But that is another matter, so I think I will leave it there on that one.

However, there are ever-growing numbers of people living with terminal illnesses who experience poverty and do not have much in the way of help – and if they do, they have to jump through hoops to get anything. It's heartbreaking knowing that my fellow cancer patients are suffering without having any moderate comfort. No person should have to choose between food and heating, let alone a cancer patient or any other patient. Thank God for Macmillan and other charities picking up the slack!

CHAPTER 33

Contemplation Time

Two cycles down, two to go. To be honest, I adapted fairly well to my new hospital life routine. I had gotten used to all the going back and forth to hospital, having chemo, as well as catching up with all my new hospital friends and coffee shop friends and the security guards. Then sent back home to recover, weekly blood test with PICC line management, then once your bone marrow starts to produce acceptable levels of healthy blood cells, off to have a bone marrow biopsy, which means another aspirate, love those – not!

Especially if you get one that isn't so experienced in doing them, like I did. That's why l only have a couple of dedicated professionals doing mine. Yes, I've got a bit *aspirate diva* about it – and rightly so. Because listen, yeah, in order to get through to your hip bone they have to use a thick, blunt needle-type instrument to pierce your skin, then break into your hip bone – bone, you know – to get to the marrow.

And as they are foraging around, all you hear is the clicking and crunching within yourself, until they get through into the bone and draw out the cells. The pain is immense – despite all the local anaesthetic. It's a bloody rotten experience!

Now, I would only have Dr. Emily, otherwise known as the bone whisperer – affectionately and aptly named by her husband. Mate, the first time she did my aspirate, I didn't really feel anything – just a bit of tugging and rummaging around under the skin and on the bone, but that was it.

I was shocked, you know. At one point, I even asked her, "Have you gone in the bone yet." My girl was like "Yes. I've got all the samples for us and the AML 19 trial team." I was like, "No. Can't be." She laughed and I laughed too, tears of laughter, in fact. You know, the type of laughter that you are trying to cover up the tragedy of the reality of it all. Nonetheless, I couldn't believe this amazingly skilled doctor could perform such an invasive procedure so beautifully.

Therefore only Dr Emily for me! Well, until one occasion.

I was scheduled to have Dr Emily for my aspirate, but on arrival I saw she was accompanied by some bloke who was going to perform my aspirate under her supervision. Apparently, he had come back to the department after being deployed elsewhere.

From the start, I didn't get a very good vibe. And I was right not to, because – oh my days – from start to finish, this man butchered me. Not only did he roughly inject me with the local anaesthetic, but there was also no 'sharp scratch' warning, he just went straight in, stabbing me with the local anaesthetic.

Poor ol' Dr Emily watched in horror and tried to guide this doctor, telling him to try to place the needle in a north, east, south, west kind of pattern, and wait a bit between the shots to ensure it gets down to the bone. My man almost pushed her to one side, as though he knew best. He didn't take one bit of notice of what she said and went straight in, digging for gold, mate.

Look, I have a high pain tolerance, but my eyes were watering from the pain to the point where I couldn't take it anymore and ending up saying, "You're gonna have to stop, mate." Man just ignored me and carried on, saying, "We're nearly in there."

The pain was so bad I had to take myself to another dimension. Even though I did, I could hear the crunching and felt the cracking of my bone as he attempted to break through it to get my blood cells out of the bone marrow. The pain got to the point where I started to feel a bit dizzy and nauseous.

I couldn't even plead with poor Emily to take over, seeing that he was apparently senior to her, and had already made a stand when I asked if Emily could have a go, saying *I know what I am doing.*

So I kept my mouth shut: *remember, you won't be thanked for it.* Besides I didn't want it to be a failed aspirate, where I would have to come back for another one in a week or so. So I just had to grin and bear it.

Then came the aftermath of an aspirate. See, the anaesthetic that has been injected in and around the bone area leaves the side of the ol' rump numb. And that numbness travels down to parts of the groin area which, for the most part, isn't too bad – until you have taken a piss.

Then that becomes an ordeal – especially if you have a bladder full of urine, like I did, and especially – like me – if you don't sit on any public or other toilet but your own. So when I am out anywhere, I am a *squatter over the pan* type of girl.

Now, after an aspirate, I can't feel the wee wee coming out, so you can't aim what you can't feel. So the inevitable happens, especially that day after I'd been butchered, because piss was going flipping everywhere except for the blasted toilet, whilst I was dancing around like a fairy, trying to aim into the pan!

Mate, it was going on the floor, on the seat, and even down my leg. Luckily, I was prepared for that. Experience taught me to have a wad of tissue in hand ready to capture anything before it travelled down my leg towards my leggings or into my flipping shoe. Because the first time I had an aspirate, I got caught, mate, what a calamity that was!

It was after I cleaned myself and freshened up when I began feeling a bit sorry for myself as I hobbled me and my numb hips towards the lift on floor 7. I pressed the button and thought I needed a little pick me up so headed to the basement, to get myself a slice of something and a large cappuccino extra shot and extra hot, one brown sugar and sprinkles (for those of you who might like to know how I like my coffee).

Coffee in hand, cake and sanger in the other (ok, I went all out and got a sanger and cake, after all it was way past lunchtime, and I was famished), I sat on a nearby seat, thinking how could that man brutally carry out such an invasive procedure in the way he did.

I reminded myself that today's test might have been a nightmare, but it is one of the most important ones, the MRD test, to detect if there are any cancer cells on a deeper level. Then I thought, *let's just hope and keep everything crossed that whatever pain I went through today would have a positive outcome tomorrow* (more like the one-plus weeks, when the results arrive).

That's the worst part, the waiting game. Even one week feels like a lifetime! During that time you can really experience some deep anticipation. Your thoughts toss between, *Will it or won't it be a clear result? Will I still be in remission or have the cancer cells returned?* (The medical term is refraction or relapse). *What treatment will I have then if the chemo doesn't work, because I don't have a stem cell donor at the moment? Will I end up on palliative care then end of life? Will I die?*

I know it all sounds a bit morbid but that is the reality of a cancer patient who is undergoing intensive treatment. Nothing is black or white, everything is uncertain. At times it can be really daunting, but somehow you have to pull yourself out of the cesspit of worry!

Many times during my treatment, I felt myself struggling so I sat myself down and had a little word with myself! Otherwise I could have driven myself to despair. No matter how hard it gets or even seems, you can't let it run away with you, you have to try to put things in perspective and keep yourself together (says she, the queen of *worst possible scenarios*). But even in the worst case, you have to accept it, because there is nothing else you can do.

But don't think it was easy for me. It wasn't, because treatment for the next cycle – cycle 3 – heavily depended on the results of my MRD test. The worst case for me is that the result comes back positive, because that would mean I need a stem cell transplant – leading to the med team having the monumental task of finding a stem cell match on their database, due to my ethnicity!

Of course I knew this was the case when I was informed, during my first consultation, that a suitable donor for me would have to be a healthy close family member, namely a sibling or child. Currently there is no match – despite the UK being extremely diverse – as there are not enough stem cell donors for many ethnic minorities to choose from. This is why I repeat my plea to those who can to contact the Anthony Nolan charity, and register, please!!

So, once again I found myself in a hope and a prayer situation! And on another emotional rollercoaster! Despite it only taking a week after the aspirate to get those all-important results back from the lab, it literally felt like forever. But finally they did arrive and the phone call came from one of the professors not known for his communication skills.

So the call went something along the lines of, "Hello, ok, well we will see you in the next week or so for your next cycle."

"Eeeer, right ok, so what about the MRD test . . . Hello, hello?"

Man cut the phone you know. Left, gone, no cheerio, no nothing, just put the phone down – leaving me somewhat bewildered.

None the wiser as to what that phone call actually meant, I ended up ringing my Sammy, who filled me in with what he left out. "NO sweetheart you don't have to have a stem cell transplant. Didn't the prof tell you?"

"No he didn't, he just said ok, we'll see you soon!"

She apologised on his behalf but, to be honest, I didn't really hear much after that – as I was consumed with elation. I felt on top of the world; man I didn't need a stem cell transplant. "Wow girl," I said as I looked down at my body, "see, we made it this far together because we were in it together. Now we've jumped over one major milestone, mind body and soul, hey girl, mind body and soul!"

It wasn't all love, light and dancing ladies though. Recovery before cycle 3 took forever. Unlike cycles 1 and 2, it took over 7 weeks for my cells to get to an acceptable level to start another round of chemo. I guess the treatment had taken its toll on my poor bone marrow. My blood had clearly had enough of it all! To make matters worse, being at home for longer didn't help making it any easier to go back to hospital, namely because I was really enjoying my time at home.

It was during this recovery that I also had a bit of an epiphany that if I am going to die, then I am going to die being happy. And what makes me happy? FOOD! And anyway, extreme dieting – cutting out almost all sugar, little to no fats, low carb and a higher protein diet – didn't stop me from getting sick, did it? In fact I often wonder if it contributed to the cancer, the extreme change in my body composition and all that. Who knows, at the end of the day many will have an opinion, but it doesn't mean it's right.

To make things worse, it was the summer – and this summer turned out to be the summer of love, the love of food to be exact. After several months of shit hospital muck together with, *you may have made it so far, but you could still die during any cycle,* I thought *fuck it*

I'm gonna have a few goodies. I didn't go silly. After all, I didn't want to undo what I'd already accomplished, so I only chose a few options to enjoy.

The first being ice cream, so after many years, I cracked out the Häagen-Dazs! So as not to overeat, I opted to buy their range of individual pots, summer berries and caramel (as I don't eat chocolate).

And the other was something I hadn't had for over four and a half years, something I consider to be one of the best things life can offer when it comes to simple enjoyment – and that is freshly baked bread (all fired up from Sainsbury's) with French butter. Oh my days, imagine a thick slice that comes from a round, crusty, browned to perfection ball of bread and unsalted President butter slathered all over it! Delicious!

This was also a time when I had something that I had never knowingly had before and that was every kind of pork, because I literally went on a bit of pork fest. I had pork everything.

Because, before then – from childhood right through to me being an adult – it has been rammed down my throat that the worst thing you could ever do as a Muslim was to eat pork. Which of course I never really understood – and which led to my family and I having huge debates over this when I was an adult.

See, most of them cheated in every other possible way, they lied, stole, had affairs, beat women, drank alcohol to the moon and back, you name it, they did it. A few of them even committed a few taboos, like marrying a close relative or two, mmm I know. Scandalous!

In fact every relative, or almost every Muslim I have met, holds pork in such high esteem, as though this is the worst thing a Muslim can do whilst justifying their poorest of behaviours with, "I might have stolen, cheated and drank alcohol, but at least I haven't eaten pork." I'm like, what mate? What an earth kind of reasoning is that. Ridiculous and delusional!

Anyway, as ridiculous as this may sound to some people, I made my peace with God by having a small conversation which starting with me placing my hands together in a prayer-like position and said, "Dear God, you know how much I love to eat, yeah, so can I just try some pork before I die? I know it's arguably a sin or haram, but I have done a lot of things that would be considered sinful! So please can I have some porky pork?"

And with that, off I skipped to porky land. So I tried bacon – yuk, too salty; pork chops – flavourless; pork belly – way too fatty; pork pies – rancid. Sausage rolls, beef ones, were so much nicer. Ham – that was ok, especially mortadella, that nice Italian ham is good but again not the best. To be honest, pork ain't all that you think. To be honest, eating pork was disappointing! I guess I expected more. That's the trouble with expectations!

Anyway, the day came when my bloods finally went back to acceptable levels and a date was set. I was dreading going back to hospital. The thought of having to go back to that terrible food and that constantly cold room was filling me with dread. Even though it was the height of summer it was Baltic in those rooms.

I also kept thinking about all the loud beeping noises, all those flashing lights in the room, the lack of fresh air, the this the that, the list is endless. But of course I had no choice but to go. So chin up and push through. There's nothing I could do so I told myself, why torture and stress yourself over something you cannot control or change, stressing won't divert the outcome. It's a few shitty weeks to save your life. So stop your moaning.

On arrival, I was taken to 5A, a slightly different change from ward 5C, but with all the usual relevant infectious testing. A few days later, the results came back and they were all negative, so I got transferred to my usual ward 5D. Into room 21. Lovely, I thought, something different. Well, of course, until I realised it was even more bloody freezing than any other room I had been in! Plus it was right next to the nurse station. Meaning noise, noise, noise!

CHAPTER 34

Cycle 3 Life Lessons

This was by far one of the toughest cycles and it is fair for me to say Cycle 3 was the one when I was the most homesick. From the day I arrived, I just wanted to go home. I missed my Mac so much. I would look out of the window thinking if I was home we would be sitting in the garden, under the umbrella, watching the bees dart from flower to flower – and seeing the many different beautiful butterflies, and the dragon flies, all flocking to my garden that was designed to encourage all manner of wildlife.

Not to mention the fact that I literally feed everything that comes into my garden. I leave sugar water on the table for the bees, and the occasional wasps. I feed the several birds each morning and – trust me – if I am late, they let me know by squawking loudly and jumping on my bedroom roof (yes they do, my husband didn't believe me either until one Sunday morning when we woke up a little later and they did exactly that. And from time to time there is this single female magpie, and some mornings after she eats, she hops on my roof and comes right up to my window and sings a little song! Not sure it's related, but I like to think it is.

Then there are the generations of foxes that I have been feeding since April 2021. It all started after my first cycle and I began leaving some bread and cakes of an evening time, so the birds got something to eat for tea as well. And of those evenings the boys came to have dinner – when I saw an animal in the garden – I knew it wasn't Mac because he was on his bed, so I thought what on earth is that. So I slowly walked towards the French doors and to my delight I saw a mummy fox eating the food I'd left on the bird table! So from that day on we have left food every single night.

In hospital, I really missed eating all that nice food I'd been having during recovery. I missed the warm garden and getting my coffee from my favourite Costa coffee drive through! Being in here was long! If it wasn't for the amazing staff it would have been so much harder. Luckily for me, I was literally known and loved all over Barts. Many members of staff even coined me as *the fitness girl*, which of course is lovely.

But there are many problems I witnessed and experienced from the way the NHS is run to how the system treats its staff. So, in turn, they end up leaving and quite often wards would be understaffed. Due to this, patients could wait for up to 20 mins for a nurse to become available. Not to mention an abundance of other issues which will unfold later.

Plus chemo treatment for Cycle 3 was flipping longgggggggg, mate. Instead of a quick 2mil shot, I ended up sitting for hours on end watching the chemo drip, drip, dripping from the top of that bag, down the tube, into the PICC line, into my vein, travelling around my body killing everything and anything. Dripping my life away, drip after painful drip. Oh and after the chemo has finished, a long ass flush of a saline bag. Because the blasted process was different on these last two cycles! Longgggggggg!

Cycle 3 was also where I had the most challenging events with my family – from my husband to two of my boys. It was a difficult time for my children to cope with. I mean their father isn't very good at all that talking stuff. In fact, he barely spoke to them when I was in hospital – unlike me, I spoke to them constantly. Which, of course, didn't help them as their family support at home had gone.

So I guess one of the easiest ways for them was to blot it out by excessively drinking and taking drugs, to mask the pain of having their mum in hospital or maybe it was just the excuse to do it even more with no consequences, because – after all – their mum may just die and they're fragile and could end up doing something to themselves!

Either way, I wasn't impressed, because for some silly reason I thought me being in hospital might have helped them understand that this is a time where I actually needed them to be strong and not to end up off the rails *Willy Nilly*, whilst I'm here in hospital, having cancer treatment.

However that wasn't always the case and many times their actions left me feeling somewhat saddened and terribly disappointed.

So with little to no feel-good factors available, together with disgusting hospital food, I temporarily turned to an old friend, for some good old-fashioned love. FOOD! And I ordered from one of my favourite places, Fortum and Masons! So did my lovely cousin Uzma. She would regularly send me shortbread, biscuits and other goodies from there. It came to the point where, most days, I was buying something to eat because I just couldn't stand that hospital slop. Whilst I did my best to prevent weight gain, eating like that had consequences! But I had no choice, so I did my best to limit the damage.

However one day, things at home took a turn for the worse during this cycle and a serious event led to it all coming to a head between me and one of my boys where it ended up with me getting quite cross – to the point where I ended up screaming all sorts at the top of my voice, which was heard by everyone nearby.

Now, I know I shouldn't have screamed like that. But that's years of parenting where all the problems are compounded, just like in any long-term relationship. Your ability to remain calm tends to melt away over the years, I know mine has to the point where my fuse doesn't exist. Not that I am known for my patience!

Soon after that call, two senior members of the med team came into my room. Initially, I was concerned because I'd already seen the team earlier. Judging by the look on their faces, I thought *shit, something's wrong!* Especially since one of them walked toward me solemnly.

Near my chair she crouched down, looking straight into my eyes with tremendous concern then gently said, "We heard you were shouting today, Sarezah!"

"I'm sorry," apologising immediately for my behaviour, "It was one of my children, we had bit of an altercation." (Not really wanting to divulge why! And still not wanting to, other that it was substance abuse related).

She replied, "Sarezah, that's not why we're here. We understand life goes on, even in here, but shouting like that, in your current condition, could lead to extremely serious effects to your health and indeed your life! You are our priority and we don't want to hear that you have been screaming like that again otherwise we will have to take appropriate action," she said, before that awkward moment of silence again!

After that, there was no need for words. I understood that stare of hers – another stare that spoke a thousand words, transporting me right back to when I was with Dr Goel all those years ago – except this time, my *fatality* is being caused by a different kind of *ticking time bomb*!

Needless to say I was upset after that whole event. I was even quite quiet for a few days, which is unheard of for me. I was polite enough, just not my usual chatty self. I really did have enough of it all, to be honest. To the point where I started contemplating many things in my life, including my children and husband, and wondered how they would be if I behaved like they have, if the roles were reversed and they were the ones in hospital. I would certainly not be behaving like they did, that's for sure.

It led me to question myself as a parent and even a wife. I wondered if I had done something wrong to make them so dependent on things like drugs and/or alcohol. Are these inherent traits, is it a nurture or nature thing? Are my children's actions and behaviour down to me as a parent? Did I give them too much? Didn't I give them enough? Was I too strict? Was I too liberal?

I soon realised, at the end of the day, they are adults, and what they do is up to them. All I can do is advise them and hope they make the right choices that are best for them. They have free will to make their own choices and choose how they want to live, by their rules, which isn't necessarily always what you hoped for them. And the hardest point about being a parent, is at some point you've just got to let them crack on with it!

For me, that point – of letting them make their own choices – came after a conversation sometime after 3am when a nurse came in to do my observation. Half asleep, I managed to let her know it had already been done over an hour ago. (Just to refresh your memory, observations are normally every four hours. So 6am, 10am, 2pm, 6pm, 10pm, 2am).

The nurse stood there for a few moments realising her mistake and apologised for waking me up again. "That's ok!" I said, as I shuffled myself to a seated position in my bed, then jokingly said, "Well seeing you're here and I am now wide awake, you can entertain me for a bit."

She laughed and said, "Ok, you are my last patient before my break anyway."

I was familiar with this nurse; she was a bank staff night shift worker (either an agency or a nurse working their day off) and we began chitty chattering. She asks me questions like, "How are you responding to my treatment? How are you coping mentally." All the usual sort of questions a cancer patient would be asked. To which I nodded a yes in response. Then she asked if I was married and had kids. Which I of course answered yes to both. She then shifted the conversation slightly to them. "How are your family coping with it all?"

As she wasn't a close friend, I would have answered a question like that with a simple *yes, they are all ok thank you,* hiding the truth behind a smile. But on that day, I just couldn't pretend, and before I knew it, I just started pouring my heart out about that call – which led to me saying, "Even in hospital I have to deal with serious family matters, whilst I'm in here battling for my life and trying to cope with the effects of having intensive chemo! What's the point," I said. "Just what is the point of fighting to survive, just to get better and to go back to the same old problems! I may as well give up treatment!"

Suddenly the nurse abruptly grabbed my attention by slamming her hands down onto the chair she was leaning on, immediately snapping me out of my rant, and said in a deep African accent, "Eh, what is wrong with you, what are you talking about? If you give up and die in this bed tomorrow, what do you think your family will do, eh?"

"Erm. I don't know?" I said, whilst looking into her fierce, widened eyes, before she bellowed, "They will carry on living their lives, doing the same as they are doing now. All of them, but this time with your money! Get better and get out of here and go and live your life, before it is too late."

Those words rang the deepest truth and, from that moment, I

changed many things – forever.

Not only did I change myself, I also began to better understand how families cope when they are separated and thrown into some extremely difficult situations. See, the nurse also told me I wasn't the first one to encounter problems at home whilst receiving treatment. So I didn't feel alone.

Even so, I still tried to see things from my children's point of view – that their mother, their absolute everything, has been diagnosed with a terrible form of aggressive cancer – and the treatment may or may not work. Mum may die from treatment. So I guess for these children all they wanted to do is run away from what was happening and the best way of escapism for them was to drown themselves in a pool full of alcohol and a bag full of chop (cocaine) or, dare I say, a bit of both. Or is it possible for them to use it as an excuse, to justify their addictions and indulge in it further? Who knows!

With that, I said to myself, when you get home from Cycle 3 you are going to keep pushing through. Whatever the challenges are now, we will face them. Whatever this shitty chemo does to my body – like the physical changes where I'd lost my hair, or the fact I was losing my body shape bit by bit due to the fact I wasn't weight training in a gym – it doesn't matter. What matters is we get ourselves through, then we can deal with whatever we need to deal with after.

Besides, it will be home time soon and it was – because before I knew it, another month had passed, and I was on that long journey back home through the thick London traffic.

A day or two after returning, I'd got back into my home workout training routine. Each day I did what I could in my little makeshift gym at home. No matter what state I was in, my mind and body came first. In fact, I love to train, feeling those endorphins release during exercise is a wonderful buzz – not just physically but mentally.

Plus I guess, somewhere inside, I have a natural fear of undoing all the hard work and sacrifices I have made over, what is now, a decade. And before you say it, remember when I said diet and exercise is a lifestyle change. Well here it is in black and white: a lifestyle change has to become your way of life.

Being home during my recovery on Cycle 3 was much the same

as all the other cycles. It had some ups and downs, some dramas and whatnots. But, luckily for me, I spent most of my recovery at home by myself with my boxer boy Mac, due to isolation, together with having to shield until my blood count recovered a bit more.

Poor ol' boy, he got to hear all my problems and incessant moaning. I tell you what though, he really is the best listener in the world. No interruptions, no judgments and no blame! If only we were like Mac and listen more instead of talking over each other, the world would be a much kinder and compassionate place.

During my time at home whilst waiting for my blood count to recover I contemplated the past few months and how my life living with cancer has changed and developed since my diagnosis. I felt I had a much better understanding of cancer and more acceptance, especially of the fact that this kind of illness will more than likely have no end date, there is no cure for cancer patients like us. The best that can be hoped for is remission.

See, unlike a cancerous lump, Leukaemia cannot be cut out and removed because it flows through the blood system, making it extremely difficult to treat. This is where you have to try to take control and manage your thoughts, so you don't end up at the mercy of this disease.

Because, believe me, it sits in the back of your mind and whispers in your ears, so if you have any little bruise or any other possible related symptom, it will torment your by saying *oooh look, the cancer is back*, and a mild panic comes over you, and before you know it things start running away thinking all sorts, believe me I know firsthand!

I also reflected a lot and went from start to finish and learnt a lot about myself and how I'd developed over my lifetime. I thought to myself how far from perfect I am, even though I would like to think I am the best thing since sliced bread!

But throughout my life I have experienced a mixture of good and bad things. I have been kind, and I have been ruthless. I have made many mistakes, and I have hurt people – some indirectly, others directly. I have done good and bad. But I never hurt anyone who didn't deserve it. I know, quite a bold statement, right?

I am not from this generation; my upbringing dictated my

actions. There was none of this '*be the bigger person*' there, it was fight of get battered. Fundamentally, I like who I am and that really is all that matters. And if I don't like something about myself I will endeavour to change it.

Another change I made was my tendency to have assumptions and certain point of view! I often thought all the good experiences or events that happened in my life were counteracted by something bad happening. For example, my 19 stone weight loss. I did all that hard work then finally reached my goal only to be told I had cancer. Or playing guitar and writing songs with my brother Ric. I gave all those dedicated years only to realise I was not going to be a rock star!

But I realised that I was so wrapped up in the negative emotions of it all that I couldn't see the positives. So I changed my perspective and made myself look at things from a different point of view, firstly with Ric, I realised I had the honour of playing and writing music with together with an extremely talented musician. I learnt how to arrange and produce my own songs, and we really did have some magical musical moments.

Secondly, if I didn't lose all that weight, and didn't have that operation I could be dead. I could have been one of those patients that went to hospital and died a week later because the cancer had ravished them to the point where they were not able to treat them. Or I could have been too obese to be treated.

And if I hadn't been so physically or mentally fit, perhaps I wouldn't have survived – which, of course, I attribute to my upbringing! Those childhood experiences made me who I am today, where I had to become resilient and had to learnt to adapt myself in any challenging environment. And I'm not the sort to just give up.

For those of you that find dealing with issues challenging, do your best to learn how to use your inner strength to overcome obstacles, rise above yourself, and find a way to get through it. Everything you need to get through life's ups and downs can be found within yourself – whether dealing with death, suicide, breakups, racism, physical or mental abuse.

Of course, there are times where this isn't always possible, especially in some domestic violence cases or abuse of a sexual nature. Sadly, a few of my friends that I met over the years have been subjected to sexual abuse. And I learnt how this can affect individuals who have suffered in different ways, like it did one friend of mine who was completely traumatised by what happened to them, and – despite having years of medication and therapy – they were still haunted by those events.

One day, during a conversation, I said to that person that whilst I could never understand what they have experienced, I can see how it has affected them and the damage it has caused. then went on to say, "This evil person has hurt you in unthinkable ways, so don't let them take even more of you, don't take over where the abuser left off. You have already been harmed, don't carry on doing what they did to you to yourself. When those thoughts or voices creep into your head, push them out. Think of or do something else. Don't let it run rings in your head.

Don't give it power!" They took that advice and, bit by bit, things changed for the better!

CHAPTER 35

Cycle Four -The Grand Finale

Drum roll! It's the 29th August, the beginning of the last cycle of chemotherapy treatment. So far so good and fingers crossed I will continue to get the same results. This cycle began with a complete mix of emotions – from its almost over, to its weird its almost over, it all seemed a bit surreal. All of a sudden you've got cancer, you've been in hospital receiving strong treatment and now it's almost over, bizarre!

Many times during treatment I would cast my memory back to that first consultation I had at St Bartholomew's hospital when my consultant said I can't guarantee the treatment will work or you will see the end of the year. So I was extremely grateful I had made it this far. Because at no point did I forget what I had and why I was here.

During this cycle I thought about the many experiences I had during my Chemotherapy treatment, which had taken up most of 2021. The whole year had been a mixture of mental, physical and emotional challenges. Having treatment in hospital also taught me an awful lot about life in the NHS, namely how nurses, doctors, professors and others work tirelessly around the clock to save lives. These people are most definitely the backbone of the National Health Service. They are the ones who give unconditionally. To which, as a patient, I am deeply grateful and thankful for all they do.

So on that day we arrived after another long journey. We took the lift with all my bags to floor 5C. I checked in, was sent to my room, had the standard Covid test and MRSA and all the others – thinking, I wish I was still home, only to remind myself it's the last cycle. *So stop your mithering SAREZAH and let's just get on with it. This is the last hurdle; we haven't got time to slip!* But even so, at times it got the better of me, after all I am still human – even though the children think I am some sort of mutant, which I think is supposed to be a compliment! But before those thoughts became oppressive, I did my best to push them aside.

Chemo began a couple of days after, later than scheduled, as there was a breakdown in communication between the pharmacy and the doctors. Not terribly common but these things do happen. However, I wasn't terribly impressed, either, because I could have spent an extra day at home, eating better foods. *Never mind, hey ho, I'm here now, just got to get on with it.* Massive eye roll.

Chemo treatment finally arrived, and I began the long hours of administration by intravenous system, continuously reminding myself this is the last cycle. I kept boosting myself mentally with phrases like *come on let's go, it's the last cycle, don't give up now – just keep pushing.*

I would tell myself to *put your house mixes on. They will keep you going.* No matter what I said to myself, at times I just wanted to go home. This cycle was by far the toughest! Look, even the strongest of rocks erode in time after the constant drip, drip, drip of water. And right there and then that's how I felt, a bit eroded with the constant battles in life so I could relate to that bit of philosophy!

But it was only temporary, as are all emotions. The best thing I have learnt is to just let them pass by as long as you don't hold onto them, because they can be damaging – as I found out for myself. So I found ways to distract myself. I would either walk or exercise and, one morning, I noticed a lady smiling at me. In fact she had been watching me for quite some time. She watched how I interacted with the staff etc. Anyway I didn't think much more of it, other than being aware.

So a few nights after I arrived, I was abruptly awoken by one of the taps going off, thinking *it can't be 2am already, can it?* So I opened my eyes to a dark room but no one there; however the tap was running. Mate, I shit myself, thinking it was some flipping ghost or some St Barts' phantom coming to haunt me.

So I put my light on, and the tap was still running. Turns out it wasn't a ghost but a dodgy sensor. So I told the nurse, who told the ward manager, who told the maintenance, who told the plumber, who said, "I can't find a fault."

I was like, "Well there is, mate, it's the sensor, it's coming on and off randomly. I know 'cos I've had to stick tape over the sensor at night to stop it randomly coming on and waking me up."

Anyway, to cut a long story short, three plumbers ended up

coming back to check the same sensor. Three of them! Who all stood outside my room on their phones, scrolling – allegedly waiting for the tap to come on randomly again. *Well you won't see it out there. will you, you c word!*

And with that, I lost my shit, flung open the door, and held it open with the big metal bin and made them watch until it came on. And as if by magic, the tap came on (perhaps that was shitting itself too!) so they fixed it in a hurry, leaving as quickly as possible – all observed by this person who I mentioned was watching me. She approached me soon after, revealing who she was.

She was one of the board directors for the hospital and simply said she wondered if I would consider being a cancer patient representative for the Barts Trust. She said she had been watching me for a reason, after someone had tipped her off about me as one that would make a difference as a representative due to my character! Initially, I didn't want to. Remember I had been a union rep, and I didn't want to bang my head against a brick wall again. So I asked her to give me time to consider her proposition!

That decision was confirmed after one of my morning walks where I had almost finished my step goal, so I cut a bit of a corner and I saw a man, who was a little older than me, pointing and speaking at me. So smiling, I proceeded to take my headphones out so I could hear him.

"I saw you cut that corner," he said, "you're cheating!!" I laughed and said, "No, I've actually finished."

He laughed back and said, "I'm only joking with ya!" then said, "How are ya, girl." "I'm alright mate. Pushing through as best I can, you know." He nodded. I mean it was obvious I had cancer. I'm in a cancer hospital with a bald head. Looking a bit worse for wear. Walking with my red patient wrist band, letting the whole world know I have an allergy, in my case penicillin.

"Do you have. . .?" I said to him, with that cancer nod! "No love, it's my wife. She's got breast cancer."

"Ah mate, I'm sorry." We both looked at each other for a few silent seconds. See, with cancer patients and their families comes a certain universal feeling and we all know what each other is going through. So I thought I would break the silence by telling him that something happened to me today and I am wondering what to do.

So I told him a Board Director asked me to be a patient representative on the St Barts Trust Cancer Board. "Oh wow," he said. I told him I wasn't sure whether to take it or not.

And to my surprise he replied, in his East London accent, "Look girl, I don't want to cause you any offence or nothing but," pointing at my tattoos and my general look, "people like me and you don't get asked to take up positions like this very often. In fact they are bloody rare. If I were you I would take that position with both hands. It will give you the opportunity to do the right thing by all of us. We need someone like you that will fight for us."

Wow, I thought, *just wow*. And with that, I smiled and winked at him, then thanked him for his opinion, wished him and his family well, and said, "I better go, before they send a search party and helicopter out for me." Then I walked away, looked back and waved goodbye, smiling away, with his words firmly placed in my head.

So I accepted the post on one condition, that the way things are run at the moment will get changed, because I don't want to fight for nothing, wasting what little time I have left with just talk and no action. And I don't want to hear we can't do that because there is too much red tape! Because, if no one has the balls to cut the red tape and get things done, then best hand me the scissors, because I will. That lovely lady looked at me and smiled and said a bloody big yes!

Yes! Yes! Thanking me, over and over again!

To this day, I try to do all I can to represent the best interests of patients and staff. But more often than not, it has been met with either being pushed from pillar to post, or we will get on with it – and never do! Together with endless excuses and, worse, the self-gratification that comes with the smallest of achievements led by the endless amount of administrative committees that exist.

I have witnessed with my own eyes where money is wasted in the NHS, and it's generally on stupid unnecessary strategy programmes that don't work. Only to discuss yet again, the same initiative, but a 'refreshed' version of something that was not worked on in the first place.

Then yet again, handed around from committee to committee, then to some subcommittee, all getting lost in translation, losing money and time and never getting anything important done, other than masking the real problems or passing the buck!

Day 6 due to the lack of availability on ward 5D I was still stuck on ward 5C. So not only was I missing home, but I was also now missing my training. Once again, I had to grin and bear it and do what I could with what I had. I continued to do my steps and mat work with the glute bands and did some light HIIT sessions, which didn't involve too much in the way of jumping as the ol' platelets and bloods would be dropping due to the chemo. So I stuck to low impact movements and walking.

CHAPTER 36

Not Again!

Finally, after finishing my first round of chemo, a room on 5D became available. And soon after, I was once again neutropenic flat – not unusual to say the least but, of course, this means you now have a low, next to nothing, immune system.

One morning shortly after, I woke up not feeling right. I couldn't say what it was because I hadn't ever felt like that. It was quite weird. Nonetheless, I got up, showered, washed etc, then went to eat a banana and a few mouthfuls of porridge, but as soon as it hit my stomach it began churning. I just put it down to being gruel, so left it in a nice tidy pile, ready for collection, then made my way to the gym.

Not long after I got on the bike I began to feel poorly, which quickly progressed to feeling nauseous, followed by waves of dizziness. Although I was unsure because the morning blood results had not come back yet, I just brushed it off thinking maybe my haemoglobin levels were low! Hence the dizzy spell.

But it got worse and worse, so I thought it's best to go back to the room and sit down. On arrival, I saw George, the stores man, standing outside my door replacing gloves and aprons etc. He noticed something was wrong and said, "Oh, are you ok, my dear?"

"No George, I feel awful, I feel really, really sick."

On entering my room I headed straight for the chair and slumped down. George, out of concern, had gone to find the lovely health care assistant, Komfort. This kind and wonderful lady came in immediately, and before she could say anything, I said, "Komfort. I'm going to be sick." She quickly got a grey paper bowl and handed it to me, and within a nano second I was puking my guts up into the bowl.

I will never forget their poor helpless, concerned faces. They had never seen me sick like that before. All they saw was a happy-go-lucky me! Komfort asked George to get a nurse whilst she stayed with me as she helped move me to my bed, because I had started shaking, again!

Moments later a nurse and doctors came in. But with each second, I was deteriorating. My temperature was soaring like crazy. And the shakes got worse and worse. I began drifting in and out of consciousness. This is when panic descended, as I thought of what happened on Cycle 1 and said to myself *OH NO! NOT AGAIN!* As they do with a temp strike, they took more bloods to the lab to discover what's what.

I was shaking uncontrollably, feeling bloody freezing – of course not helped by that stupid air conditioning unit above my bed, which I lay helplessly watching, feeling it constantly spewing out freezing cold air, almost laughing at me – like it was there to finish me off.

I felt fear and dread come over me, because for some stupid blooming reason, I needed a wee wee, but I couldn't even move, let alone stand up, because I was extremely wobbly with legs that felt like jelly. Therefore, with no coordination and with the room spinning, I thought it was best to hold it in. Honestly, it was getting worse and worse, and I felt like I'd been on a complete bender – a feeling I totally loathe. Remember, the reason I no longer drink alcohol is because I got so drunk on my 40th birthday party and ended up being sick and humiliated. So no more after that. And no more has it been. Not that it was a bad thing. Booze really wasn't my thing.

But it got to the point where I couldn't hold my wee in any longer, so I pressed the buzzer. I knew it wouldn't be a long wait, as I was on high alert due to the temp spike meaning I had an infection. Before I had time to think the worst possible scenario (WPS), my lovely ward manager came in. And I said I needed the toilet.

To which he responded, "Sorry, but I am the only person available." I was like *Noooooo, I've got to go.* Now man is going to see my Mary (my private parts). So I hesitated a bit. Then he came over to help me up, because he could see visibly that I was wobbling.

"Hold onto me," he said, followed by, "I really have seen it all before so please don't feel embarrassed."

I was like, "Well you haven't seen mine!" But I literally had no choice, it was either go with him or piss myself. So I took his arm, and off we went. Mate, I was really shaking and wobbling like a good 'un.

Now, because I'd held onto my wee for too long already, just before I got to the toilet wee wee started to come out. Mate, the ward manager saw – but said nothing. I mean, for goodness sakes.

So quickly, he helped me pull my trousers down and looked away as I hovered over the toilet bowl. Mate, wee was going blooming everywhere, worsened by my uncontrollable shaking. Realising it would be easier if I sat on the toilet, he said, "Sit down."

"I can't," I said. "I don't sit on the loo," so he pulled the disabled bar down so I could hold onto it so I wouldn't fall down.

A while later the doctor came in with the results of my blood test. He came towards me with a pensive look on his face and said, "I'm really sorry but it's sepsis negative. We are not sure where the infection started, although microbiology suspects it's your PICC line. Or it could be something else. Additionally, your infection markers are very high, and your potassium levels have dropped dramatically. You will need antibiotics immediately and a potassium bag."

My eyes held his but with a completely blank stare, no words. But a look of *well that's fantastic. Bloody marvellous. That's the stuff. Just what I need hey. Sepsis! Beautiful!* Bang goes my theory that I'd be in and out, with no hiccups or spikes in temperature like the previous cycle! *Hey ho!*

However, luckily for me, the infection was under control within two days, and I was back in the gym, but was only permitted to do gentle exercises along with soft walks and no power walking or stomping. The reason was that they didn't want the infection to be bouncing around my body and I was still neutropenic flat, where the neutrophil count is still zero.

The worst thing was that I wasn't going home any time soon, which wasn't ideal, because all I could think was that in a few weeks' time, it's my baby Azim's birthday. Even though I was prepared, I was hoping and praying I will not be in here.

This cycle was long, each day dragged by, and every day there was something new to deal with, be it rashes, nausea, actual sickness, tiredness, then not being able to sleep, night or day. In fact, sleep was almost non-existent, because every second, night and day, it was bleep bleep bleeping of the nurses' buzzer. Long, long, longgggggg.

Even though Cycle 4 was a real challenge for me, I just kept telling myself to keep going. *Get up and just keep pushing. We're nearly there.* So I kept myself busy and stayed focused on the end.

Somehow, you just have to find the strength to get yourself through, otherwise this disease will completely consume you. Not just physically but mentally. You have to bounce back after every problem, by any means necessary and with whatever you've got left. You have to dig deep and find the determination and will to fight your way through! You might not win, but you know you gave it your all and didn't give up. Be that true fighter who never gave up even in the face of adversity!

People have often said to me, "You are a fighter, you're strong. You've fought and won against cancer."

My answer is, "Well I appreciate what you are saying, but I have witnessed people in this hospital giving it all they've got, and they still lost."

So it's not always about beating or winning. In my honest opinion, surviving cancer is pretty much down to being lucky. And you either respond to treatment – or you don't. Yes, certain elements come into it, like health and fitness, but the bottom line is… Fate!

At the end of the day, if we're going to die we're going to die. When it's your time it's your time and that's that. There's nothing you can do but just accept it. The only thing you can do is fight until you can't fight anymore. It doesn't mean you are not strong or didn't have a strong mental attitude, or you weren't positive, it just means that you just couldn't fight anymore.

Besides were all going to die, some will die at 8 months old, 8 years old, 18, 28, 88. We all have an expiry date written on our foreheads. We just don't know when that date is.

CHAPTER 37

September 2021

Whilst the infection did clear up, I was still waiting for my cells to recover. By now it was mid- September and in a couple of days it was to be my son Zee Zee's birthday. I resigned myself to the fact that we will probably be spending it in here, just me and him. Like I said, I already brought a few gifts, together with some banners and balloons, just in case. Not ideal, but it is what it is.

Inevitably, the birthday arrived, and I was still in hospital. But instead of being all doom and gloom I felt elated, because it seemed like I was the one who got the presents that day as my blood test came back, and I had a reading of 0.1 neutrophil. This meant my bone marrow was recovering and starting to produce healthy blood cells again. And as soon as I got to at least 0.5-0.8 I could go home. Fingers crossed, for the very last time. But for now, I had a room, albeit a hospital room, to decorate for my son's birthday.

So after the tests came back, I began to get things done and started to wrap the few presents I brought with me, then decorated the room with the help of one of the nurses on duty. Mate, she had to blow up the balloons, because I didn't have much in the way of puff due to the low haemoglobin levels, meaning I had very low oxygen levels in my body as the count was 81. Any less and it would have meant a blood transfusion, again.

Together, my nurse and I put up a few happy birthday banners and some balloons on my hospital door so when my Azim came in, he would see it. I had a cake, a Victoria sponge from M&S, as the ward clerk went completely out of her way to get it because that is the one I wanted.

We couldn't light the candles in my room as there were oxygen tanks in there – which I didn't know until I had asked a nurse if I could light a candle as my very dear friends Kevin and Karen Bentley had bought one for me. Thank the Lord I asked first, else ward 5D could have quite easy gone *boom.* Nevertheless, we managed to do what we could. It was a simple fact of adjusting to your situation and making it as special as possible.

When my little Azim came in, I will never forget his eyes. He looked so happy, but the eyes don't lie. The sadness of it all couldn't be hidden. Here we are, mummy and youngest son, celebrating a birthday under the saddest of circumstances. No child wants to come into a hospital to see their mummy, let alone at a time when it's your birthday.

By 22nd of September, my cells had recovered just enough to give me hope that the doctors might say I could go home. We all anxiously waited, and in the meantime, they topped up my platelets via intravenous drip. I sat painfully waiting a decision and before I knew it, it was lunch time then early afternoon. I told myself *it's just the waiting game now, let's see whether the med team will be happy to let me go home.*

Whilst I was waiting, I managed to escape with the ward clerk, with the permission of the ward manager, to get a few bits for the girls – meaning the nurses – just in case I was going to go home. I wanted to get a thank you card and some cakes and biscuits from the one and only M&S, which wasn't so far from the hospital. It was so nice to get out, I almost felt normal like I wasn't a hospital patient anymore. I was just ok, walking around the streets, buying bits and bobs.

As soon as I got back from my little excursion to the shops around St. Paul's, I was immediately informed by several very excited staff the all-important news that I was going home. I made a squeaky-like noise that I didn't even recognise, let alone imagine I could get that high. Delighted was an understatement.

But whilst I was feeling so happy to go home, I also felt a bit sad too, because whilst I was leaving hospital for the foreseeable future, I was also leaving behind all those that I had grown close to over the past eight months – and it dawned on me I wasn't going to see the people that took care of me. Bonds like this grow strong even in what was a very small timescale of my life.

After a few moments chit chatting, I went into my room with the bags of goodies, then sat down to write in the card I had bought.

I began by thanking everyone for all they did and continued to fill it with words that were truly from the bottom of my heart. Once it was all written and sealed, I gathered the few little treats I'd bought, I opened my ward room door, for what would be one of the last times ever and made my way towards the nurse station.

Some of the nurses on duty that day gathered around and began to congratulate me, saying things like, "Well done, you've smashed it." One nurse said, "You have completed this tough treatment with the best possible outcome and least problems that we could hope for."

I guess when they say *the least problems*, it's because at a drop of a hat you could spike a temperature – and before you know it you rapidly decline and next thing the crash team are in and somehow you get through. Others, end up in ICU (intensive care unit) or worse, dead.

I put the bits on the table and thanked my team for everything they did for me to help get me through my time as an in-patient with blood cancer. "Thank you, Mama Lake," it's our pleasure.

One of the nurses, Natalie, took the card and opened it and, to my astonishment, she started to read the card aloud. That's when I said. "Oh no, read it later when I've gone," because, for some unknown reason, I felt really shy.

To which she said, "Don't be silly," and began reading. But before long, her little voice began to get emotional, and her throat began to get a bit croaky. I looked at the other nurses and their little faces began to change as she continued to read, and their eyes filled up. Now, remember I said I don't cry, because I'd become hardened to showing my emotions from childhood. Well, I did that day. My eyes were overflowing with tears, of sadness, of happiness, of appreciation, of relief, of fears, and of making it through.

The transport came to pick me up, unfortunately much later than I anticipated, which made things even worse. I began to think maybe it won't turn up and I would be in here another night. Or even worse, I end up staying the night, somehow spike a temperature and end up staying for a week! I know me and my WPS's. But it did arrive – and as soon as it did, we all hugged and said our goodbyes.

The ward clerk came down with me and we had one last hug.

I looked around for what I was hoping would be the last time, got into the car, put my seatbelt on, and waved – teary eyed – at Raz, the clerk. As we drove off, still full of emotions, I took my phone out and videoed us leaving the hospital that had been my home for the best part of that year. And we began our journey back home.

On arrival, it was much like any other cycle after Cycle 1. Just normal. There were no *welcome home* banners. *You've smashed it.* Hey ho! There I go again with the expectations. Thankfully Mac was happy to see me.

Back home after another month of recovery, my cells stabilised, and an appointment was set for my last biopsy and consultation. On arrival at that consultation room, the same consultant that I met on that fateful day that seemed like an eternity ago who'd said, 'I can't guarantee the treatment will work or that you will see the end of the year,' said, "Well you snuck through Cycle 4, didn't you?"

I wasn't sure if that was just a rhetorical question, so I didn't actually answer. I just sat there with a bit of a sickly grin on my face – the grin you have when you are not quite sure what is meant by that comment, 'snuck through'.

The consultant then sort of tossed his pen onto the table as he leant back into the swivel chair and said, "In fact, you've come out of this relatively unscathed, haven't you?"

"Oh what does that mean? That's it, is it? I got through," I said.

"Well no, you're not out of the woods yet."

"Oh, ok then," bringing me back down to earth, in one big fell swoop. Just as I was starting to feel like I was a bit invincible, I'm clearly not!

He went on to say, "You have to continue with a maintenance treatment for one year." Which I kind of knew, to be honest. He went on to say, "It's Midostaurin, you've been taking that already. Oh yes. For two weeks at a time. The inhibitor. That's right. Except this time you will take the same dose but back-to-back for 365 days."

"A year! Well that's going to batter my stomach, right? And I'm going to gain a lot of water retention right?"

"Yes, but we will keep a close eye on you as you will be monitored monthly for blood tests and ECGs as it can seriously affect your heart!"

Oh that's just bloody fantastic! Goody! Fat and a heart attack waiting!

CHAPTER 38

Another Year

Cycle one arrived via courier to my home address as arranged by the AML 19 trial, along with the usual diary to fill, a page with boxes to tick for each dose taken and a comment box to describe how you feel in general.

The start of the first cycle wasn't too bad – especially as I was now given the big green light to go back to the gym. Obviously, I had to take precautions, like wear a mask when people were around etc. I cannot tell you how excited I was to go back to the gym.

So off I went back to my gym for the past 18 odd years, Bannatyne. Cast your memory back to my initial weight loss. It was there at my local Bannatyne where that journey began. And now another journey was about to start, post cancer treatment.

Once again, the staff did everything they could to ensure I was looked after – and at any time I needed anything, they provided it without delay. I cannot thank them enough for all their support, kind words and help. Especially the support of the PT's. They were always on hand to push, and kept an eye on me to make sure I was ok and motivated me during the days when I started to gain weight, which more or less started a month in.

My first day back to a proper gym came in the last week of October 2021. I hadn't been in since my diagnosis on 26th February 2021. I was so excited. I could barely contain myself.

Despite having my own home gym, it was still very limited. So once I was back in the gym I was like a kid in a sweet shop. Even so, I didn't go silly, I took it nice and easy and gradually built back up.

Besides, I was still on treatment for a year, so I had to be cautious, because each month for that year I had to have a blood test followed by a consultation. The blood test was necessary because Midostaurin is a targeted therapy which destroys any FLT3 mutated cells that might pop up. The downside of that is it will also impact and affect the good cells too, leading to lower blood counts.

But again, I was extremely lucky, as I more or less stayed within the normal range right throughout my treatment. The side effects I had were minor too, such as nausea, tummy issues and, at times, laboured breathing, along with a few headaches.

My ECG results were always within the normal range each month with no issues. However the worst effect was the rapid weight gain, where I watched myself putting on weight again. And boy, oh boy, did I grow bigger and bigger. It was absolutely devastating to watch all my hard work get undone!

Over the months as I got better, I became stronger and fitter because slowly I built my training back up to five days a week, mixing it up with 3 to 4 days of cardio in the afternoon – sweat pouring! I painstakingly watched my weight gain. Each cycle, each month, I saw myself getting bigger and bigger and bigger. No matter what I did, how I ate, I got bigger. It was painful watching myself become something that I had left behind all those years ago. I was becoming more and more upset and frustrated with this situation. I even began making awful comments about how big I was getting to anyone who would listen.

Each time I spoke to my new and allotted consultant, the most wonderful Dr De Vos, all I did was complain incessantly about my weight gain each and every single monthly telephone appointment. To the point that I forgot the very thing that was giving me back my life and keeping me alive and killing that mutated genetic gene called FLT3. At one point he even said to me, “Look, you are alive,” which of course I understood. But it felt like in order to have my life, I had to give something back in return.

I am sure many people with the same diagnosis would be grateful to be in my position. But in this situation being grateful wasn’t the issue. It wasn’t just how the weight made me feel mentally, it was how it was making me feel physically. I could feel my hard work and what I had achieved was slowly slipping away since I’d been at my biggest, a whopping 32st. I had no idea then of what I could achieve and what I would look like. Because I went far and beyond the goal I initially set of size 18. I went from a colossal size 32-34 – and carried until I bought my first pair of jeans at a size 10 and not 12 like I had anticipated.

I estimate I gained around 20 kilos (44lbs), because I couldn't even bring myself to get myself on the scales! Even though my internal organs were all ok, due to the amount of training I did and still do, that extra weight gain made me heavy again. I felt uncomfortable and not as light on my feet.

It was only at this point I actually had something to compare and understand the difference of carrying excess weight, as opposed to being lighter. Because my initial weight loss was a slow process, I adapted to the reduced size as I went along. But now I had quickly gained weight, I saw how carrying that kind of excess weight affected my body – which was in a very negative way.

After several months into my maintenance treatment, my clothes began to get tighter and tighter. Even though I was stretching my clothes over my body, some items had gotten so tight it was cutting into my skin, forcing me to go out and buy the next size up. I went from an 8-10 to a 10-12 and then towards the last few cycles a bloody 12-14, and that's bloody well and truly snug and some shitting items of clothing were a pissing size 16.

Not only that, but the weight gain from the medication also began to cause a bit of breathlessness. To be honest with you, it was really starting to get me down. I mean there is only so much 'positivity' a girl can have. It's fair to say I'd been through the meat grinder and back again and through it again to the point I was almost paté.

But no matter how hard it got, I just carried on. Even after cycle 9 when my weight gain really started to take a huge toll on me. I reminded myself of what a dear friend Eldon said to me, "Razor, the grave doesn't care how much you weigh." And he was right. The grave doesn't care. Cos once you're dead, you're dead.

But even to date, I am struggling with the long-term effects of that weight gain. And no matter what I do, I can't seem to shift the weight I gained. That – and with several other factors against me and the fact I'm an ageing female, meaning perimenopause – it just seemed like many things were stacked against me (including Palmiers from my local M&S, ok that's my bad, but they are so good and once a week isn't that bad, and for months I haven't had any and still the weight is not shifting!).

During recovery, I also focused on my new role as a patient representative on the cancer board. Having done so and delving a little deeper into the way things are run, it didn't take long to realise that the administration side of the NHS is a bit of a shit show. Most meetings I attended led me to question their philosophy of why, when you make cuts, is it in patient care and staffing and not white-collar jobs? I mean, do you need a manager for a manager? Is this really necessary?

Get rid of all these irrelevant positions and stop milking the NHS fund on things that are not important. Like a meeting that includes 76 members of administration to discuss anything but actual patient care. Instead it was utter nonsense questions, all funded by the taxpayer, on shit like, "Does Poona need an interpreter when she arrives at the hospital?" I was like, "What for, she's in a cosmopolitan London hospital mate, I'm pretty sure Poona can point to what's wrong, hun, or use Google translate! All Poona needs is a doctor!"

Anyway, I keep pushing with what little voice I have through all the bullshit and bureaucracy. I do not hold back or back down. I corner whoever I can for answers, despite being pushed from pillar to post, lied to, stalled, delayed, you name it they've done it.

It seems like they just flush public money into all the wrong places with no recourse. But because I am stubborn I won't give up nor let them pull the wool over my eyes. Many times I have told them I will keep going until I get what is needed for the comfort of us sick patients and help the staff have a safe pathway to air grievances. And each time I do, my little voice gets that little bit bigger and that little bit stronger.

Consequently my presence on the board, or should I say big mouth, has spread across the Barts Trust and to other communities, where I am told, I'm either much loved by some or a nightmare to others! I also give regular talks to nurses about being a cancer patient. It helps develop better understanding between patients and nurses as I am open to any type of question. I have also been invited to talk on the executive board, which resulted in them making some minor changes, but not the changes I was hoping for.

November 2022 was one of the saddest times of my life, because I had to say goodbye to my best friend, my beloved Mac, to the worst thing ever – cancer. Heartbreakingly, as I got better he got sick. I had to make that truly crippling decision that many pet owners have had to make to end their beloved animal from suffering. That time came when Mac could no longer eat.

In his last moments, I sat on the floor holding him in my arms until his very last breath. The only comfort I have ever had is knowing at least he went before me. Because I know he is never coming back. Whereas if I went before him, he would still be waiting for me. Whilst it may get easier with time, there still remains a massive hole in my heart. I will always miss my little friend Mac and – who knows if I ever will – I hope one day I get to see him again.

CHAPTER 39

The Road Ahead

Living in remission has its ups and downs. Life can, at times, certainly feel a bit 'raw' due to the nature of remission's uncertainty. At times it can feel like life is on death row, where you've been sentenced to die, but you don't know when. For me, it feels like someone is pointing a gun at your head (a situation I am not unfamiliar with), whilst following you around with a finger on that trigger – and at any moment they might squeeze the trigger and boom, gone.

It can be very easy to slip into dark thoughts. In fact many times I have had to pull myself out of negative thinking, especially when I see any little bruise, or every tiny little cough, or anything else that could pertain to the cancer returning.

It's difficult not to become paranoid about these things, but it can easily end up at a place of torment and fear. And remember, at the end of the day, what can you do if it does come back?

Nothing! You can't change, nor are you in control of what is going to happen. You just have to deal with what's in front of you!

In fact, no matter if it is cancer or another disease or anything else in life, at some point you have to try to accept what you have gone through and learn to live alongside it and adapt to your situation. For me, I let cancer become part of my daily life and accepted cancer is now part of life and who I am. Even though at times it is difficult, I try not to hold onto the anguish, no matter what has caused it, otherwise it will end up weighing you down!

I will try to give you an example of something I learnt during one of my conditioning training sessions, where I would take a 1 kilo dumbbell in each hand and raise them to shoulder level, 1 kilo, being a fairly small object and not heavy for someone like me. Until I held onto it for a significant period of time!

So the longer I held on, the heavier it became. For example, if you held it for a minute nothing much would really happen; after a few minutes, it will start to get a little harder. After several minutes, my shoulders would be burning to the point I was sweating and shaking, and eventually my shoulders would start to ache so much that I would just give up holding them and drop them.

Now imagine holding onto that for a day, or a week or a lifetime; by the end of it you would feel numb and paralysed. So what I am trying to say is, the weight of the object hasn't changed, so what matters here is how long you are holding onto that object.

See, the longer you hold on to something, the heavier it becomes. And the heavier it becomes, the more you will suffer, the more you suffer, the more that will spread that sufferance around others, and the more that happens the more others close to you will suffer too. So the best thing to do is – put it down.

CHAPTER 40

Final Chapter!

There is this expression I have heard over the years, and one I have touched upon earlier, and that is *positive mental attitude.* Whilst I do understand the sentiment behind it, I am not terribly fond of it, similar to expressions like *you're a fighter, you're strong, you've done it before, you can do it again,* or *it's all up here, you know,* with someone quite often pointing at their head. I'm usually standing there, biting my tongue (till it bleeds) because I know they mean well, so I don't want to be rude and say, as if *being positive* affects the outcome, but if it gets you through the tough times, then that's all that matters.

In my experience, it's not always the case of just have *positive thoughts* then you will be ok, especially in a cancer ward. Because what about those who died, who had a strong *positive mental attitude* but didn't make it? Therefore the reality here is, whatever your attitude, it won't have an impact on the way your body will respond to chemotherapy treatment. In the grand scheme of things, your body either will, or it won't. And there is nothing you can do. You just have to accept what fate lays ahead!

In my experience of being a cancer patient, the most important aspect is acceptance – acceptance of your fate. I knew I would either survive or I would die. Whichever one it may be, my advice is to prepare for it. I told myself if I ever got to a point where I couldn't bear the suffering any longer, then I would say goodbye to my family, then let fate do the rest!

And for those who are affected by that kind of decision, try to understand that no matter how much we smile or say we are ok, sometimes we just can't take it anymore. Pain can be relentless, and it can be tiresome dealing with those agonising effects of treatment, together with the countless list of side effects. But we will often fight to stay alive just for those few extra moments with our loved ones.

At some point in life we will have to accept death, death is inevitable to us all! We will all live and we will all die – when, who knows? When it's your time, it's your time, and there is nothing you can do about it!

Funnily enough, I recall a moment when I said exactly that to one of the taxi drivers on the way to a hospital one time. We spoke about cancer and death. During that conversation I ended up saying, "At the end of the day, mate" (in my best Essex accent, of course), "we all have an expiry date on our foreheads, we just don't know what that date is."

He paused for a few moments then said, "Yeah, but you can still go past the expiry date though, can't you?" I did smile at that *positive mental attitude* response, because he has a point, and what he said was coming from a good place. But I said to him at the end, you can't cheat death, because one day we will all close our eyes for ever!

After a short pause I continued saying, "And until that day, we can't let those fears and thoughts drag us down and suffocate our soul. Especially when we are faced with life threatening challenges. We must try to find ways to occupy ourselves away from being a prisoner of words inside our heads. We must do our best, not to allow fear to spread through our minds. Because fear of what we think, may not always be the reality!"

Remember my fear of spiders? I have learnt not to fear things I cannot control, not even death. For me, it is an honour to die as it is an honour to live. And, until that day, we must find comfort in whatever we can to get us through the dark days in life!

My comfort that has gotten me through every stage of my life is music and food! These two have been with me through everything. They are my lifetime companions. They are powerful, and not just for me. They can unite complete strangers together, like music did that New Year's Eve night when I worked on the doors, when we all raised our hands together to see in the New Year.

And that humble cup of coffee the young lady bought for me, as we all waited together for my ride home one cold summer's night after my shift in a nightclub.

See, no matter who we are, or where any of us come from, these two go hand in hand, throughout the world. These two can even help heal. Food can nourish our bodies and make us better, and music can change your emotions in an instant – it can make us happy, or it can evoke feelings of sadness, and it can even give us the feeling of hope.

I have experience of this, where music went from feeling sorrowful, then changed into hope, hope that led for a better day. This happened soon after I began composing songs on my guitar. And sometime after my mother's death, I wrote a piece of music called *Sound of Tears.*

This mirrored how my mother's suicide affected me, reflecting the pain I felt within. So from the start this song had a melancholy, sad feel to it. Until one day, whilst recording the track, when a moment of clarity happened and changed that song forever – which ironically took place on a rainy gloomy day, somewhat befitting for a song like that.

As the song travelled through the verses and began approaching the end, I decided to look out of the window, and saw a small break in the blackened sky, where a thin sunbeam had broken through the clouds. Soon after that, the clouds parted and the sun began to brighten up the sky. I instantly felt the glow of the sun that shone through the window straight onto my face. I closed my eyes to embrace that moment whilst I continued to play my weeping guitar!

Until unconsciously, something happened, because I unknowingly changed the feeling of the melody of that song, as the warmth of the glowing sun soothed away that dull ache in my heart, blending the sorrow away into what was to become the next track I named *Better Days,* a melody that now reflected a different emotion, this time of hope, hope for a better day. It was in that magical small moment, I realised no matter what we go through in life, no matter how dark the days are, one day those clouds of sadness will be lifted and those tears will melt away – and the sun, will shine again! Because sad days don't last forever.

Talking of songs. Almost all of us have a song that is close to our hearts. I myself, over the years, have collected many songs that are memorable, especially with my children. These songs range from Indian to classical music, from house songs to metal and rock.

And when we are cooking together, we sometimes even play

some traditional Mauritian Sega music! We even have a selection of our own songs that we've written and composed, be it one of my songs I have written, or a piece beautifully composed and performed by my incredibly talented pianist son, Azim. Or, even when I had the absolute pleasure of jamming with my son Khaliq, when he played drums. And, of course, listening to those fantastic DJ Mixes created by my son Rahim!

Songs can evoke all sorts of memories that can remind us of many different occasions during our lifetime. Perhaps a birthday or that first dance at a wedding. It can remind us of a Loved one, or family members. Or even when we've been in clubs and the DJ drops a song that we all love!

Songs can also make us happy and they can make us sad, they may remind us of someone we lost or even something we regret. Regret, gosh, that's another word isn't it? I tell you what, I have had a few of those over the years. Some make me cringe, some laugh, and some have even made me sad.

But there was this one time, where I felt the impact of that contrived word 'regret' – until something inside of me snapped, enlightening me to change my perception of regret!

This took place in hospital during my last cycle, as I lay awake in my bed, late one evening unable to sleep, due to the incessant noise in the ward. So rather than suffer it, I put my headphones on and decided to listen to one of my son's mixes. I flicked through the playlist until I landed upon a mix I hadn't heard for a while, so I put it on, got myself comfortable, lay my head back onto my pillow, and closed my eyes to shut out the flashing lights in the room and began enjoying the mix, smiling from time to time as the mix moved from song to song, evoking certain memories of better times.

As I continued to listen, my mind wandered to my present situation, reflecting on what I had been through the past few months. Then I heard what was to be the last song of the mix blending in, which immediately made me feel emotional. Those emotions intensified as lyrics of that song resonated through my headphones, and soon I felt a huge lump in my throat, swiftly followed by tears forming in my eyes!

I felt them overflow, rolling down my cold cheeks. Whilst a mental lifetime picture story began to unfold before me. And for a few moments, I felt consumed by remorse, as everything I had ever known – and ever knew – flashed before me, and regret began to fill my heart.

I started to regret things I didn't do, like the things I left, waiting in vain for tomorrow to come. Then I started to question certain things in my life. Like why did I do this or why I did I do that, why did life always get in the way? Then I asked, why did I always do the right thing by others when, most of them, really didn't do the right thing by me? Why was I always loyal to the wrong people? And now, it feels like it's too late because, here I am, in a hospital bed, fighting to survive, hoping to live another day so I may do one or more of these things I have always wanted to do.

I really did feel my heart aching as I felt myself spiralling towards the bottomless pit of hopelessness that regret brings! Almost everything began to consume me, and I wondered *has my spirit finally broken, has life finally beaten me?* as I continued drowning deeply and feeling the full weight of sorrow and hopelessness.

Then I reminded myself of something I learnt many years ago, that hope comes from hopelessness and, with that, I offered my hand to myself, and pulled us out of that hole of despair! I said to myself, *that is enough Sarezah, there really is no point dwelling or having any regrets. What we have been through and what you've learnt has made you who you are today. Life is life, where good things have happened and bad things have happened, and this will continue to be the case, until one day we do close our eyes for forever. Yesterday was yesterday. Today is today! And if we're lucky, there will be a tomorrow!*

I wiped the tears off my face and sat up, then raised my arms up in the air, closing my eyes, and in that hospital bed I then danced – just like I did for cake as a little girl – but this time, I danced to save myself from drowning in the sadness of my reality, as I sang the words of that song, over and over again, until that familiar sound of a thunderstorm effect echoed in the background, that signified either the beginning or the end of each and every one of those magical mixes made just for me by my son Lightning Rahim, that connected us four together in songs, mother and sons my Rahim, Khaliq and my Azim!

As the words of that song faded, the sentiments of those lyrics reminded me that, no matter what happens, we still have today! So make the most of what we have, so we don't regret the things that could have been!

"Oh friend, we don't need to see the end… So let's stay, dream, the things that could have been… Oh friend, we don't need to see the end…So let's stay, dream, the things that could have been… Dream…!"

(Julio Bashmore 'Kong' feat BIXBY).

Finally Finished 21/10/23. And revised and edited until 10/05/25.

Special Thanks

To my husband and my best friend Guy.

To all my die-hard girls! Janie my bestie, an inspiration to us all. To my beautiful stunning sister Kate, my rock and my heart.

My dear friend Jan. The kindest sweetest soul ever. My 'Shirley to my Pepsi' Lisa forever Diles.

To Natalija Dolgova my warrior, my sister and my mentor.

Thank you to my Cathie 'keep your mouth shut, you won't be thanked for it'. To my beautiful one and only Aunty Rashida my ma' til the day I die.

And of course to my amazing cousin and baby sister Uzma. 'Big doctor in big doctor world'. 'Wages'

To my dear Turkish/Cypriot brothers Kader and Savash.

And my lovely girls Lisa Ali and my beautiful nieces the biggest joys, my little Zara, and baby Sophie.

To the entire Harvey family. Love you all Aunty Razor. To my brother Ric. Forever we rock!

To my dear friend Rob Russel, for always listening to me moan and teaching me the true concept of 'do the right thing'.

To my dear friend Colonel Tony "be better than you were yesterday" one of the best life mentors.

To Kevin and Karen Bentley, thank you for proofreading my book and for being kind and supportive friends for over 20 odd years.

To my mate since I was 11, Martin Mcglyn. (That's what? ten years now). To my dear brother Farhad. Somehow we got through that mess!

To my dear friend Mat Ottley one of the best guitarists ever.

And a very big special thank you to all the staff past and present at Bannatyne's Kingsford Park. Thank you for all the love and continued support throughout my weight loss and Leukaemia journey. You all mean the world to me. Thank you to everyone in the spa and to all the trainers past and present. A special thanks to Tim the GM, nothing is ever too much. Thank you Charlotte for always looking after me and to young Pat for helping with those deadlifts!

Thank you to everyone who helped me with my journey.

Thank you to my lovely Meg, from Pump Gyms for getting the best out of me in the gym, as well as cheering me up with those lovely messages from you and the horses, whilst I was in hospital!

Thank you to my friends and staff at David Lloyds Colchester, during the summer of '23.

To David Kearns, The Dreambody Coach. My dear friend. Thank you for offering your guidance and help.

Thank you to the wonderful Ash and all my friends at Audi Colchester who have gone above and beyond any customer services are expected to do during the past 15 odd years. Love all you guys.

And of course thank you to Mr. Miles Banwell. For making me look like Jlo (for about 7 minutes) but mostly, if you didn't do what you did, I would not be here. Thank you for saving my life and being my hero!

Not to ever forget my honest and amazing Doctor, Sonica Goel. Thank you for all your continued support and dedication to making sure I get the best help I have ever needed.

And last but not least. My beautiful lifesaving med team in St Bartholomew's Hospital and the Collingwood Cancer centre in Colchester. You are the all the real heroes.

A massive thank you to all my friends over the years. Those who have loved and supported me throughout my life, past and present. Your kindness, and support, taught me many life lessons and got me through. Hope you have enjoyed reading my life journey. A tale of an ordinary girl with an extraordinary life.

Acknowledgements

Wonderwall Oasis; Julio Bashmore 'Kong' feat BIXBY.

A very special thank you to Karen Ainley and Linda Green for your invaluable support and help.